Bruce Willis

The Unauthorised Biography

John Parker

First published in Great Britain in 1997 by
Virgin Books
an imprint of Virgin Publishing Ltd
332 Ladbroke Grove
London W10 5AH

A catalogue record for this book is available from the British Library.

ISBN 1 85227 652 5

Typeset by TW Typesetting, Plymouth, Devon

Printed and bound by
Mackays of Chatham, Lordswood, Chatham, Kent

Contents

Acknowledgements

Bruce Willis, perhaps more than any other actor in the film capital, epitomises modern trends in today's Hollywood. The brash, cocky screen manner for which he is best known combines with an evident subcurrent of insecurity and ordinariness which is also forte on screen, most notably in the *Die Hard* trilogy, though no longer in real life. A man of modest training and slender CV, he has had a bumpy ride after his classic overnight rise to fame and great fortune, then came perilously close to the ejection seat after a bad run of off-beam movies until he was rescued by Quentin Tarantino. He resumed his place among his peers, friends and enemies, in a craft whose basic requirements have undergone a drastic change in the nineties. More often than not, his co-stars have been the pyrotechnics rather than great actors and his associates are the producers rather than stylistic directors. His power has grown with his wealth, derived not merely from being a pace-setter in the Hollywood earnings league but from shrewd, expansive investments in business and real estate, as will be revealed in these pages. His wife Demi Moore commands similar status and around them is a veritable ring of steel, managers, publicists, lawyers, aides and minders aplenty to guard them and their privacy. In spite of that, it will be evident from the ensuing chapters that a large number of people have been willing to assist me in my endeavours to chart the life and times of a blue-collar boy who made up his own version of the American dream.

Thanks to all those who gave their time with interviews or answered my correspondence, either specifically for this work or in past interviews from which some recollections have been drawn. Thanks are also due to the staff and administrators of the Film Department of the University of Southern California, Los Angeles, the American Film Institute Library and Archive, the British Film Institute for video and film facilities, the Tasiemka

Archive, London, the Academy of Motion Pictures Arts and Sciences, Los Angeles, and the Oral History Collection at the DeGolyer Institute of American Studies, Southern Methodist University, Dallas, Texas.

1 Local Hero

CARNEY'S POINT, said Bruce Willis, was a cool place to grow up. It was, and still is, a blue-collar town, male orientated, with strong and tough men for whom Friday night is sacred. The place had a kind of split personality when he was a kid. On one side, it was semi-circled by the larger municipality of Penns Grove, which edges out towards the Delaware River in southern New Jersey. The waterfront, once the scene of great activity, had an old pier that jutted into the river at the point where it begins to widen towards the mouth and then flows into the Atlantic Ocean. The urban landscape that clings to both sides of that famous waterway was punctuated by the chimney stacks of the factories and chemical plants, pumping out smoke and fumes – notably those of the Du Pont Company, then the chief employer in that locality and the base of economic life. Grimy and smelly, it was hardly an inviting place.

Half an hour's drive in one direction the scenery was that of an urban jungle, heading towards the heavy-metal territory where Robert De Niro filmed the early scenes of *The Deer Hunter*. A half-hour drive away in the opposite direction and you could be in open countryside and farmland, smelling some fresher, cleaner air. The draw of greener grass was always strong, especially when this hefty manufacturing industry went into a nose dive and the diverse ethnic communities, with large Italian, Irish and Afro-American populations, were confronted by the harsher realities of modern times. By 1993, Penns Grove was listed by the Office of Management and Budget as the second most economically depressed municipality in New Jersey.

Once it was a prosperous, thriving community whose better times were lodged in the earlier part of the century when a gunpowder factory was built at Deepwater, a few miles south along the river. The Du Pont Corp held huge tracts of property, at one time employing 15,000 at Deepwater alone. The company built a railway line to Penns Grove, just to transport workers to and fro. In those days, there were steamships and coal barges visiting the Penns Grove pier. Fishing boats came too, unloading caviar for a canning factory that was also built there.

Thus, from those beginnings it became one of the traditional heartlands of American blue-collar male domination, of Friday nights with the boys, bar-room brawls, hard-drinking men who spoke in expletive-ridden sentences and whose women knew their place and seldom attempted to challenge it. Men behaving badly on payday was as normal as it had ever been. The same environment produced several other famous names whose attitudes were noticeably anchored to those traditions – like Frank Sinatra and Jack Nicholson, both New Jerseyites.

The toughness of its natives, whose famous sons also included a fair smattering among the higher echelons of the Mafia and organised crime, has long been a joke on the stand-up circuit. Penns Grove and its surrounds had a reputation for various illicit activities dating from the days of its early prosperity which had attracted the underworld element. There were discreet and illegal gambling joints and a colourful riverboat life that had attracted high-rollers from New York and Philadelphia. It was also, conversely, a family place, with bungalows along the river where the city folk came for their holidays.

By the time Bruce Willis arrived on the scene, a lot of the community's affluence was already in decline, jettisoned in part by the building of the Delaware Memorial Bridge which meant that the area was now being bypassed by the very traffic that had once helped sustain it.

Quite apart from the physical influences, Willis also had to deal with some confusing, predetermined tendencies emanating from the Zodiac. He was born on the cusp between Pisces and Aries. According to one eminent stargazer, his birth date of 19 March 1955 placed him in the middle of some difficult conflicts, pulled this way and then that by the distinct characteristics of those signs. Pisces people fell into the 'obeying' category while Aries produced a strong 'commanding' nature; put together you get a natural-born rebel. In his case, the pull of Aries seems to have won – but there would be a mix of influential trends to disturb the psyche, says our friendly astrologer, consulted for a reading without knowing the identity of the subject.

Aries, the Ram, is powerful: vernal, dry, fiery, masculine, violent – hot in temper, bold in character. Pisces, the Fish, is cold, watery, feminine, phlegmatic and nocturnal – 'extremely fruitful', but its people are often devoid of energy and have a tendency to lounge around. The Pisces-born native often develops an ill-shaped body, fleshy if not corpulent, with thick round shoulders and a large head and face. Add the metaphysical to the physical, and the character and form of Bruce Willis actually emerges in quite predictable fashion.

The two aspects of birth date and location converged when he was two years old. His parents moved to New Jersey from Germany, where he was born and named Walter Bruce. His father David who, according to his son's own description, came from a 'long line of welders and mechanics', was, at the time, a twenty-year-old in the service of Uncle Sam – as an army engineer at the flashpoint of the burgeoning Cold War. In the best traditions of Yanks over there, Dave Willis started dating a local girl, nineteen-year-old Marlene from Idar-Oberstein. It was no big deal, according to Willis, and might only have been a fleeting romance, one more girl in one more town where servicemen were stationed, had it not been for the fact that, as in every one of these towns, a girl gets pregnant.

Marlene, who barely spoke English, announced she was with child and Dave did the decent thing. He married her before Bruce was born and eventually brought them both back to New Jersey. The world was on the change and a number of significant historical signposts were being set in stone as he entered it, in the same year, incidentally, as several other future luminaries of his profession: Kevin Costner, Kirstie Alley, Debra Winger, Isabelle Adjani, Willem Dafoe, Bo Derek and Ray Liotta were born in 1955 – and of course, it was the exit year of James Dean.

Nikita Krushchev had just become the undisputed master of the Soviet Union, with eyes on the universe. The Eastern Bloc nations had joined to form the Warsaw Pact and so hammer down the lid on personal freedoms. Vietnam, a subject on which Bruce Willis would become an avid student in later life, had erupted into civil strife (less than three months after the uneasy truce in the Indo-China War) which divided the nation along the 17th parallel.

In America, the postwar era of affluence and materialism, of big gas-guzzling autos, fridges big enough to hide a body in and that little flickering screen in the corner of every living room, was showing the early signs of its own metamorphosis. The problems that were to come alive in the second half of the century were already smouldering, and no better confronted and illuminated than in *The Blackboard Jungle*, the film version of Evan Hunter's powerful novel, premiered in New York the day after Willis was born.

The movie, forty years on, is no less powerful, though it was a mild precursor to the violent swing of things and in which Willis himself would be caught up during his own schooldays. At the time, it was a statement of the day, cautiously handled by MGM because of its then socially sensitive plot of unruliness in the classroom, where Glenn Ford faced a melee of young thugs who called him Daddy-O, ignored his teachings, threatened his wife and raped a woman colleague. Sunday school stuff, compared to the 1990s, but the script was at pains to point out that the vast majority of youth was polite and conforming to the rules of society. Yet, when the movie was shown, kids were dancing in the aisles to Bill Haley's 'Rock Around the Clock' and were soon ripping up seats in the rock 'n' roll revolution it foreshadowed.

Fast forward to New Year's Eve, 1987: Glenn Ford, then a frail 71-year-old, was introduced to Bruce Willis at a party:

'I read these articles about you and Sean Penn and the rest of you guys. Kicking ass and raising a storm. Man, Henry Fonda, Bogart, Bob Mitchum and me, we raised more hell than you guys ever did. We tore this town right up.'

Then he laughed: 'Just keep smiling, son. It don't mean a thing – I promise you.'

In Glenn's day, it didn't. Not to the stars, anyhow, because when those names were young bloods, the paparazzi were in short trousers, the tabloids were *sotto voce* and the studio PR men cleaned up the mess. They made movies that had no bearing on youth, no affiliation to the younger generation and the art of the spectacular hadn't been invented yet. As the *New York Times* noted in the mid-fifties, 'time has caught up with most of the front line stars . . . the rapport between them and the broad mass of film audiences which ranges from 15 to 25 is virtually nonexistent.'

Ford, Bogart, Mitchum and Fonda were already tinting their greying temples and adding weight to their thinning hairline. Even *The Blackboard Jungle* kept its foot in both camps of the generation gap. The styles, the postures and the mannerisms of youth that eventually caught hold of Willis as they progressed through the years and made him into a star were just edging through. Back then, in the year of his birth, disorientated kids in search of idols had nominated Marlon Brando, Montgomery Clift and James Dean as the acts to follow – their riders in the sky. By the time Willis caught up, those guiding forces were in other hands, developed and modernised by the likes of Jack Nicholson, Robert De Niro and Al Pacino.

In the March of 1955, the new breed was in full swing. Clift had already tackled socially taboo subjects, like getting a girl (Shelley Winters) pregnant and ditching her for the rich kid (Liz Taylor) in *A Place in the Sun* and then got cut up by Ernest Borgnine in *From Here to Eternity*. Brando won an Oscar for his memorable role as Terry Malloy in *On The Waterfront*. James Dean had just burst onto the scene in his first major movie, *East of Eden*, and was working on *Rebel Without a Cause*, though he would not live to see it.

There were other milestones.

In that week of Willis' birth, Tennessee Williams was shocking the theatre zone with his new play *Cat on a Hot Tin Roof*. Coincidentally, eighteen years later, Willis himself made his acting debut in a production of that same play, by then considered safe enough, innocuous enough, to be staged at the Montclair State College. At that point in his life, Hollywood was far away and not even a consideration, but the changes that would provide him with the route, the way through, began more or less in the year of his birth.

Then, Hollywood was coming apart at the seams and heading down the road that changed the ballgame and the players. The old studio system was dying on its feet. The moguls of the Golden Age were heading for their mink-lined coffins and Jack Nicholson spent his lunchtimes laying on the grass at MGM, where he was a 17-year-old postboy, trying to look up Lana Turner's skirt as she came out of the commissary. Turner, Gable, Garland and the other great names of that place, where there were more stars then in heaven (as Louis B. Mayer liked to boast), were already facing a not-so-golden goodbye.

The newer arrivals were turning the movie industry on its head, aided by the side-effects of Senator Joe McCarthy's anti-Communist purges and the US Supreme Court which ruled that the major studios should divest themselves of their monopoly on cinema chains. Artistic upheavels that would reshape the future of movies, and in time gather up the boy Willis, were falling into place. As the foulmouthed but, in his day, brilliant film-maker Harry Cohn, boss of Columbia, wailed dolefully just before he was felled by a fatal heart attack: 'The lunatics are taking over the asylum.' In the 1990s, those in Hollywood who hanker for the good old days reckon he was absolutely spot-on in his prediction.

Meanwhile, back at Carney's Point, Dave, with his young German bride Marlene, settled down to the anonymity that goes with the heritage of welders and mechanics the world over, never imagining for a second that they had a son who would, in just a few years time, bring posses of paparazzi and wagonloads of writers searching for a record of their roots.

Bruce was the eldest of the four Willis children – three boys and a girl – born over the ensuing five years. Dave resumed his career as a self-employed welder, setting up shop with his father and brother at nearby Camden and making enough for a relatively comfortable, if fairly basic, life for his family in a small, cramped home. There were few thrills or frills. Just a straightforward blue-collar existence, along with thousands of others in the same routine. But this is America, where childhood dreams, every once in a while, come true, throwing up a snot-nosed kid from some unimagined corner of the social structure and setting them on the road to discovery and fortune.

Psychologists tell us that childhood is the place to discover the beginnings of many traits and idiosyncracies that emerge later, and this seems especially true of those who make it in Hollywood. Behind many stars is a background of trauma, anguish or some kind of drama in early age, often connected with parental problems: Clift had an overbearing, possessive mother who tried to control him to her dying day; Brando had an alcoholic mother;

Dean carried the grief of a mother who died from cancer when he was nine and, for some childish reason, he blamed himself; Nicholson's 'mother' turned out to be his grandmother and his 'sister' was his real mother; De Niro's parents split when he was two and several times he had to rescue his artist father from the depths of despair. Stallone's was a similar tale.

It was forever thus; life stories of the rich and famous or the artistically inspired invariably involve some elements of quirkiness in their upbringing, to the point that it seems an inevitable ingredient, the driving force behind any successful career. In the case of Bruce Willis, his early life was small-town normality although there were a few problems arising out of his parents' marriage, which had been made in the passion of a moment rather than out of any true romance. Dave, still a young man, kept up the traditions of the locality with his penchant for nights out with the boys and a general liking for a party whenever there was one going.

There were also a few interjections of drama involving Bruce himself that were usually self-created. Like most new stars, pressurised by fame and the need to keep ahead of the game, once you're in play, he revisited his childhood when, in 1987, he went into therapy soon after being arrested and thrown in a cage by the Los Angeles police department.

He took therapy, he said, because he needed to challenge himself at a particular time when fame struck and he was living the life of a carefree, rich bachelor to the full, enjoying all the trimmings that came with it – women, drugs, alcohol etc., etc. He had just been offered $5 million for his first big movie, *Die Hard*, and the pressure was even heavier. He was a big television star by then, after several series of *Moonlighting*, and was hitting the newspapers for all the wrong reasons.

His therapist brought him to attention, made him go back and look at the things he had refused to look at for a long time – beginning, of course, with his infant days. Between them, they concluded, in terms of psycho-speak, that he had been building walls around himself, to protect himself.

This, in his younger days, had more to do with the fairly tough urban life of New Jersey and difficult school days than any particular dysfunctional elements of family life although, as he admitted, there were problems on that front which eventually led to the separation of his parents.

The paternal side of the family was fairly close knit, with grandfather, father and uncles always around and generally working together at their machine shop, until it would no longer support them. Relationships within his immediate family group were not especially demonstrative. He had no memory of a great deal of closeness; 'not a lot of hugging', he admitted. There was isolation too, and from the discussions he had with his therapist, he identified this as resulting from insecurity – 'a fear of the world and my place in it.' In a way, that insecurity actually put him on the route to an acting career.

At the age of eight, he developed a severe stutter and it was in his efforts to overcome this, a few years later, that put him on the stage. One day, when forced to make an appearance in front of an audience of his schoolfriends, the stutter went. Once he stepped back into offstage life it returned and, as with many who suffer from speech impediment, it remained with him until his late teens. He has spoken often about the disability and to this day winces when the painful memory of his own experiences resurfaces, when he sees others afflicted in the same way: 'When I see others like it, I see myself as a teen-years kid,' he once recalled. 'I could hardly talk. It took me three minutes to complete a sentence. It was crushing for anyone who wanted to express themselves, who wanted to be heard and couldn't. It was frightening. Yet, when I became another character, in a play, I lost the stutter. It was phenomenal.'

In an effort to conquer it totally, confidence building exercises, encouraged by schoolteachers, a speech therapist and his parents, led him towards taking a more extrovert place in school life and among his friends. The stargazers would tell us that the Pisces elements of his character which had seemingly prevailed in his early years were to be overtaken by the stronger Aries characteristics and, according to his schoolfriends, he gradually developed into a tough, mischievous character; a 'born leader' among the school pranksters and, eventually, as his courage blossomed in junior high, the scourge of the less forceful among his tutors.

He ditched his first Christian name, Walter, in favour of Bruce, and that eventually became Bruno, a nickname which has stuck to this day. Willis's own reluctance to discuss his childhood in the probing interviews that confronted him in later life was, as he frankly admitted, due in part to the fact that his adolescent years were not especially happy. Apart from the personal difficulties of the stammer, for which he was ribbed unmercifully at times, home life was not exactly a bed of roses either, with difficulties arising between his parents. Friends still abound in Carney's Point and Penns Grove who remember him well, and can chart the progression from a shy, almost backward boy through to his transformation into a high-profile school-prank activist.

Bruce Alissi, who grew up with him, remembers the earliest days. 'At about eight or nine,' he recalls, 'he was a scared little guy who hardly ever talked for fear of being teased. He just kept out of the way, back of the class, never getting involved unless he had to.'

That lasted into his early teens at Penns Grove High School, but within a couple of years he was fighting back, literally, in what became an interesting adolescent precursor to the hell-raising, brawling, boozing and wenching character the world came to know from exaggerated tabloid headlines during his rise to fame a decade or more later.

Anthony Rastelli, one of his early high school teachers, watched his progress with interest. At first glance, he was still a retiring, fairly respectful boy, well turned out and evidently well controlled by his parents. His hair was cropped to a respectable length, even when long tresses were in vogue in the sixties and early seventies. The change to a sharp-witted, devil-may-care attitude was gradual. Rastelli recalls:

'At that age where boys begin to find their feet, Willis had a hard time. The stammer was a problem and in the end, he began to compensate for it by his antics. He had to establish himself among the pack, and unable to do so with fluent speech, he did it another way – making himself stand out in the crowd by becoming the joker, the mini-tearaway. What he was doing was saying "Yes, I stutter – but that doesn't mean I'm not as good as the rest of you, better even." He made the others like him – and they did, although you could never eliminate the cruelty that exists when youngsters have someone in the midst who is afflicted by impediment or some other setback. I nearly died for him when he went on stage to make a speech. The kids were all laughing but somehow, he stuck it out and finished his piece, which was fairly typical of his spirit. And eventually, of course, he discovered that in front of an audience, he could overcome his disability.'

His academic progress was patchy and generally undistinguished. He was a C student, said Rastelli, because he spent so much time avoiding lessons and cutting class. He was soon making a name for himself by his escapades which are still remembered. He was the one who organised the breaking in of a new substitute teacher. Every time her back was turned, Bruce and his cronies sprang silently out of their desks and changed places, and then snigger while the poor woman tried to sort out who was who. Then there was the educational trip to Washington. One of his classmates, Cheryl White, recalls that they stayed in a small hotel and on the first night, Willis threw a party in his room. 'He'd filled a dozen balloons with water,' said Cheryl, 'and we hung out of the window and everytime Bruce spotted someone walking by, he'd bomb them with the balloons from six floors up. The police were called, but by then we'd all disappeared back into our rooms and they couldn't prove who'd done it. Junior class trips were cancelled for years after that.'

Other memorable Willis exhibitionist antics included streaking, for a bet, through the town, naked except for sunglasses and sneakers. One of his friends dropped him off in the centre of town, on the corner of Broad and Main. A local newspaper photographer had been tipped off but only managed a blurred image of the kid making his dash through the crowded streets. Willis ran like the wind. Once again, the police were called and, although they and the teachers knew who had performed this terrible act, again he escaped any formal retribution.

Next, he turned up at the school fancy dress party wearing just a baby's nappy. 'It was freezing outside,' said his friend Michael Whipkey, 'but he didn't care as long as he got the laughs. That's what it was all about – the humour. He had to be the centre of attention.'

Several of his tutors pretty well gave up on him and have no fondness in their memories of his attendance in their classes. Chemistry teacher Craig Martynian would describe him as 'rotten to the core.' He recalls: 'He had shifty eyes and I felt I could never trust him. He was a real handful at times. He mixed up chemicals wrongly and I was always on edge, expecting a fire to break out at any moment.'

Willis had a short attention span when it came to subjects that bored him but overall, he was good at subjects that appealed, like sports, music and drama. The discovery that his stutter vanished when he got on stage gave him the courage to join the Penns Grove Drama Club and he took small roles in a number of school productions. He was never a serious student of the performing arts, however. Influences that might have provided the basis for a future in the precarious profession of film and theatre did not come from watching old Brando, Clift and Dean movies.

Current heroes of the big screen were Robert Redford, Paul Newman and Dustin Hoffman. Jack Nicholson was just edging unexpectedly towards overnight stardom, after fourteen years in the business, with a supporting role in the 1969 movie *Easy Rider*. De Niro and Harvey Keitel – a future friend and near neighbour – were on the brink of it. They were eagerly followed, as and when they arrived, but only from the standpoint of, 'What's on at the local cinema?'

In Willis's circle, there were no heavy discussions about movies or the performances of a particular star, merely boyish wonderment and hero worship, and his knowledge of the theatre could have been written on the back of a book of matches, with space to spare. If there were performers who made an impression on the young brain, to be ingrained for future reference, they came not from the higher orders of modern Hollywood or Broadway but from old movies and comedy shows, relentlessly churned out on American television during his childhood and youth.

Films made in the 1930s and 40s to cheer up a depressed nation, were his early evening fodder. He would especially single out the Three Stooges, Danny Kaye, Jerry Lewis and Bob Hope as the ones he most enjoyed. A cherished poster of the Stooges was, in later years, carted from dressing room to dressing room, trailer to trailer, as he became a more serious student of his childhood heroes and Hollywood's silliest funnymen, with a respect that approaches reverence.

At the time, however, they were there to be laughed at, enjoyed and only subconsciously taken in. In the quiet of his bedroom, he read a lot. Dickens mesmerised him but he could never get to grips with Shakespeare, although he came back to it later. He devoured modern novels and Elmore Leonard was a particular favourite. By and large, however, learning was not high on his agenda of priorities, especially when puberty and sex appeared on his horizon.

At around fourteen, when the spotty ugliness of his childhood years was subsiding in favour of quite a handsome young man, his eagerness to lose his virginity was finally and boastfully achieved with the glee of all young men – and with the willing aid of an older girl. He had an evening job at the local Holiday Inn at the time, employed as a bellboy. One night, there was a party and he was invited: 'This chick scooped me up; she snagged me. I had a pass-key to the service rooms and we went down to the laundry and she kind of led me through it. I was amazed at what happened. I walked out of the laundry room with a whole new step and whistling nonchalantly.'

The shy boy had acquired a bolder personality all round. The challenging pursuits of getting laid, hanging out in the malls and listening to soul music were the natural basics for him and his comrades. He grew up with the Philadelphia and Motown sounds and became a proficient, self-taught harmonica player. He also bought a second-hand saxophone and struggled to teach himself how to play. 'He drove us all crazy,' his father Dave recalls. 'We lived in a small apartment at the time and there was no way he could play it there. So he'd climb up the hill behind the building and play his heart out.'

Humour was his forte and still the way of overcoming the speech difficulties, the mounting problems on the home front and the normal pressures of growing up in an unpromising environment. At the age of sixteen, he was beaten up badly by a gang of white kids who decided they were going to teach the show-off a lesson. He went home bruised and bleeding. His father, a sombre, taciturn man, was philosophical: 'Don't get into fights – but if you do, fight to win.'

By then, Bruce Willis's bravado among his schoolfriends was also hiding other traumas. In the previous couple of years, the situation at home had become increasingly fraught. His own personal adolescent difficulties were overshadowed by warring parents. The relationship which had begun so tenuously seventeen years earlier in Germany had run its course and virtually broken down. Just after Bruce's sixteenth birthday, Dave and Marlene Willis split up, and the family was carved down the middle. The split affected him deeply, and he always refused to discuss it when interviewers later came to call.

Bruce chose to live with his father while his brothers and sister stayed with their mother. From that moment on, he was pretty much taking care of himself. 'It was a rending, tearing thing, as it always is,' he admitted in reflection years later. It would be left to the passage of time to heal and, though split, the family would eventually remain in close touch. His popularity with most of the kids was a compensation and was sufficient to make him a kind of local hero. As he headed towards his last years at Penns Grove, he ran for the presidency of the student council. He treated the election with the offhand, glint-in-the-eye, smirking-lip humour that made him so popular.

He struggled through a hammy, tub-thumping campaign speech which was cheered uproariously as he promised 'We're going to have fun next year . . . we're going to play music in the cafeteria.' Naturally, with that kind of manifesto, he beat his more serious-minded opponents hands down and became student president, which was the pinnacle of his achievement at Penns Grove. Those last months of his high school education were marred, however, when he was expelled for supposedly being one of the ringleaders of a race riot in the school complex.

Racial discord was merely an excuse for a fight, although Penns Grove High had become an integrated school when it was still a controversial issue. Around half the student population was black, and there were also other ethnic groups whose families came mainly from Europe, notably Italy and Ireland. At times, passions ran high: 'It was a tough place,' Michael Whipkey remembers. 'A lot of kids, white and black, didn't know how to handle it and, of course, there had been a lot of media coverage of the problems in integrated schools at the time, and a lot of copycat activity. There were few years while we were there when the tensions did not flare up.' That year, there was a particularly nasty incident in the summer which erupted after a minor fight between a black boy and a white boy in the cafeteria. Rumours soon spread that the black guy had pulled a knife, and very soon battle lines were being drawn.

A full-blown fight broke out involving more than a hundred boys – strong seventeen-year-olds in a pitched struggle that needed a large contingent of police in riot gear to break it up. Police with guard dogs patrolled the school corridors for the rest of the year.

In the aftermath, Willis was identified by staff as being one of the instigators – a claim which he hotly denied. Even so, he was expelled from the school along with about 50 others. Bruce Willis stuck to his story that, sure enough, he had been in the thick of the action but he and some friends had been trying to calm the riot, rather than promote it. Father Dave believed his son and appealed to the school board for them to reconsider their decision to expel him. When that failed, he dug deep into his savings to hire a local attorney to prove the case.

The lawyer, a soft-spoken Perry Mason-type, visited the school, took statements from a number of Willis's friends and then interviewed members of staff who had accused him of helping to start the riot:

'Did you actually see him . . . ?'

'Well . . . not exactly . . . I . . .'

'Thank you very much,' the lawyer would say, scribbling his notes.

Two months later, he submitted his report. There was no direct evidence or clear identification of Bruce Willis to support the claim that he was among the ringleaders, or even personally involved in the riot. He maintained that the accusers had merely 'assumed' he was, because of his record as a troublemaker. With implied threats of further legal action, the school withdrew its charges. Willis was exonerated, received a letter of apology and was promptly reinstated. He returned to complete his otherwise undistinguished time at Penns Grove and left a message in the school graduation book which more or less summed up his cavalier approach to his time there.

Of his ambitions for the future, he wrote with now-typical zany nonchalance, 'To become deliriously happy, or a professional harp player.' The harp in question was not the stringed instrument of classical orchestras but the mouth harp, or harmonica, with which he had become proficient.

It didn't add up to any great promise for the future.

2 Aggression

FOR A WHILE, an anonymous life in Carney's Point and the daily drudge of a seven-to-five attendance in one of the local grime factories beckoned. For a stuttering youth with an uninspiring school record, there was little on offer. At the time, with family finances low, he had no route to college, no particular interests that pushed him towards a career, and the possibility of becoming an actor was something that came up in his thoughts only occasionally. It was like a mirage, and it vanished just as quickly.

There was nothing to grab hold of and tie down in a structured way. Looking back on high school, he would say that the only thing it taught him about acting was how to lie with a straight face. Above that, acting was but a distant dream, and one that seemed so unachievable that he barely considered it.

Instead, he followed his father into heavy industry. Dave himself had joined the herd by then, giving up his attempts to make a living as a self-employed welder and taking employment at the Du Pont factory in nearby Deepwater, New Jersey. Dave scouted the employment scene and the only job available for Bruce was an undemanding one, driving a truck that ferried work crew around the plant. Once inside the factory, and getting a first-hand glimpse of the workplace, he knew he couldn't last there. The shopfloor talk of the men was narrow and glum, of hard, problem-filled lives and a future that, even at the start of the 1970s, looked dismally insecure.

As each day passed, Willis built up a loathing of the place and when weeks turned into months, the longing to get out increased. He was shocked into quitting one day when a fellow truck driver was killed. He was driving past a drum the size of a house, in which chemicals were being mixed, when it exploded – the same point that Willis himself drove by ten times a day. He was about a mile away at the time and heard the explosion: 'They found parts of him all over the place,' Willis recalled. 'I wasn't all that shook up by it. What made me think about quitting was the way the other guys, the older ones who had been there for ten or twenty years, took it. They were gone; just white. That's me in twenty years time? No way. I left at the end of the week.'

His next job was just as much a dead end, metaphorically speaking. He became a security guard at a nearby nuclear power plant, then under construction. He worked nights, from twelve to eight, patrolling the plant with a bunch of keys, making sure everything was secure; in the quiet of the nuclear container, 300 feet under ground, his harmonica sounded terrific; he discovered it sounded even better on the company's PA system and there are plenty of workers in Penns Grove today who remember being ear-blasted by the youth who became Bruce Willis.

The job was nothing more than the provider of $2.80 an hour and he was soon bored with that, and left. For a while, he just hung around in bars, sometimes tending for a few dollars but mostly just drinking. At nights, he played the occasional gig with a local blues band called Loose Goose. The languishing did him no good, except to eventually direct his thoughts to going back to school and trying to recoup the once-missed opportunity of an education. The thoughts crystallised when, by chance, he ran into one of his former teachers at Penns Grove, Grace Dilks, who taught Latin.

She was one of the few who had believed he had potential, possibly as an actor. Others, knowing the impediment that still troubled him, might have laughed. Grace suggested that he should enrol at Montclair State College, where the fees for state residents were low and where they had a particularly outstanding performing arts curriculum.

Grace was so persistent that she even offered to drive him to the college to enrol, knowing he had no transport of his own and very little money. It was at the time of petrol rationing following the Middle East oil crisis of 1974/75. Grace knew she would probably not have enough fuel to get there and back but took him anyway, having convinced herself, and Willis, that it was his only hope of progressing. 'It was like driving into the desert without water,' she admitted. 'I knew we were going to run out of gas and sure enough, we did on the way back. Bruce kept up a running banter while we waited for the state troopers who carried emergency supplies.'

So from that moment when fate took a brief hand, Willis was at least pointed in the right direction. Immediately thereafter, he was gripped by the acting bug and it never let go. Suddenly, there was something to jolt him out of the ambling, pointless journey of his early youth.

Acting.

The thought grew in its importance, to the point that everything else was unimportant; all he cared about was getting a gig on stage, and heroes and style-leaders were already forming in his brain. Pacino, who he had seen in *The Godfather*, De Niro, in *The Godfather Part II*, and Paul Newman were especially singled out as the acts he would follow.

He moved to Montclair that year and began his studies, principally under the guidance of drama professor Jerry Rockwood. He was impressed by Willis. He saw in him a certain charisma, and it was with his help, along with a college therapist, that the stutter was finally ironed out. Now, with the opportunity of doing drama readings and actually performing in meaningful plays at a place where it was all taken very seriously, Willis discovered that by diving into other characters the speech impediment could be totally eradicated.

This was completely evident when he took his first major role in any stage production, when he appeared as Brick in a Montclair presentation of *Cat On A Hot Tin Roof* – the character played by Paul Newman in the film version. His performance, according to Professor Rockwood, was competent, though not brilliant by any means. There were many students around who Rockwood would place well above him in terms of acting potential. What Willis possessed, according to the professor, was an impatient, simmering aggression combined with sharp, off-the-wall humour that came through in his stage performances and readings.

His street-life experiences in New Jersey had at least given him some grounding. That quality, harnessed and developed, Rockwood presumed, would more than compensate for his lacking in other directions and at some point in the future, might become his prime stock in trade – as indeed it did, almost to the letter.

The impatience was not merely a quality of his acting. He felt it offstage, too. Willis wanted to be away, to challenge himself in the real world. He began his old Penns Grove trick of cutting class, but now the reason was to take the train to New York, to attend auditions for off-Broadway productions.

With less than eighteen months' study at Montclair under his belt, his fellow students judged it nothing short of arrogance that this randomly educated, ill-read young man of 21 imagined that he could walk into the New York theatre world and expect to get work – in a city with a thousand and one trained actors scouring the jobs section but spending most of their time 'resting'. But it happened.

Coincidentally, he'd just had a run-in with the law over the possession of a small quantity of marijuana, still a sacking offence in those days. He was picked up by the police in Montclair, New Jersey, on 10 May 1976, for possessing less than an ounce of dope. At the time, he was wandering along the street to a friend's house, with a bottle of beer in his hand. He had just rolled two joints; he was smoking one and had put the other behind his ear. A patrolling policeman stopped him, told him not to drink beer in the street and then spotted the roll-up behind his ear (Bruce having already ditched the smoking one).

'What's this?' cried the officer.

'Ooops . . . a joint,' Willis admitted.

'A *joint*?'

There was no point trying to hide it: a joint is a joint and it looks like a joint, and the officer was no fool. Willis was hand-cuffed and taken down to the police headquarters where he was charged with possession of an illegal substance, for which he got six months probation, a lecture and a warning that next time, he would be thrown in prison. He stopped smoking the stuff for a while but soon returned to it when he got to New York.

It caused a few ripples at Montclair, but it didn't matter anyway. Willis had already decided to quit college and take his chance in the big wide world of New York. That winter, he landed work in Manhattan. It was a modest job, as an assistant stage manager understudying the lead in a now-forgotten play which was set to open well off-Broadway in January 1977. It was sufficient for him to brush aside the cautions of his tutors. He packed his bags and waved goodbye to Montclair for ever. With the minimum of credentials and a good deal of bluff, he was off to New York to become an actor with the resolve to work at any job in the theatre, from backstage to front of house, to get experience.

The euphoria, as every advice-giver had warned him, was short lived. The job, and the play, had a limited run and barely provided him with the rent. There were problems, too, back at Carney's Point. One of his brothers had been in a road accident and his sister Florence was also ill. He returned to his roots penniless, tail temporarily between his legs and worried about Flo, who was then nineteen. 'She was the dearest person in the world to him,' said his father. 'And like the rest of us, he was mortified when she was diagnosed as having cancerous Hodgkins disease. The doctors told us she would be lucky if she lived to see 30.'

The incredible coincidence was that Florence was engaged to a local boy who developed the same kind of cancer. He died later, after a long and painful struggle. Bruce stayed on in Carney's Point and when Florence was at her weakest, and hope seemed to be fading, she made him promise that he would go back to New York and work at his dream to become a movie star. 'He said he would do it for both of them,' said Dave. 'And he was determined to make it. Personally, I wasn't that optimistic. But I thought he had to get it out of his system.'

Bruce stayed at Carney's Point for about five months. Florence underwent a long period of treatment, eventually made a remarkable recovery and is today the mother of four healthy children herself. While he was at home, Willis took work as an attendant at the European Health Club, trying to get enough money together for a second attack on Manhattan. The owners also had a similar place in New York and by the end of 1977, as Flo improved, Willis left for a job with that outlet.

He rented a squalid little 'railroad' apartment in Hell's Kitchen, the infamous address of struggling souls and assorted other semi-vagrants whose previous, but later famous, residents had included Sylvester Stallone, Richard Gere and Al Pacino. His was a fifth floor walk-up on West Forty-Ninth Street, close to the Broadway theatre district. It consisted of a single long room, almost like a hall, with virtually no natural light. It cost $170 a month unfurnished and, he suspected, was previously occupied by a Satanist. Everything was painted black, even the bath, and decorated with moons and crescents.

He furnished it with second hand and junked pieces picked up from tips and trash lorries, including a desk that had no knobs on the drawers, so he improvised using bent nails. His standing joke about the place was that there were so many cockroaches he had to put timber pallets on the floors to avoid walking on them. Dave sent him a do-it-yourself book and he worked at it whenever he had some spare cash, which wasn't often. He lived there for six years and kept on the lease when he became rich and famous, just to remind him of the bad times.

He became a denizen of the actors' waiting room, scouring the new starts and the jobs pages of every magazine associated with the performing arts and possessed by the New York Public Library. The auditions came and went.

It was a meat market: lines of hopefuls who turned up at every call and became familiar faces – the wannabes, the has-beens and never-will-bes, all trying to control the swarms of butterflies in their stomachs, peering anxiously into the darkness of a gloomy, daytime theatre or rehearsal hall after giving a reading, and then feeling their hearts sink when the shout comes in an identifiably dismissive tone . . . 'Next!'

It had been the lot of every actor, lusting for the breakthrough that lay beyond the next hill. Fame was hardly even a concept let alone a dot on his horizon. He stayed with the European Health Club for a while and then moved on to the Paris Health Club, where he made better money selling membership. But at the first smell of a theatre job he was off again, into the realms of poverty – this time, working as an electrician-cum-bit player in an off-off-Broadway production.

Members of his family came up to see him when he took his first real acting role, in a play called *True West*. Dave was impressed and changed his mind about his son's future possibilities; the kid had talent, though, unfortunately, no one else recognised it yet. Work was spasmodic, with long gaps between theatre jobs. He was forced to seek help from the traditional support system of resting actors, the New York eateries.

There, he began a long association with the restaurants and bars around Manhattan, on the other side of the counter. His first employment in such surroundings was at Artie's Warehouse, a popular drop-in that attracted a varied crowd ranging from tourists to leather jacketed diners from the local gay community. One of the partners was a former lawyer from the Bronx named Lenny Angelo who was, quite coincidentally, a friend of Ed Hayes upon whom the character of Tommy Killian in *The Bonfire of The Vanities* was loosely based, the film version of which Willis, of course, starred in a dozen years later.

Lenny, when his former employee became famous, used to dine out on Bruce Willis stories. He always found him a bundle of laughs, a happy-go-lucky, whistling character – and eventually overly so. Angelo's favourite tale is the one about Bruce's 24th birthday party. About sixty people were crammed into the tiny apartment when he arrived. Music blared from the stereo and the bring-a-bottle drinks flowed merrily. Then Angelo noticed something familiar about the crockery on which the food was served. Most of it had been 'borrowed' from Artie's Warehouse, along with some of the food. He even recognised the birthday cake which Willis had secreted out of the restaurant under his trench coat. Willis left Artie's soon afterwards, but remained on good terms.

He had become a familiar figure in the sub-theatre culture which existed around the bars and restaurants. He also had little difficulty in getting small roles in the theatre and walk-on parts in television shows and commercials, though none amounted to a great deal. There was even the briefest whiff of the big time, in 1979, when he secured a tiny role – blink and you missed him – in the Frank Sinatra movie *The First Deadly Sin*, which was set in New York and for which local actors were hired in the bit parts.

It was heavily panned and turned out to be Sinatra's last film, but for Willis it was A MOVIE – something for the CV: a credits list that began with Sinatra and ended with himself, albeit as 'figure in long shot'. The film did, however, provide another important key to his future: it was that work, for which he appeared in the movie credits, that finally gave him the necessary qualifications to obtain his Screen Actors Guild card, opening up wider opportunities.

In the summer of 1979, he began to get regular work before

live, if small, audiences when he was invited into the six-member workshop group of actors who made up the nucleus of the Barbara Contardi First Amendment Comedy Theater which was based in West Twenty-Fourth Street and where Willis had been taking classes. It paid very little, but the experience mattered. That was his theme. He'd do anything, go anywhere, for the chance to act – and often for no money. For the time being, he remained a star of the bars.

Cafe owner Larry McIntyre hired him to tend his hostelry at the Chelsea Central. One of Willis's former colleagues there, Stephen Eads, who went on to beat him to Hollywood (but in the music business), described him as 'outrageous . . . he used to roller skate into the place dressed in big baggy pants, a ripped T-shirt and a headband . . . then he'd start . . . his work was a performance, absolutely.'

McIntyre was so impressed that he moved him to his more popular bar uptown, called Cafe Central. 'He had class,' McIntyre remembers. 'He was also very entertaining, very funny and acerbically witty which the customers enjoyed.' Cafe Central suited Willis even better. It had become a busy, core venue for the theatre crowd and a lot of showbusiness celebrities and almost-stars hung out there. Cher, Sting, Robert Duvall, Richard Gere: Willis could name-drop all day. To them, he was Bruno, the sharp-talking, entertaining bartender who, as the evening wore on, was having a high old time and might just spring on to the bar and play his harmonica and then, later still, jump the other side of it to sort out any high jinks among the more lively clientele. 'Biff, bash, quick as a flash,' they used to say as he cleaned up any troublemakers.

'It was a late night spot and we usually ended up having to throw people out,' McIntyre said. 'There was always somebody in there who Bruce could relate to. Often, some of them would stay on after we'd gotten rid of most of the clientele. Bruce was in his element. He would talk with people like James Taylor or Treat Williams who were two of our regulars. Treat and Bruce used to talk for ever. Or James would sing while Bruce played his harmonica. They were great times.'

Willis used his contact with celebrities to scout for work and soon discovered that Treat Williams was not only a useful font of knowledge in this direction but also that he and Willis had very similar ideas. With his rugged, dark Irish-American good looks, Williams was himself a rising star whose origins were on Broadway. He followed Richard Gere as both understudy and, later, star of the Broadway musical *Grease*, and by 1979 was a leading-man choice for several films, including the movie version of *Hair*. The following year, he was offered his first major dramatic role in a new New York-based movie, *Prince of the City*.

Alerted by Williams, Bruce Willis dashed off to auditions for the supporting actors. He won only a small uncredited role, but the greater significance was that that provided him with the opportunity to watch and learn, and this one was important. It was in the hands of one of Hollywood's finest directors, Sidney Lumet. The film, a powerful semi-documentary on police corruption, was not one of Lumet's best but, having established the contact, Willis kept watch. When Lumet came back to New York a year later to film *The Verdict*, Willis was once again among the bit part players. This time, he had the chance to see one of his personal icons, Paul Newman, who headed an impressive cast which included James Mason, Charlotte Rampling and Jack Warden.

Around the same time, he had high hopes for a role in a new play by black writer Dennis Watlington. Again, it was no big deal in terms of money or prestige, merely the opportunity to test himself with a strong and meaty character role. A young director was casting for a group called Theater for the Forgotten, a small company which put on plays in prisons, rehabilitation centres and lesser colleges.

The play was called *Bullpen* and Willis was to take the role of the only white prisoner in the holding cage of a New York jail who tries to tough-out the toughest of the black prisoners. As Watlington, of similar age and disposition to Willis, describes it, the company 'really roughed it . . . people talk about low-budget shows; this was a no-budget show.'

He first met Willis, along with one of the other actors, when they were called for a reading at the director's loft apartment in Little Italy. Watlington, who turned up during the reading, was suffering from the hangover of a heavy night and promptly fell asleep. He was awakened by Willis, loudly proclaiming that the rehearsal was not going well. He wanted to know what the author thought.

Bruce Willis

Willis thrust his face into Watlington's and said, 'Hi, I'm Bruce.' It was the beginning of a four-year collaboration on the project, and a succession of drink-sodden adventures within the lower regions of New York social life. The young director was, in due course, fired, and Watlington took over. They rehearsed the play in the cold, damp basement of a community hall in Harlem and, in the beginning, a few kids started to come in off the street to watch. Word got around, and more people began to wander in. It attracted such interest that they began to perform the play upstairs in the community hall and it ran off and on, now and again, for six months.

Watlington recalls that Willis, at the time, was a struggling actor in every sense. He badly needed the work, any kind of acting work, to get his confidence. The plain fact was that he had not mastered any of the dramatic techniques of the kind that an actor establishes himself with. The brash, loud, macho joker who seemed fearless in real life could still melt on stage through inexperience and lack of power. As Watlington observed: 'Although his tremendous presence and natural comedic timing were evident from the beginning, he had trouble harnessing his fear on stage. He was a great rehearsal actor but he would shrink under the heat of the actual performance lights. In front of an audience, he was raw nerves. At times, he could be very disapppointing, but flashes of unique talent showed through, no matter how badly he screwed it up.'

What the Theater for the Forgotten produced was a scenario more akin to street acting, and as Willis acknowledged it was a tough, hard grind that provided him with the chance to extend himself, merge the character with his own personality and eventually find a route forward. In Harlem, according to Watlington's own description of his brethren, 'hard niggers in their big pimp-daddy hats' lined the walls and everyone was sniffing coke. They were saying out loud, 'Bad white boy . . . baaad white boy' as he challenged the black guys in the play, and in a place where most white folk wouldn't dare be caught in.

In between the spasmodic performances of *Bullpen*, it was back to the Cafe Central where he resumed his performances as the loud and active, cocktail-shaking, bottle-tossing, harmonica-playing barman, a model, surely, for Tom Cruise and Bryan Brown in *Cocktail*. On free nights, Willis and his coterie tore up the town, as best their finances would allow. 'Bruce and I loved to go out drinking,' said Watlington. 'On a good night, we would just turn a bottle to our lips, we'd turn up the whole bar. When it came to hanging out in the city, he was fearless. We drank till we dropped.'

Slam dancing was all the rage then, and they often wound up being physical in late night punk rock joints – 'wild and crazy nights' that never seemed to end. When he was neither acting nor bartending, he would seek out other recently acquired pals, including musician Robert Kraft who played regularly at the Greene Street Cafe which provided live jazz to accompany its customers dining on 'the finest American and French cuisine'. Some nights, Willis sat in and played. Then, it was off to some other joint, drinking until dawn.

That Willis had a propensity for the good times is evidenced by the accounts of a dozen or more friends who were around him at the time. Without exception, however, they would all end their accounts of their exploits with the telling phrase that provided a more serious undercurrent: 'He would go anywhere, do anything for an acting gig.' But five years or more had passed swiftly since he had left Montclair, so determined to find fame, and his CV looked exceedingly bleak.

He looked up to other New York actors whom he had served at various bars in recent times, notably Richard Gere, a year older than Willis and whose own journey from Syracuse, in the northern reaches of New York state, had followed a remarkably similar path, only with considerably more success. Gere, more handsome and naturally charismatic, had been in New York for ten years and had passed through the poverty and pain barriers and the restaurant sub-culture, although he'd always had a rule never to 'go public' in the service industry.

He stayed in the kitchens, doing the washing up.

His break came in the musical *Grease*. He garnered an impressive theatrical background and, in the late 1970s, won acclaim in a series of movies for outstanding directors such as Richard Brook's excellent *Looking for Mr Goodbar*, Terence Malik's enigmatic *Days of Heaven* and John Schlesinger's *Yanks*. In 1980, Gere finally hit the jackpot with *American Gigolo*. Willis would have given his right arm for a role in any of them, whatever it was. By comparison, he was still at the starting gate.

The fact was, Willis met more Equity-card holders in the bars than he did in the theatre. In that environment, he was the star. Mickey Rourke, John Hurt and Peter Weller were hanging out and just starting to get work. It was a boys' club, although not exclusively. Among Willis's close friends at the time was Linda Fiorentino, the now voluptuous and reclusive star of *The Last Seduction*. The relationship was, Willis insists, purely platonic. It had to be, according to him, because for a while, Linda and her sister Terry shared his bed. The two girls came into the bar one night and told Bruce their story of woe. They had just been evicted from their apartment and were homeless. Bruce, being the laid-back, well-met fellow he was, offered them a helping hand.

'You can stay at my crib if you want,' said Bruce.

Linda and Terry, with nowhere else to go, accepted his kind offer, and stayed for almost nine months. Bruce insists to this day, 'We were just friends. Sure we slept in the same bed, but nothing happened. I promise you . . .'

His friends are inclined to believe him, thousands wouldn't. It was the kind of camaraderie that existed at the time. The fun and the laughs were interspersed with the lows and the disappointments and everyone supported each other. By and large, his work had been so low-key that he had not even been able to get on to the books of an agent, and without representation in New York, the chance of prestige work was pretty near impossible.

In 1982, the first signs of a breakthrough appeared. He landed the part of a tycoon in a play called *Railroad Bill*, staged for a limited run at the Labor Theater. Soon afterwards, he joyfully secured his first ever lead, in an off-Broadway production, *Bayside Boys*, which at last brought him some modest critical acclaim in Village Voice for his performance as a domineering construction worker with a failing marriage.

When that play folded, Willis returned to bartending. He had moved on to a new place, the Kamikaze, opened by the former maître d' at the Cafe Central, Kirke Walsh. 'He helped me build the place,' said Walsh. 'And when we opened, he worked the bar. He was a great attraction in himself, jumping around and playing his harmonica. But I knew, there was no question that some time, he would make it.'

Another year of small roles and TV commercials passed. He was approaching that landmark birthday of 30. Linda and Terry had departed long ago and he had the anchor of a serious relationship in his life, which for a time quelled his roaming nightlife tendencies. She was the writer Sheri Rivera, former wife of Geraldo, the investigative television reporter and eventual chat show host. Sheri enjoyed his party-time approach to life, but also saw his serious side which she encouraged.

Their relationship was the subject of a good deal of discussion among friends of both. Sheri's marriage to Geraldo had come through some turbulent times. She was a fiery excitable dark-eyed beauty, a year older than Willis and the mother of a five-year-old son by her former husband. Her life with Geraldo had attracted microscopic attention from the media. It followed the flamboyant television reporter's own rise to fame, accompanied by a well-documented social life as he became noted for his many controversial investigations. He tackled everything from the death of Elvis to Satanism. He was often branded the originator of 'tabloid TV' before he was given his own, and now long-running, hour-long participation show on which the present author had the dubious pleasure of appearing.

What Sheri saw in Willis, a wannabe actor going nowhere at the time, was something of a mystery in her own circle. She was an aspiring writer who flitted around the Manhattan scene with ease, roving through the uptown parties, the Broadway theatre crowd and yet equally at home in the arty Greenwich Village community, which she preferred. They met at a party given by a mutual friend. To Willis, she was a classy lady with connections in the right places.

Their relationship was set to run and, like her marriage to Geraldo, it was, according to one friend from that era, hot and heavy. The irony was that Sheri herself provided the introductions that set Willis on the road to the fame and fortune which she would not be part of; it would take him to the West Coast and out of her life. One other ironical touch came much later, in 1988, when Willis was hitting the headlines for all the wrong reasons. Geraldo himself sprang to his defence:

'Bruce is a very decent guy. When he and Sheri were together, he treated my son in a fatherly way and that's all I cared about. Like me, he gets a bum rap in the press. If he's having fun, or gets arrested for being slightly tipsy, or having a seed of marijuana in his possession or going five miles over the speed limit, it's major news. My son noticed. He said they were doing to Bruce what they did to my dad.'

Sheri was there to guide him through the one break that can be identified as the true starting point of Willis's route to better times. It appeared out of the blue in 1984 and, once again, it was transmitted through a friend. One night in the Kamikaze, the actor Will Patton revealed that he was quitting his stint in the long-running off-Broadway production of Sam Shepard's *Fool for Love*, the role of Eddie.

Willis crashed the theatre and demanded to be heard. He was invited to read and, having been well primed by Patton, was called back for a final run through. The role was his although, for safety's sake, Willis kept a foot behind the bar at Kirke Walsh's place. The play was scheduled for a limited remaining run.

His galaxy of New York friends who boosted the theatre audiences for days after he opened were all pretty well agreed that Willis was finally on his way. The performance was widely applauded and Gene Parseghian, a key man in the New York office of the Triad Theatrical Agency, was dragged kicking and screaming to the theatre by Sheri Rivera, protesting snootily that seeing replacement actors in an off-Broadway show was not something he normally agreed to do.

Parseghian was impressed. A couple of days later, Willis was in his office putting his signature to his first ever agency representation contract. Within the month, Triad had booked him a screen test in New York for the movie *Desperately Seeking Susan* starring Madonna. The part was for a punk rock musician and Willis intended to make absolutely certain that at least his physical appearance fitted the director's requirements. He bought a tattoo kit and put a couple on his arms. He had his hair shorn to differing lengths and added a couple of earrings for good measure.

He didn't get the job, and legend has it that he left that audition to be snapped up immediately for the role that was to launch him, finally, to stardom. In fact, soon afterwards, armed with an introduction to Jenny Delaney, head of Triad's Los Angeles office, he flew out to California to take a look at the 1984 Olympics, and combine it with his first reconnoitre of Hollywood, still with the punk appearance he had adopted for the Madonna audition.

Before he left, he called in on Kirke Walsh at the Kamikaze. There was more than a touch of apprehension about him. The bravado facade had once again melted.

'I'll be broke when I get back,' Willis told him.

'No problem,' said Walsh. 'Your job will still be open.' Willis took a slug at his beer bottle, and pondered for a moment.

'I don't think I want to work the bar anymore.'

'Okay,' said Walsh. 'But I was thinking about making you manager.'

Willis pulled out his harmonica and blew some bluesy notes, then dashed off into the night.

3 'Hi, I'm Cybill'

THE TIME AND THE PLACE were right and fate was on his side that week. A day later, and the moment would have passed.

Producer Glenn Gordon Caron stood up despondently, took a swig of his cold coffee, stretched his arms and loosened the crutch of his pants, having just dismissed another batch of applicants who had given him a reading for a new television role he was casting:

'Jeez! Where're all the men in this town,' Caron moaned. 'They've all gone soft. They're whimps. They sit around drinking white wine and are wiped out if they meet a real woman. I want a guy who is sharp, glint-eyed and isn't afraid to be sexist.'

Everyone was doing the laid-back Alan Alda routine, oozing sensitivity and calmness. So, there was an intriguing background to the scenario that, unknown to Bruce Willis, was waiting to gather him up and turn him into an international face. Two years earlier, Caron, then a 30-year-old aspiring producer/writer began working on his idea for a new television series. Caron and a small writing team had pored over it for months. Something different, they said, based upon the perennial battle of the sexes; something in the mould of the old Cary Grant comedies but updated to account for the streetwise, sexual overtness of the 1980s. Above all, they sought a total departure from the typical sitcom or cut-to-the-chase formula fare that adorned the US television channels as they battled for ratings.

They wanted bristling, witty dialogue, sexy and sexist, between the two stars which, according to Caron, would 'take them out of the social and political consciousness prevailing at the time.' In short, he wanted to revert to some old-fashioned male chauvinism and get out from under the subduing pressure of the conscious-raising feminist movement that rose up in the seventies and had such an impact on the output of the performing arts.

During the embryonic stages of this project, Caron screened hours of romantic comedy classics, like *Bringing up Baby* (Grant and Katharine Hepburn), *The Philadelphia Story* (Grant, Hepburn and James Stewart) and *His Girl Friday* (Grant and Rosalind Russell). The show they came up with was entitled *Moonlighting*, loosely hung around a private detective agency, although the plot hardly mattered.

The two stars and the hip, almost randy, banter to be assigned to them were the key figures in their scheme to storm the television ratings.

Caron had already cast his leading lady. She was, of course, Cybill Shepherd, the big and beautiful fast-talking blonde whose film career had blossomed from her involvement with two of the most enigmatic of Hollywood directors, Peter Bogdanovich and Martin Scorsese. But she had then taken a spectacular nose-dive.

Her on and offscreen relationship with her Svengali, Bog-danovich, brought her into the limelight in the early 1970s as the petulant teenage coquette, Jaycee Farrow, in *The Last Picture Show*. He also put his protégé in two movies for which she was somewhat out of her depth: *Daisy Miller*, co-starring with Bryan Brown in 1974 and *At Long Last Love*, a musical with Burt Reynolds a year later. In 1976, Scorsese temporarily revived her fortunes by starring her in his most famous movie to date, *Taxi Driver*, and made her the subject of Robert De Niro's cringe-making advances. But, after a couple more pictures which took her nowhere, her career came to an abrupt halt.

By 1980, Shepherd was reduced to a supporting role in a cheap sci-fi movie called *The Aliens Return* and, filled with despondency, she sought the advice of her friend Orson Welles who told her: 'Go home and reinvent yourself. Come back a new woman.' She did exactly that, retiring to Tennessee to seek regional stage and theatre work. The break worked well. She discovered a latent and quite natural flair for comedy. Three years and a broken marriage later, she went back to Hollywood with a spring in her step and a new determination to regain past glory. Unfortunately, big screen directors showed a distinct lack of interest in her return.

She found nothing of a challenging nature, until she was approached by Glenn Caron, seeking a leading lady for his planned new series. Shepherd was apprehensive. Moving into television at that point in her career had a certain finality about it from which she might never escape.

In Hollywood, television was a place to be coming from, not going to; movie stars did not, as a rule, appear on television until the silver screen no longer provided the work. Once the transfer is made, there is usually no going back. As Shepherd discovered on her return, however, Hollywood had become even more cut-throat for women actors. The rise and rise of male-dominated adventure movies, virtually the only arena left where men could be men, had made it worse. A mere handful of leading female stars clung to their status like grim death and the rest indulged in a highly competitive, and sometimes unseemly, catfight for lesser roles. She had lost her place in the scrum and, as she herself admitted, simply 'couldn't get arrested.'

When ABC offered her large amounts of money to switch to the small screen, Shepherd anguished for a second or two and then accepted. She was to play Maddie Hayes, the model turned sleuth, in the new show for which they had high hopes. She thought the script was fabulous and, for a slightly struggling single girl, the rest of the package was brilliant: she was the star and earning $50,000 an episode. If it ran and ran, as she was assured it would, they were talking in millions with all the spin-offs. It would, producer Glenn Caron promised, turn her into a bigger name than she had ever been.

Caron had begun, simultaneously, to scour the nation for his leading man and he had a clear picture in his mind of the type he was looking for: a modern male, young and sprightly with the curling lip irreverence of Jack Nicholson and the darker humour of Sean Connery's James Bond. In short, he wanted an actor who could restore some of the machismo which he believed had been knocked out of the current male heroes of television as the networks followed the trend towards non-sexist plots. He wanted to get back the kind of humour that the networks had banished: they were even worried about rerunning old movies that had 'offensive' scenes, like James Cagney smashing a grapefruit into Mae Clark's face in *The Public Enemy*.

The search had so far proved fruitless. Caron took his casting team out on the road. They visited ten cities, and saw around 3,000 possibles for the role of David Addison, Maddie Hayes's sidekick and verbal sparring partner. By then, his eyes were beginning to glaze over. He was nearing the end of his tether and ABC were demanding a decision.

Bruce Willis knew nothing of this when he dropped into the Los Angeles office of his new agents, Triad, for a chat with one of their executives, Jenny Delaney, who did know about the casting net for the new TV show. Caron had alerted just about every agency from east to west about his search. Delaney took one look at Willis and picked up the phone. 'Bruce was not expecting to be sent out to an audition,' Delaney confirms. 'He basically just wandered in off the street. I sent him out immediately to see Glenn Caron.'

Caron describes Willis's arrival at the ABC studio as 'rather shocking but pleasantly surprising.' He was late and had his hair closely cropped, almost shaven, with those bits that stood up like an angry cockatoo's feathers. He had a couple of earrings and was wearing battle fatigues and dirty sneakers. Above all, the New York strut was entirely evident. Willis was given a few sheets of script to prepare and sat reading them in a bar on Pico Boulevard, laughing his head off. Willis told himself: 'I can do this . . . I can do this.' He went back to the studio to join the line-up of actors that Caron was seeing that day. It was definitely going to be the last day of interviews and after that, it was decision time.

Willis was called to give his reading and he has told the story of that moment often enough: 'There is a certain etiquette that happens at auditions. You walk in and – especially if you want the job – you're very polite. I knew I could do this man's material, but partly because I didn't think I would get it, I just went in and said "Hi. I'm Bruce Willis. Let's do it." I recognised the off-beat character, a guy on edge, horsing around out there where the air's real thin. Then I just said "Adios" and walked out.'

No one stopped him and he half expected not to hear from them again. In fact, the casting team were quite happy to let him go. Not one of them considered Willis right for the role – except Glenn Caron himself, who said in words that could have been taken out of a Hollywood movie: 'That's the one . . . the guy who just left. There's something edgy about him. Scary. He's David Addison.'

His aides thought he was mad.

'What the fuck are you talking about,' they chorused. 'Him? No way.'

Caron persisted. 'When he opened his mouth, I sensed that here was exactly the kind of sarcastic, arrogant New York wise-guy that I always had in mind. For a moment, it didn't even matter if he could act – but of course, it did matter and, what's more, I knew I would have a helluva job getting him cast. He wasn't the kind of guy the network executives at that time would willingly hire. He just didn't look anything like a leading man. But to me, he had a personality that was something to behold.'

Willis was called for a second reading and then a third with Cybill Shepherd who eyed him from a distance and drawled: 'He's cu-u-u-te.'

She wandered over and introduced herself: 'Hi, I'm Cybill.'

For a moment, Willis's stutter returned – and then it was gone again as he confronted the tall, formidable figure before him who began chatting which put him at ease. He began flirting with her, because that's what the producers wanted and, anyhow, it helped relieve a nerve-wracking situation from his point of view. In any event, they had to have a certain 'chemistry' – as the PR people would insist on it for the next three years and their onscreen relationship really had to have its foundations in real life.

'I'm kind of embarrassed talking to you,' Willis told her, 'because you are so beautiful to look at it's hard for me to concentrate.'

'Don't worry about it,' said Shepherd. 'That's what this is all about, isn't it?'

The reading went well. Caron was convinced and told Willis he would get back to him as soon as possible. Others around him were less sure and a battle royal loomed as the young producer dug in his heels and said: 'I want Bruce Willis.'

The struggle he would face in trying to hire Willis was as fraught with trouble as he had predicted. As he explained, the ABC Network was heavily influenced by the hugely powerful producer Aaron Spelling, creator of a host of top-rated television shows. He had a reputation for casting traditional leading men, clean and classically handsome with chiselled features. Bruce Willis did not fit that mould at all and the network executives howled their protests.

They were laying out the biggest budget ever for a television series, and Caron was putting it at risk, they said, by wanting to cast an actor who was not only a complete unknown; but was also a hooligan. A stalemate was reached. Willis, meantime, went off to perform another new and prestigious task, having won a part in an episode of another new and virulent television series, *Miami Vice*. There he met DJ – Don Johnson – who was to become his early drinking pal in Hollywood and his lifelong friend; they would remain close through all the trials and tribulations that would, in the ensuing years, encompass them both.

Johnson himself was in the process of revitalising a fading career as he, too, moved to centre stage in the top-rated show that, like *Moonlighting*, heralded the post-feminist fight-back by, what would be termed by the pundits as, 'the soulful machismo of America's new New Man.'

Whether or not Willis would join him in that vanguard remained to be seen. At that moment, it looked doubtful. The *Miami Vice* shoot completed, Willis flew back to New York, unaware that Caron had given ABC an ultimatum – if he could not cast Willis for David Addison, he would pull out and take his script with him. In fact, a week or so later, Willis received a call from his agent, Gene Parseghian, who told him: 'It's over. You're out. The show's not going to be done.'

For about 24 hours, the prospect of returning to the bar at the Kamikaze loomed ever closer. Then, the next night, Glenn Caron himself telephoned Willis and apologised for the delay: 'Look, I think I have beat them. They're going to humour me. Get on the next plane to LA for a screen test. I think you'll get the part.' And he did.

A few concessions had to be made. Willis should work on his presentation; the Alcatraz look and the aggressive punk style should be calmed down. ABC wanted him smartened up – normal length hair, wear a suit, shiny shoes. They wanted style and panache that was akin, sure enough, to Connery's Bond, complete with tuxedo and red carnation in the buttonhole when the occasion demanded it. Women wouldn't go for a guy in dirty denims and three days stubble on his chin. Caron had accepted these pre-conditions because he did not think it would affect the Willis bravado coming through.

Willis himself, of course, said 'Yeah, yeah . . . where do I sign' to everything, including a five-year contract and more money than he had ever dreamed of possessing, which was actually about a fifth of what Cybill was receiving. And finally, Caron now had all the ingredients for the show that had taken two years or more to put together.

It was to be an original, a trendsetter, with a script that was razor-sharp and full of combustible humour, more like a stand-up talk show than a crime series. The plots were almost incidental to the rapid-pace dialogue, dripping with sexual innuendo, between Maddie Hayes and David Addison, each completely ignoring the other's point of view.

It would set the pace in US television for the rest of the decade and create a cult following that remains internationally strong a decade or more later, when barely a month passes without an episode of *Moonlighting* being shown on television somewhere in the world. ABC executives had no idea that Caron was creating the kind of television monster hit that every one of them prayed for in that ultra-competitive ratrace ruled by the ratings and the advertising-space bookers. Few appreciated or foresaw the impact it would have on their balance sheet.

In that autumn of 1984, Caron and his team were working on a pile of scripts that would see them through the first season. Willis moved to Los Angeles. His feet never touched the floor. He went straight into rehearsals with Shepherd for the 90-minute pilot show, scheduled for its first airing in March 1985, to be followed immediately by five one-hour shows.

They began by analysing the two characters, as actors and directors do. The whole show revolved around a basic premise, the 'sexual chemistry' between them. Cybill's character was worked out: a strong-willed, petulant woman, used to getting her own way, nervous of a deep relationship and whose confident facade hides a deeply insecure and emotional woman. She is drawn to David, but then continually rejects him. It was not a million miles away from Shepherd herself.

Willis's job description, as perceived by Caron (perhaps unsurprisingly), also had more of a passing resemblance to the actor. From the distance of time, it is interesting to look back on the way Willis himself outlined his perception of the character, and it becomes clear why Caron chose him:

'I saw him as a kind of modern Peter Pan. There was a party

going on in his head and behind his eyes all the time. He had a code that was sometimes mystical, sometimes devious. He hides behind his humour and uses it as a weapon and a shield. And ultimately, he never wants to grow up. The innate part of me that is him is that fun-loving, chance-taking, risk-taking guy who in the face of insurmountable odds or adversity, laughs and finds a way out of it. He was beyond cool . . . in other words, he doesn't give a shit whether people think he's cool or not. That lack of caring is the ultimate cool. Just be yourself.'

The characters were mapped out and the 'chemistry', a polite way of describing raw sexual attraction around which the show had been hung, had begun to gel from the moment Willis and Shepherd met. Curiously, however, they had different views about it. He, being the man that he was and a past master at the famous lies that men tell women in certain situations, reckoned the chemistry was totally faked: 'You betcha,' he told *Playboy* interviewer Lawrence Grobel in 1988. 'Its something that's created out of two personalities, two fictional characters. But I'm not David Addison.'

Cybill had a completely opposing view. Around the same time, she was telling *Newsweek* that the chemistry between them, Bruce and Cybill that is, was potent. 'People misunderstand the chemistry thing,' she said. 'The chemistry's not between your screen characters. It's between two real people, Bruce and Cybill, and can't be faked or acted. That was there, it existed from the start. What we didn't have at the beginning was friendship and trust and that was important. There were a number of shows on television where the actors hated each other's guts, and there's no way of stopping that coming across. The chemistry was there, there's no question about that. But it didn't mean it was the start of a big relationship. No way. I went to a therapist to make sure that kind of guy wouldn't be in my personal life again. I'd had it with enigma.'

So he was faking and she wasn't. Anyhow, it was all grist to the mill, part of the hype. In the beginning, when they first came together for the real thing, the speaking of lines and acting their roles, the offscreen 'chemistry' that was supposed to fire the show never stood a chance. It was hard work. The scripts that Caron and his writing team had produced were daunting enough for any actor. Though packed with other characters, they were on screen virtually the whole time. Rehearsals were hot, temperamental and long. They were called to the set at 6 a.m. and did not leave until late at night.

Often, their lines were being rewritten as they went along – to fit the improvisation – and it took a while to fall into place. Other emotions also came into play. Willis and Shepherd were strangers when they met, as Kirk Douglas would say, and, between them, they had to build the fiery flirtation that would be extended from one episode to the next, taking the viewers to the very edge of some hot passion that never quite materialised until well into the series.

The whole, underpinned by the banter, would eventually translate to worldwide audiences as the longest act of foreplay ever filmed, and in the end have them on the edges of their seats, asking when are Maddie and David going to get into bed. That eventuality was a long way off, but carefully contemplated and plotted by the writers.

It was easier written than acted. Both were nervous. It was almost five years since Shepherd herself had appeared in front of any camera other than the screen tests she had taken and failed. She had been told from the outset that she was the star and Willis was her feed. Like all stars, and especially in the hothouse environment that existed for women in Hollywood, she jealously guarded the status as she battled with a script that was distinctly chauvinistic and in which her position was challenged by Willis who had been set up as a kind of post-feminist hero in a role that had echoes of Cagney, Bogart and Wayne. Shepherd, fighting on two fronts, was spitting her lines with fire, and determined not to let her costar get the better of the action.

Willis found her powerful and intimidating. He had never in his life faced this type of work pressure – or this kind of woman. She was stunningly attractive which, as he admitted, was a distraction to him and at the beginning he was certainly the lesser of the two personalities as Caron's crackling dialogue began to explode from their mouths.

The star of the New York bars may have been the master of quick-fire repartee on his own territory, serving drinks to half-plastered customers but here, in the controlled yet frantic air of a film studio – lights, camera, action – it was a totally fresh experience for which he was ill-prepared by his eight years of modest roles in the nether regions of Broadway. Impromptu humour is one thing but speaking written lines and achieving the same effect, as every comedy actor knows well, does not always have the desired results.

Willis found it hard going and pretty well followed directions. Mr Supercool, he of the natural smirk and expressive eyes, took some time to adapt and produce those mannerisms to order, although he wasn't alone in that regard. They were all on edge, racketing around with a new show on which so much rested. It was so new, so off-the-wall that it could go either way: a smash or a flop, pulled at the end of the first season, or sooner, if the ratings did not score well.

It arrived at the point of screening as something of a dark horse, a surprise entry into the spring schedules for 1985. The reviewers, given the customary previews and opinions, were not whole-heartedly supportive, although most welcomed its freshness and complete diversion from the traditional fare. The pilot went on air in the first week of March, the scene setter for all that was to follow. Its plot line had Cybill as the wealthy former model, Maddie Hayes, who discovers one morning that her business manager has stolen all the money she had in the bank.

All she has left is her BMW, her house and the money-losing companies which were maintained as tax write-offs – one of which is the detective agency run by David Addison. The trouble is that it has no clients and no income. Maddie meets to inform him that the company is to be shut down but he persuades her to keep it open by convincing her that the detective agency can make money. To prove it, he draws Maddie into the investigation of a murder case involving $4 million worth of smuggled diamonds.

And so on.

They had a party after the first television airing. It looked good and they were all congratulating themselves. The reception had been encouraging and Willis's performance, so doubted by ABC executives, was good enough for Caron to retort, 'I told you so.' They still weren't convinced until the second, third and fourth episodes went out, and favourable reaction began to build.

Bruce Willis, the unknown from Carney's Point, was poised to become the classic overnight star, an international celebrity. Unlike the movies, where there is a slow build to reach that status and an even slower one to confirm it with many months passing between films, Willis was able to enhance his profile week by week and was on the brink of elevation to front-page recognition. As with the role itself, he was ill prepared for that too, although he had received some early caution on the effects. The day after the pilot was aired, he bumped into one of his new Hollywood friends, Paul Michael Glaser, who had been part of that duo of actors who experienced similar fame in the 1970s with the equally innovative *Starsky and Hutch* cop series.

Glaser grasped Willis by the shoulders, looked into his face and said sternly: 'Enjoy your anonymity while it lasts, man, because in a finite number of days it will be gone and you will never get it back. The paparazzi will be camping on your doorstep and every move you make will be scrutinised.'

Until that moment, Willis had no idea, no conception of the consequences or the pressures that were heading his way. He simply hadn't thought it through and, as with royalty, there was no training school for the suddenly famous. 'In my wildest dreams,' he admitted, 'I had never connected being a success in acting, by which I mean getting a regularly paid job, with public notoriety and loss of privacy. I hadn't looked that far ahead because, for one thing, it was tempting fate.'

4 'Booze, Brawls and Broads'

H E WAS BASKING in the afterglow. Everyone was predicting *Moonlighting* would become a sure-fire hit. Willis liked to trot out a statistic that summed up his discovery by television audiences and the media: so far in his life, his work in the theatre had been seen by less than 5,000 souls. It seemed to be a self-denigrating understatement, but probably not by much. By contrast, *Moonlighting* would, at its peak, be avidly watched and awaited by 180 million viewers around the world.

Although the arrival of the new show on the television screens was an incredible milestone, the launchpad of his career, it was not the instantaneous hit that Caron and ABC had hoped for. The pilot and the first five episodes, screened weekly in the spring of 1985, attracted ratings that were, in fact, a disappointment.

The doubters and the detractors among the television network community, of whom there were plenty still, were saying that *Moonlighting* and its dotty, machine-gun dialogue was destined for, at best, no more than a cult following. The slow-burn reaction, prodded furiously and anxiously by the ABC publicity department, began to take off when the first season's six shows were repeated in the summer of 1985, ending in the last week of August.

By then, production of the next sequence of nineteen shows was well advanced. The quick-fire production schedule had ensured that, through those early months of 1985, Shepherd and Willis were nailed down to a gruelling fifteen-hours-a-day routine in order to meet the air dates for the new 1985/86 season.

Production aide David Goldman recalls: 'I promise you, they did not know what hit them. The work was intense, the dialogue huge and the show as a whole was a tremendous taskmaster for all concerned. It was basically a two-character, one-hour show and there were so many words to learn for the principles that they had to do it in short takes, and even then they might come in the morning only to discover that changes had been made overnight.

'It wasn't easy to make that kind of dialogue seem spontaneous and offhand, which was its secret. In the beginning, Bruce was, quite frankly, like a fish out of water. Apart from a couple of bit parts and a television commercial, he'd simply had no experience of it; he had never been in a situation of prolonged work in front of cameras. He was fairly nervous when filming the first series, intimidated by the whole scenario and would get a lot of retakes, often of his own volition. I think also he is basically a shy person who tried to hide it with his over-the-top, hip humour. The network people were still worried about him and weren't convinced he could carry it off, but gradually, he began opening up.

'By the time they began filming the second season's shows, he was far more relaxed; like the character, he was growing as an actor. He was starting to stand up for his point of view instead of accepting all that was laid before him, as he had done to a degree in the first few shows. He was on a high, now you could see it. He was rolling. If anything, I think that worried Cybill simply because of his competitiveness and the demands that were being made on both of them, first by the producers and then by the public and the media. It wasn't just a case of onscreen fights. They were soon arguing among themselves, about the lines, the jokes, even their appearance: "Your hairstyle's old fashioned," Bruce once told Cybill. "Well at least I've got some," she screamed back. The only thing that brought them back together was the sheer weight of the filming routine itself. It was like an arranged marriage. They simply had to stay friends, and just do it. I don't think Bruce really had any concept of what it would be like, or how it would develop. And, of course, when the media – and especially the supermarket tabloids – began to get interested in him, he was totally deluged; absolutely knocked out of his socks. But let's remember also, it had it benefits, and how . . . he was on the brink of huge fortune and lots of good times. Whatever came with it, the bad things and the scandalous headlines, he more or less invited in.'

The summer repeats established *Moonlighting* as the show to watch and in the wake of that, ABC launched a huge publicity build-up for the new season which opened on 25 September 1985 with an episode entitled *Brother Can You Spare a Blonde*. *Moonlighting* just grew and grew. There were some brilliant episodes ahead along with some curious titles, such as *The Lady in the Iron Mask*, *The Dream Sequence Always Rings Twice*, *My Fair David*, *Somewhere Under the Rainbow*, *Atlas Belched*, *T'was the Episode Before Christmas*, *In God We Strongly Suspect*, *Every Daughter's Father is a Virgin* and *Witness for the Execution*. They began inviting in guest stars, often friends of Shepherd and Willis, like Orson Welles, John Goodman, Robert Weller, Tom O'Brien and Ray Charles.

Media interest progressed in three stages, and in part manipulated by the ABC publicists who were wringing all they could out of the Maddie/David and Cybill/Bruce situation. At first, they focused on the return of Cybill Shepherd, the former teenage teaser turned fiery New Woman. She willingly honoured her ABC publicity commitments with a number of magazine interviews.

She adored being the centre of attraction again, although there were one or two unwelcome aspects. The revival of press interest in her led writers to her past life and relationship with Peter Bogdanovich, who had lately been in the news over the tragic death of Shepherd's successor as his lover and star, Dorothy Stratten.

He had starred the former *Playboy* centrefold in his 1980 movie *They All Laughed* and they were locked in a passionate affair until Dorothy's estranged husband burst on to the scene, shot her dead and then turned the gun on himself. Cybill refused to connect with that for anyone, and concentrated her interviews on her new role, though the tabloids were not averse to recalling that, back in the seventies, when Bogdanovich split from his wife for her, she was branded 'home wrecker'.

Then, as the second series began to take off, the show itself became the focus – and the subject of some fairly hefty analytical pieces in newspapers and magazines, interpreting the reason for its success. What intrigued the writers and reviewers was that the show had no set form to it. It changed week by week through flighty, dreamlike scenes to out-and-out slapstick comedy. The dialogue broke completely with the routine of normal prime-time shows. It never took itself seriously. Although it was ostensibly a comedy-drama about a detective agency dealing in murders, robberies and other familiar elements of such series, Caron had set up plot lines that, as he described it, 'put the principle characters in emotional rather than physical jeopardy.'

They conducted their verbal wrestling matches, cracked insider jokes and introduced one of the show's most innovative features – breaking the 'fourth wall' – by talking directly to the audience with unconventional asides unconcernedly acknowledging that this was only television:

When she says, 'David, you're in my seat,' he replies, 'Please, Maddie, there are children watching.'

And when David attempts some physical contact, she chides, 'Be serious.' He replies, 'I only had my hand on your behind,' and she says, 'If you're not careful they'll move us to cable.'

Harry Walters, the *Newsweek* critic, described it as 'an intriguing reversal of the psychic direction of our cathode heroes.' A *New York Daily News* article concluded that there was nothing new in having two very different principle characters who engaged in sexual sparring because they were attracted to each other. 'What is new,' the piece continued, 'is that there is a certain political and social consciousness from Addison's side which is a necessary part of the whole social equation today.'

All serious stuff for a show aimed at providing 60 minutes of animated stand-up routines. One of the *Moonlighting* producers, Jay Daniel, reckoned the secret lay in its spontaneous, improvisational feel and he attributed that to Willis himself: 'I've been on TV shows where the actors come in, hit their marks, say their lines and ask what time's lunch. Willis, new to it, was still on the set late at night when everyone else is exhausted, still trying to attack a line he'd already done a dozen times, trying to find a new way. He worked at it so that it did sound spontaneous.'

Cybill had won the early rounds of attention-getting and a revitalisation of her career. The show itself had been dissected and analysed. Now, the focus turned towards Willis as his Addison character edged gradually to the foreground. His cocksure arrogance on screen soon had women literally swooning. The instant acclaim that only television can provide came rushing towards him, and as with most television stars – unlike in the movies – he became the character he was playing, to fans at least.

Just as Larry Hagman was forever JR and Raymond Burr could never be any other than Perry Mason, Willis's own identity was overwhelmed by his television role. Crowds formed wherever he went. Women, and men, shouted to him across the street and from cab windows. Bruce Willis no longer existed. The moment it struck him personally was when two oriental women tourists, screaming 'David, David' tried to run up a down-moving elevator just to get him to sign something.

Willis's alter ego quickly assumed the role of sex symbol. Never mind Don Johnson's hairy-chestedness in *Miami Vice* or that other leader among the new breed of unashamed lechers and chauvinists, Ted Dansen in *Cheers*, or the out-and-out machismo of George Peppard in *The A Team* – Willis climbed high and fast in the sexual attraction league. What was old was new again. Macho, in a funny ha-ha sort of way, was backlashing against the feminist era and the cocky sorts (and Willis in particular) were swaggering back into vogue on television – just as they were on the big screen, where Sylvester Stallone (*Rambo*), Harrison Ford (*Indiana Jones*) and Arnold Schwarzenegger (*The Terminator*) had left some guiding footprints.

Other things were happening, too. Bruce's silly sayings and expressions, soon to become known as Addisonisms, very quickly caught the imagination of the audiences. His catchphrase of 'Great Googlymoogly' swept the nation. *Moonlighting* parties became all the rage. Within a year of its launch, the show won a regular high spot in the top ten ratings, and was ABC's only entry.

That year, 1986, *Moonlighting* and its team received sixteen Emmy nominations, for writing, direction and acting. Cybill Shepherd went on to collect three Golden Globe Awards for best actress in a television comedy, four People's Choice Awards and was jointly named with Willis as 'Woman and Man of the Year in Broadcasting' by the Hollywood Radio and Television Society. Willis himself won an Emmy award for best actor in a television comedy in 1986. The effects on him personally were incredible, shocking to a degree.

The first effect, of course, was rewarding; the financial upgrading. When he was cast for *Moonlighting*, he was being paid a fraction of Cybill's weekly cheque. Step forward Arnold Rifkin, head of the Triad agency and today one of Hollywood's most powerful managers. He personally took over the management of Willis. 'Do you know,' he said, 'when that guy first came to us he didn't even possess a credit card? He was broke.'

Rifkin soon took care of that. He renegotiated Willis's contract to $50,000 a show, and later it went higher still, to $65,000. Film scripts were already being hurled at his door, and by mid-1986, after the end of the second series, he had firm offers on three projects.

Commercial companies were clamouring for his services too, and Rifkin, master of the big deal, selected only one and kept the fees high. It was a ground-breaking deal with Seagrams, the drinks people, and in the summer of 1986 Willis signed a two-year contract worth $5 million to promote Seagram's Golden Wine Cooler, an ironic choice considering the way Willis's personal life was shaping up.

The company's president, 31-year-old Edgar Bronfman, happened to be one of his most rapturous fans and selected him personally for a drink that was being directed to the heart of 1980s Yuppiedom. 'I could see that Bruce was more than just hip,' said Branfman. 'He could be irreverent, funny and charming. He could also be serious. He could do all those things in a way that was infinitely appealing: the glint in his eye, or the curling lip smile allowed him to get away with a lot.'

The commercials, like the show, took off and before long the bars and the liquor stores faced a hefty demand for what quickly became known as Bruce Juice.

Another approach that gave Willis great personal pleasure came from the head of Motown Records who, noticing that David Addison routinely broke into song and occasionally played the harmonica (as he did in Episode One, with his rendition of 'Blue Moon'), offered him a recording contract. During the summer of 1986, he began recording tracks for an album entitled *The Return of Bruno*, filled with bluesy numbers and soul standards such as 'Under the Boardwalk' and 'Secret Agent Man'.

He surrounded himself with top line musicians and employed original members of the Temptations for the harmonies. The album was poorly received by the critics and the music press, some dismissing him as a poseur with a pretty ordinary voice which, but for his fame, would never have made it on to that most famous of soul labels. But it did well, selling more than half a million copies, and threw up a hit single of the old Mauves Staples number, 'Respect Yourself'. An HBO television special and a number of one-night stand gigs followed. Soon, he was playing to audiences of 20–30,000 people.

Back at ABC headquarters, executives, now happily reviewing the ratings and the overseas sales, were ready to give Willis virtually anything he wanted. Chauffeur-driven limos, helicopters at his disposal and a huge trailer dressing room which he adorned with his favourite posters of the Three Stooges, a signed photograph of Frank Sinatra and a sticker which read: 'Protect wild-life – throw a party.'

The ABC publicity department had a section devoted entirely to *Moonlighting*. They had rushed out a mass of photographs of the stars and had the one-time punk now dressed up James Bond style, looking smart and wholesome, and leerily chauvinistic.

That was the appeal, and that was the way they sold him. Kelloggs could not have promoted him better. They more than hinted at offscreen repartee between Willis and Shepherd and then kept the action going by suggesting that they were fighting like an old married couple on set, knowing full well that a 'best of friends' story had nothing like the clout of one with a few broken chairs and the occasional smack across the mouth.

Willis was rapidly elevated to the number one spot as America's newest sex icon. As such, and as Paul Michael Glaser had predicted, the media and the tabloids bore down on him like an advancing division of storm troopers.

But Willis wasn't playing.

He had already been heavily front-paged with Cybill and the network people were tearing their hair out trying to get him to do interviews and chat shows. Cybill had obliged, so why not him? Intrusion of Privacy? It's all part of the game. You accept it, they said.

Willis did not. He turned them all down flat, even the supportive magazines like TV guides. He was, said one of his close friends of that era, concerned on two fronts. The quality journals and newspapers would want to delve into his past, as in *What makes Bruce Willis run?* His CV was a problem. It could be written on a single sheet of A4 with space to spare. Unlike most of his peers, he had no real formal training, no famous mentors or tutors, none of the usual New York credentials, like studying at the Actors Studio or with Stella Adler who had between them produced screen heroes like Brando, Dean, De Niro, Pacino, Newman, McQueen, Hoffman, Beatty and so on.

Even his modern pals, like Treat Williams and Sean Penn could muster some very decent acting history. Penn in particular, who was better known for his mid-eighties offscreen exploits and bar-room brawls than for the gallery of morally corrupt young men he had portrayed on screen, was an actor of some depth of experience and training.

On paper, Willis was not in the same league. He had virtually no track-record that might impress, apart from one Sam Shepherd play. His background was blue-collar and unremarkable, aside from a few wayward incidents. He didn't particularly want to talk about his upbringing or the fact that his parents split when he was sixteen. Although in one sense this lack of qualifications and experience made his story and rise to fame all the more remarkable, it was not the kind of thing an aspiring star of the silver screen – his ultimate ambition – would want to boast about; he simply had no rosy apples to set at the front of his stall.

The mass-selling magazines, on the other hand, would want to grab at this aspect: the classic tale of local boy made good and go on to open up his private life, his love life and his misdemeanours. He had already made a study of tabloid treatment of television and movie stars. He remembered how Richard Gere had been iconised after *American Gigolo* and *An Officer and a Gentleman* and had since been crucified as the most arrogant young man in Hollywood, a reputation, incidentally, which he lived up to for a while.

De Niro, who was also a media recluse, had been pursued over his apparent fascination for black female company. Another of Willis's pals, Don Johnson, now unconcernedly flaunting the good life and the array of stunning young things who populated his love life, had taken some nasty hits when he edged back into the television big time after his promising career of a few years ago crash-landed in a cloud of white powder and smoke from best Mexican grass. He faced a mass of headlines like 'Miami Vice Star's Drug-Haze Past' and 'How Don Johnson Seduced Underage Melanie' in huge black and yellow type – Melanie being Melanie

Griffith whom he first married when she was in her own wild youth.

Nothing had changed in that regard. Willis knew the history; he had read all about the Tabloid Lunch and the beginnings of modern-day obsession with star scandal. The old *Hollywood Confidential*, run by a pretty despicable blackmailer named Robert Harrison, started the trend back in the 1950s, running sensational stories about the stars. The most famous included: Errol Flynn and His Two Way Mirrors; The Best Pumper in Hollywood? M-M-M-Marilyn Monroe; Robert Wagner A Flat Tire in the Boudoir; Johnnie Ray: Is it True?

The magazine became the scourge of Hollywood for seven years before it was wound up following a collective law suit for $10 million libel by Errol Flynn, Robert Mitchum, Lizabeth Scott and heiress Doris Duke. Eighties tabloids, controlled by hugely more wealthy men and conglomerates, one of whom was also on the brink of buying up a large chunk of the movie industry, never ran scared of such possibilities. Willis realised that he would be a target, and made a conscious decision not to get involved. Whatever he said would be taken down and used in evidence against him. That was his view, and he supported it with a few choice quotes about modern popular journalism being venal and mean, and wasn't it Paul Newman who said: 'Candour? Fuck candour!'?

He could see no upside to sharing his inner thoughts with a reporter with a tape recorder. He became almost paranoid about it as the press became hungrier for his story. When a journalist clutching his tape recorder appeared on the *Moonlighting* set one day for a pre-arranged chat with Cybill, Willis spotted him and yelled, 'Get that fuckin' spy outta here. He's recording my rehearsal.' He wasn't, but Willis wouldn't go on until he had left.

In the first eighteen months of *Moonlighting*, he gave only three major interviews outside of normal press conference situations, at which he barely spoke. The PR people were tearing their hair out. He finally agreed to the first interview in April 1986, a year after *Moonlighting* began. He opened up in a limited way for a magazine he knew he could trust, *Rolling Stone*. Later, he sat for Lawrence Grobel, veteran of dozens of celebrity interviews for *Playboy* in their searching Q and A sessions that were traditionally likened to spending a week in a psychiatrist's chair.

Playboy's reputation for the probing, analytical interview was, of course, famous. Its writers had performed the same data-extraction operation on countless stars, some of whom – like Jack Nicholson – later wondered how on earth they had been persuaded to be so candid and open. Above those two, and a few selected magazines whose writers he had checked out, Willis simply said, 'No thanks and goodbye', or words to that effect, to the dozens of requests he received.

He shunned television chat shows altogether. The PR people tried to persuade him, countering that he would only antagonise the more virulent strain of media if he refused to co-operate. He only needed to do the 'I was a teenage lecher and pot smoker and I come from a broken home but I'm a good boy now' routine a couple of times, and it would all go away. It would be an old story.

That might well have won him a smoother ride with an increasingly hostile media – except that he didn't want to do that; neither was he yet ready to adopt the image of a reformed pothead or whatever else he might be accused of having been on the way up. He had a deal more partying left in his young bones yet, and a little spending too, spreading bonhomie and goodwill among the hedonistic and spacey crowd he ran with.

Money, lots of it, more than he had ever imagined possible, was there to be spent. He acquired the familiar trappings of instant wealth and fame. He'd taken a large house in Nichols Canyon where he gave, according to one neighbour, 'defiantly noisy parties', sometimes with live music and at which he also played and sang. It was his first sortie into the era of carefree, rich young bachelor. In the garage he'd parked a snarling '66 Corvette Convertible, the car that every young American dreamed of owning. Later, he added a '48 Buick Roadster, a '62 Chevy Impala, a Mercedes for restoring and, predictably, a couple of husky Harley Davidsons on which he roared around with the wind blowing through the declining strands on his pate.

Skiing became a passion, and at weekends he was off to Aspen. Night times, he was hitting the clubs and bars, often ending the evening doing not very good stand-up routines in the comedy clubs with his limited range of Colonel Gadaffi jokes. By his own admission, he was also 'like everyone else, a multi-substance abuser.' As the tabloid spies began to follow him around, the headlines became a succession of exaggerated exposés on his life and wild times: 'BRUCE'S THREE Bs – BOOZE, BRAWLS AND BROADS' blared one famous account quoting a well-known Hollywood veteran as saying, 'This guy believes his own press releases. He's so big-headed, we'll all have to get larger television sets. He'll ruin himself in a year if he doesn't die first.'

Further 'evidence' was acquired from a string of girls and women who claimed to have joined Willis in his wild parties. If sexual harassment suits had been as popular then as they are in the 1990s, he would – according to their testimonies – have collected dozens of writs. His policy of non-co-operation with journalists, an expletive barrage and the occasional physical response to that posse of paparazzi that now followed his every move, ensured that Willis received a worse press than any other single member of the Hollywood power group in recent times – equalled only, perhaps, by another of his good friends, Sean Penn.

The media knock-about was over the top and much of it the product of modern 'creative' tabloidese. But it wasn't all lies and invention; far from it. There were wall-to-wall women and a running party-time theme to his life which led to a painful split with the one person whose presence he had so far managed to keep out of sight – Sheri Rivera. She had been at his side, encouraging and advising, as he made his entry into the television super league.

By the end of 1986, Rivera was history. She walked out of his life and, like Willis, refused to talk about their 'tempestuous' relationship. The pressures of Willis's fame on her were very evident to his friends. Sheri was caught up in the side-effects and saw him zooming away, almost out of control. However much he hated the popular media for its persistence in tracking him down at the most inconvenient moments of his off-duty hours, he continued to provide a very ample and active contribution toward the stories of his waywardness for which, incidentally, there were also plenty of apologists among his friends.

One of them who knew Willis in his early days, speaking anonymously for this work, recalled: 'I think what his friends knew about Bruce at the time – and the media didn't – was that he'd never really changed. He was, and is, a pretty genuine guy at heart. The fact that he walked down the street as if he owned it was the way he'd always been. Bruce has always had a wild side. Overly cheerful, you might say, compensating for the troubles and disappointments.

'He did all that was going in New York and the only restricting factor at the time was the same as we all faced – poverty. But it was the old story, repeated in this town a thousand times. When he got to Hollywood, it all changed. He was still the same guy, but the opportunities that confronted him were amazing and confusing; in that first wave of success, he went wild. Within days, they were throwing money and everything at him by the bucketful. Within months, he was getting it by the wagon load. He was also working at a terrific pace; the emotional and psychological strain was quite heavy. Everybody wanted a piece of him. Just everybody ... publicists, managers, film people, fans and especially the media, all tearing at him. It was something of a phenomenon, even for this mad, bad town. He couldn't handle it. I suppose the best analogy would be the old sixties scene, where the rock bands entered the hell of instant celebrity, got spaced out and started beating up their instruments and throwing television sets from their hotel room windows out of sheer frustration.

'After working a sixteen hour day, we'd be sitting in some bar somewhere at four in the morning, trawling the meaning of life. It sounds corny, but Bruce was actually saying, "Why me? Why have I suddenly been given all these things, all this money? Why was it that they pulled me out of the pack?" It puzzled and shocked him that he was receiving this kind of attention. Then he'd grab a cab and hurl off into the dawn saying, "Another day, twenty grand" – this from a guy who less then two years earlier was gladly picking up 20-cent tips. It sounds almost pathetic to say that, for a fleeting moment, you could actually feel sorry for the guy. That's a ridiculous thought, isn't it? Who could, really? He had choices now, and as Michael Douglas once said, power in Hollywood means having choices. But I could understand his confusion. As everyone knows, such a malady is not uncommon in this God-awful town. Ask Betty Ford.'

As the pressure became heavier and more hostile, Willis's agent, Arnold Rifkin, while slicing his cut from the take, actually offered his condolences: 'I tell you honestly,' he says, 'at one point I did actually apologise to him for contributing to his fame. He was so upset.' Oh dear!

Meanwhile, the studio publicists were staking their claim on the image of the unco-operative new star, pumping out the stories that helped promote the show and keep the golden eggs coming forth. By the third season, that was more important to ABC than it was to Willis himself. *Moonlighting* had become the network's biggest earner and, according to some close observers at the time, Shepherd and Willis were carrying the whole studio on their backs.

The network executives, however, seemed to want to distance themselves from their attention-grabbing series, and most certainly from its mercurial star. Willis, in one of his rare moments of going on public record, began to complain: 'I don't get it. ABC doesn't give a shit about this show. The president, Brandon Stoddard, has never come over to say hello – not once. They are moaning about the cost. Given a choice between quality and consistency, they would choose consistency, and that's not our way. They just don't understand.'

More and more articles filtered through of tensions on the set, of the behind the scenes battles between the two stars. Showbusiness writers and syndicated columnists were being fed the 'inside' story, often from the mouths of the network publicists who were devoid of new promotional ideas and faced the task of counteracting Willis's hostile press.

It made good copy to record that Maddie and David, i.e. Bruce and Cybill, were fighting, throwing things at each other and storming off the set. One report said Willis actually hit her, which they both subsequently denied. But there was trouble. Bruce had developed a habit of what one columnist described as Cybillbaiting, especially when she became pregnant in real life: 'His idea of fun is to joke non-stop about her looks, her age and her acting ability. When she put on weight, as she did, Bruce would say: "Widen the doors. Bring in a crane. Cybill's coming." He claimed she was a prima donna who thought she owned the show, and who hated it because he had become the star.'

Soon, there would be a follow up, tit-for-tat tale from Cybill, in which she described Willis as a pig. 'There are times when I hate and detest him. He's disgusting and sometimes I just want to hit him,' she fumed. It was the eighties equivalent of the nineties

Charles and Diana saga, though with tongues decidedly in cheeks. It turned into a weekly soap opera of its own, a sub-plot beyond what was appearing on screen in *Moonlighting* itself, with the television magazines, the tabloids and the publicists merely using the dynamics of the show to find parallels in real life. In the process, Bruce and Cybill were portrayed as offscreen monsters with massive ego problems.

With the benefit of passing time and reflection, Cybill today concedes they were difficult times, simply because of the pressures of the show and its uniqueness. 'To use a well-worn phrase, tempers flared,' she said, 'but I don't think we ever actually came to blows. What it was really about was two creative people trying to get the best out of the material, trying to keep it fresh. The basic premise that we launched around could not go on forever. David Addison could not continue to rely on just being sexist. We had to find new dimensions all the time.'

As time went on, *Moonlighting* became notorious for its production delays, rescheduling and missed episodes, sometimes completing production of a show only hours before it was due to go out. Some never made it on time and repeats were slotted in their place. By the end of the third season, it was already showing signs of trouble and it faced yet another challenge and, as most *Moonlighting* fans will agree, perhaps the turning point from which it never really recovered.

Cybill Shepherd's personal life suddenly interjected into the series. On a personal level, she had sought a much quieter life away from the freneticism of the show. She had met and married Dr Bruce Oppenheimer and surprised her wedding guests by announcing she was expecting twins.

Hasty discussions among the producers and writers concluded that the only way to prevent the show from going off the air for a prolonged period was to write Cybill's pregnancy into the script, a decision which many, including Willis and Cybill herself, later regretted. The plot lines that followed, with Maddie disappearing, going home, being pregnant, announcing the baby wasn't David's and that she was in fact married, caused an aberration.

It took the show into a direction that it was unprepared for, and away from the concept of light-hearted banter and into the danger zones – for them – of socio-drama. Audiences protested. Letters

came in by the sack load; the phones never st...
millions of viewers wanted to see, ultimately, w...
David happily married with children; now that poss...
dream for women viewers, was about to be demolished.

The show went off the air for three months while Cybill had he...
twins. Meantime, there was a lot of catch-up writing to be done
to get the show back on track. Coincidentally, it came at a time
when Willis himself had reached a certain crossroads. He was
already becoming bored with television, and found the effort of
maintaining the ever-smiling, gag-littered dialogue an increasing
strain. Arnold Rifkin was already touting for other work, in
mainstream Hollywood – the movies, the big time.

H__ ___ _IN! The upheaval caused by Cybill's pregnancy ___ __e fourteen weeks that *Moonlighting* was off the air to _ccommodate it gave Willis and his managers the opening they needed to get him greater exposure. He just had time to fit in a movie and out of several on offer from directors anxious to cash in on his television fame was one being launched by the renowned and multi-credited Blake Edwards, best known as creator of the Peter Sellers' *Pink Panther* movies.

'I saw in this television actor,' said Edwards, 'a humour that was in some ways similar to Peter Sellers' in its naturalness, straight out comedy, although Peter had huge depth, of course, that few could match. Willis was totally new to film but the success of *Moonlighting* was sufficient to hold my interest and I liked what I saw. I told Julie, this guy has a future.'

Edwards, married to Julie Andrews and with a list of films as a writer, producer or director dating back to 1947, had worked with dozens of Hollywood's major stars of modern times, and gave many of them their first international success, including Dudley Moore in his huge 1979 hit, *10*, with Bo Derek. Although it must be said that Edwards was reaching the end of a prodigious and prolific career, his selection of Willis was a prestigious first for the actor himself, and Arnold Rifkin was certain it could launch his now famous client towards the silver screen.

Edwards had written a comedy script based upon the vagaries of drink. It was familiar territory for him: one of his finest films was the brilliant shocker on alcoholism, *Days of Wine and Roses* starring Jack Lemmon and Lee Remmick. Another, less well received, was *The Party*, a 1967 glossy comedy starring Peter Sellers as an accident-prone Indian actor accidentally invited to a swish Hollywood party and who then proceeds to wreck it.

His current project, *Blind Date*, was about the same kinds of social embarrassment. Grapevine gossip claimed that Edwards saw Willis as filling the gaping hole in his stable that had existed since the death of Sellers in 1980 – he could go on to build a succession of modern comedies around him. He had initially cast Madonna in the female lead, thus planning to bring about the meeting Willis had missed when he didn't get the role in *Desperately Seeking Susan*. However, she had to drop out at the last minute and was replaced by Kim Basinger.

The script of *Blind Date* was even aligned to *Moonlighting*, inasmuch as it centred on the banter and the adventures of the two principle characters, played by Willis and Basinger – his blind date in every sense of the word. One glass of champagne and she's running wild. It was a relatively low-budget production compared with some of Edwards' past offerings, but for Willis it was one more milestone, his first $1 million, a one-off pay cheque and the bridge to cross over into the real Hollywood.

The other distinct advantage was being cast with one of the most appealing and, at the risk of sounding sexist, decorative actresses of the moment. Kim Basinger's uninhibited style had attracted a large male following. In those silly magazine or television vox pops, she scored ten out of ten when young men were asked the question, 'Who would you most like to date?' Such was the unfortunate triviality that, even in the 1980s, ran as a ridiculous parallel to the careers of movie people.

Coincidentally, she had given perhaps her most convincing performance to date in an otherwise dreary 1985 movie version of Sam Shepard's *Fool For Love*, which had begun Willis's road to fame back in New York. Since then, she had been dragged screaming through alligator infested swamps by Richard Gere in *No Mercy*, but made her name and mild notoriety for stripping for Mickey Rourke in Adrian Lyne's soft-porn bore *Nine and a Half Weeks*.

The problem with *Blind Date* was that it was based upon one long joke, about a girl, Basinger, who has the misfortune to go berserk after a couple of drinks. The plot must be familiar to all, since it has become one of the most oft-repeated movies on television, where it was perhaps best suited. Willis, trying his hardest NOT to be David Addison plays Walter Davis, a nerdish character who needs a date to take to the company dinner given in honour of visiting Japanese businessmen.

His brother fixes him up with Nadia Gates (Basinger) but warns: 'Don't let her touch alcohol. She goes crazy if she drinks.' Around that line, Edwards strings his comedy of errors. In their ensuing adventures, Nadia gets Walter fired, beaten up, chased, shot at, arrested and through the adversity shines a romance. There were some inspired moments of comedy in this movie, as funny and laughter-inspiring as anything Edwards had done. But in the main, the set-piece gags did not allow the actors, perhaps deliberately so, a great deal of scope for developing their character.

Basinger, acclaimed until then for her looks, suffered the indignity of drunkenness, never a particularly attractive scenario for women, even in a comedy. Seemingly not wishing to drag her down to the deepest depths of a woman stoned, Edwards kept a tight control and, though at times hilarious, Basinger was never quite able to convince us of her unpredictability.

The laughs came from the slapstick set pieces rather than the characters and if there was a lesson in this for Willis, it was to show how difficult it is to make comedy work successfully, and that any part of it that doesn't can pull the rest of the movie down. In a way, it also confirmed that while *Moonlighting* had been an excellent showcase for his talents, they did not necessarily transfer to the big screen with the same electrifying effect. The movie reviewers had clearly been expecting that, and better.

They doled out some sniffy notices, and occasional outright panning. The reception did not augur well for Willis personally because it was being said that he was one more television star who would have difficulty making it in the more competitive world of the movies. Commercially, it did better than the notices implied. With Willis and Basinger on screen for virtually the whole movie, *Blind Date* transcended its critics and quickly established itself at the box office. It took $87 million gross, and with considerable overseas interest, video sales and eventually television, turned in a very healthy profit.

Willis himself recognised some of the shortcomings of the film. 'When I was offered the part,' he recalled for Lawrence Grobel, 'I felt I'd finally arrived, starring in a major film. And a first film. I was very happy with it, even if it was a one-joke movie about a blind date. I thought the first hour was good, then it became strained. My role was one of a reactor, not a motivator. I'm better at driving a scene than I am a reactor.'

The truth of it was that it was no great shakes of a movie, and a pretty ordinary show by Willis's standards, as seen on TV. But on the strength of it, Blake Edwards immediately offered him another movie, *Sunset*, co-starring James Garner, which would go into production as soon as he was free. He was also sought out by one of the acknowledged masters of movies, Stanley Kubrick, to star in his new Vietnam war film, *Full Metal Jacket*. Willis was 'crushed' when he had to turn it down. Kubrick's production schedule clashed with the start of filming another six episodes of *Moonlighting*, to which he owed contractual allegiance.

All in all, 1987 was developing with incredible pace and amazing new possibilities for Willis. Mainstream directors were looking at his work. Money was pouring in from all angles – *Moonlighting*, the Seagrams commercial, his Motown album contract, the two Blake Edwards movies and the hint of another big project in the offing, unknown then, but later confirmed as *Die Hard*.

It was exactly at that point, much to the chagrin of his new sponsors, not to mention his managers, that he almost blew it with one more potentially damaging intervention from his now well-documented offscreen activities that gave the tabloids a veritable feast.

It was Memorial Day, and the scene was his house in Nichols Canyon, a quiet residential district of the Hollywood hills off Mulholland Drive, not far from the compound which contained the mansions of Jack Nicholson and Marlon Brando. It was the first property he had ever owned and was surrounded by neighbours of a certain standing and prosperity. With Sheri Rivera gone from his life, he was in the middle of what he described as 'my swinging bachelor days.' He had searched for a place where he could party and play loud music and the Nichols Canyon house, set in six acres of grounds, complete with large pool, seemed to fit the bill.

He used to fantasise about the conversation he might have with his neighbours:

'Oh, hi Mr Willis. Nice to see you. By the way, what are those structures at the bottom of your canyon. Guesthouses?'

'No, they ain't guesthouses . . .'

'What are they?'

'They're SPEAKERS.'

His work schedule did not permit him too many parties to begin with, and his neighbours welcomed the new young celebrity to their midst. 'When he first moved in towards the end of 1986,' said Sam Loch who lived across the road, 'we didn't even know he was there. He wasn't noisy, there were no scenes; normality itself. A nice, regular guy, we all thought.'

Within a couple of months, however, the same neighbours were complaining about the noisy parties. The first couple of times, Willis obliged and turned down the stereo. But not for long; the noise pollution soon reached the highest levels his expensive electronics could blast out.

On 25 May 1987, a memorable Memorial Day party he threw for Sean Penn was in progress and the soul sounds could be heard streets away. His crowd were mostly outside, swimming and dancing around the pool. Around ten o'clock, one of the neighbours summoned the local constabulary and within minutes a couple of officers in an LAPD black and white drew up on Willis's front drive.

They got no response from the front door, so they went around the back and into his garden, and then on into the house through the glass doors. Willis and the others were by the pool and hadn't heard the bell.

According to Police Lieutenant Neil Zachary who compiled a report on the incident for the Los Angeles Police Department, Willis came 'rushing at the officers, arms outstretched and yelling abusive language at them . . . demanding to know why they had walked into his house without being invited . . . he said he wouldn't talk to them until they got out of his house . . . and then attempted to push one of the officers out.'

Willis, according to the police report, was using randomly selected vocabulary to invite the officers to leave. What actually transpired was this:

The two officers were standing in his sitting room when he rushed in from the pool area.

'What the fuck are you doing in my house? Have you got a
search warrant?'

'Nossir . . . we're following up complaints about the noise.
Don't you have any consideration?'

'And you haven't got a search warrant?'

'Nossir.'

'THEN GET THE FUCK OUTTA HERE.'

'Why are you saying "fuck" so much?' the leading officer asked.

'What is this, courtesy class?' Willis responded. 'That's the way
I talk. I'm from New York.'

'I've arrested more important people than you,' the officer
replied, and in an aside to his assistant, used those immortal words
that came straight out of a cop movie: 'Read him his rights and
book him.'

At this point, Zachary reported, the two policemen 'subdued
him and handcuffed him after a brief struggle.' As they did so,
twisting his arms behind his back, Willis let out a mighty yell and
more curses. A few months earlier, he had fractured his collarbone
in a skiing accident. It was still tender and as the police physically
restrained him, he heard it go 'snick, snick' and the shoulder
seared with pain.

His friends gathered round and began to protest, shouting to the
police that Willis had a broken shoulder. He was dragged protesting outside, wearing only pants and shoes, yelling: 'You're going
to be out of a job tomorrow.' Other party guests surrounded the
officers.

By then, the LAPD had reacted with overwhelming enthusiasm,
despatching a manpower strength more akin to an armed hold up.
Half a dozen police cars had arrived bearing a dozen or more
officers and, a little later, a police helicopter flew over the house.
Willis and four others – including his younger brother Robert –
were arrested and ferried to the local police department, where he
was caged for two and a half hours and charged with assaulting
a police officer.

With his shoulder now in agonising pain, the police agreed to
allow him to go to the Queen of Angels Hospital for treatment,
which was perhaps fortuitous. When Willis was summoned to a
closed pre-trial hearing on 9 June, his lawyer, Jacob A. Bloom,
countered that the arresting officers had been over-zealous on their

arrival at the Willis house and had reinjured his damaged collarbone. One of the policemen, he said, appeared to have a particular dislike for celebrities.

He pointed out that Willis had been entirely co-operative since the incident and had tempered his home life so as not to upset the neighbours again. The hearing was behind closed doors and thus the detail went unreported. There was, however, speculation that the Willis lawyers had mentioned the possibility of a law suit over the injury sustained by their client which might well have had a damaging effect on his career. The hearing officer, Deputy LA City Attorney Robert Pingle listened to the evidence, deferred his decision for a week and subsequently announced that the police would not be pursuing their charges against Willis. The decision brought an angry response from the policemen who had attended the disturbance, claiming that the whole business had been covered up.

The headlines were not done yet, either. Willis moved out of the Nichols Canyon house the night of the bust and never went back. He had recently completed the purchase of a magnificent $3 million beach-front home in Malibu, next door but one to Larry Hagman and three away from Harvey Keitel. Within weeks of moving in, the police descended on his new abode after a young law student named Cameron Pagter, who was living in the locality, went missing. His body was found eleven days later, floating face down in the sea.

According to one witness, the dead man had been to a party at Willis's house just before he went missing. Others said he had simply been repairing one of the star's jet-ski craft. The star himself said he hardly knew him. But Willis's weighty presence in the media projection of the story was assured when one of the leading investigative officers in the case announced to an assembled posse of reporters that the body would be tested for drugs and that 'there are more versions to this than a *Moonlighting* script.' It was a God-given headline.

The eventual outcome declared that the boy had died accidentally, though this did not deter 'the mystery' being included in any story concerning Willis for months to come as the mass-market writers stuck on his heels, waiting for the Willis crash-and-burn story that they were certain was to come.

One other breaking-news story came out of the close attendance of the media on the Willis beach mansion, and it heralded a development that was ultimately to achieve a wholly settling effect on the life and times of the man currently in the spotlight. On one occasion, the front door had been opened by a certain young actress named Demi Moore which, of course, set the hounds sniffing around the private life of the *Moonlighting* star once again.

It was the beginning of one of Hollywood's longest running sagas of relationships under the microscope, set to run and run. Willis had met Demi just a month earlier at a screening of *Stakeout*, starring her former boyfriend Emilio Estevez, eldest son of Martin Sheen, brother of Charlie. Emilio's own relationship with the up and coming young actress had been the subject of much gossip and acres of media coverage for months. Her association with Estevez, who had adopted his father's Spanish name, had ensured Ms Moore's position in the spotlight at a time when she was a relatively unknown actress.

Demi was unimpressed by Willis at their first meeting, but he rapidly sought to rectify that situation. She apparently saw in him some of the troublesome traits that had haunted her own past and from which she had taken a timely and exacting recovery in order to save her own career from crashing, almost before it began. The fact that she had been there and come through it was to have a life-altering influence. Her arrival in his life came at a point when he was forced to concede a dramatic turnaround in his own attitudes and social behaviour.

Like him, Demi Moore, nee Guynes, had been taking chances since her early teens and had come through the pain barrier of alcohol and substance abuse. Born in November 1962, in Roswell, New Mexico, supposedly the daughter of Danny Guynes, a salesman of advertising space for a local newspaper, and a heavy-drinking mother, Virginia, she had a deprived and chaotic childhood. She reckoned that, on average, the family moved house every six months, from the time she was five until she went on her own at sixteen. Her education suffered because she 'never went to less than two schools in any one year.'

In the meantime, her parents divorced and remarried and, in the early 1970s, moved to Los Angeles, renting a small apartment in

West Hollywood. When she was thirteen, Danny, whom she has described as a self-destructive, gambling con artist, walked out, leaving Demi as the mainstay in her mother's unstable life. It was only then that she learned he was not her biological father anyway, but she was the product of one of her mother's earlier, and hushed-up, liaisons. She had found the Guynes's marriage certificate in a drawer; it showed they were married on 19 February 1962.

Some time later, she went to Texas to visit an aunt, and there discovered the truth. Her real father – 'this Charles character' – was dumped by her mother before she was born. When he heard of Demi's birth, he tried to make contact but Demi's mother refused to allow him back in her life. He had never even seen a photograph of her. When Demi went to the aunt's house, her real father visited her briefly. She described it as 'a bizarre experience' which was apparently never repeated. The discovery hit her badly. She saw her mother's cover-up as a 'tremendous betrayal', especially when she discovered that her entire family knew the truth.

Now, Danny, too, was gone and she hardly saw him again before he committed suicide just before her seventeenth birthday. Alone with Virginia in a seedy, low-rent apartment, the parent-daughter roles were reversed.

Her mother's own drinking problems overwhelmed her own emotional troubles. She attended Fairfax High School in West Los Angeles until she could take it no longer and dropped out, both from school and her mother's house. She was barely sixteen, a teenager on the very fringe of Beverly Hills, like a child looking through the window of a candy store, but Los Angeles was full of kids in her position – on the periphery of the phoney atmosphere of a city where the wealth and opulence enjoyed by a minute segment provided the inspiration for ambition.

She had no money, but managed to join the graduate crowd which was experiencing the throwback of Dr Timothy Leary's tune-in, turn-on and drop-out era. In the seventies, marijuana had become the dope of childhood – older kids got through school on amphetamimes, Quaaludes and liquor. It was in this atmosphere that her own ambitions began to take shape. She was drawn, through necessity, to the candy store window of Hollywood, first as a model, then trying for bit-parts.

At sixteen, she had spoken three words on television and sought greater exposure, literally, by agreeing to pose provocatively and in scant attire for a freelance photographer who got her on the cover of the titillating men's magazine *Oui*, plus a spread inside. It did not provide her with the big break she had hoped for and, like Willis himself at the time, she remained as anonymous as a thousand other young girls trying for the same lucky break.

She survived on small, irregular roles in daytime television soaps which she interspersed with casual work as a telephone debt-chaser, having the ability to make her husky voice sound menacing. She was already firmly in the wild-child arena when she met British-born rock musician Freddie Moore, then pushing 28, who played in a going-nowhere band called The Cats in the clubs and bars of Los Angeles. 'I wanted him,' Demi would say, 'and there was the added adrenalin rush from the fact that he was married.'

According to him, they moved in together after their second date. Freddie went home and told Lucy, his partner of ten years, he was leaving. Demi conveyed the same message to her boyfriend, Tom, who promptly threatened to beat up Freddie if he ever set eyes on him, not realising that it was she who had engineered the affair.

They married a year or so later, in February 1980, and, looking back with some bitterness on the eventual outcome, Freddie recalls: 'Before we were married, her friends would pull me to one side and say, "Listen, don't take this the wrong way, but get out. She's a user. She's desperate to get into showbiz, and you're her ticket." I didn't believe them at the time, although she was very insecure.'

The marriage lasted little more than three years and by then Demi had entered her wildest phase of parties, drink and drugs, running with the Hollywood crowd, edging perilously close to becoming a second generation alcoholic. She was also enjoying the early taste of fame, with a regular part in *General Hospital*, in which she appeared for three years from 1981, and a couple of small movie roles. Freddie Moore says: 'She started out on the fame trip when the producers of *General Hospital* wanted her to do talk shows and media promotion. They began flying her all over the place, and in the beginning I went too, since they were paying for first-class air tickets. She had tapped into the rich vein, and she didn't need me any longer. She was staying out later, four and five in the morning, and turned into a totally different personality.'

Beyond the drink and drugs, however, the potential was emerging, and spotted by astute Hollywood directors. Moore's distinctive voice and earthy style were attractive qualities.

Trevor Wallace, a British expatriate producer in Hollywood, remembers her arrival: 'She had the makings of a future actress of character, even then. She had an alluring quality that directors and casting agencies look for. The voice was incredibly sexy. She had the type of appeal that could translate to the younger male audiences who, not to put too finer point on it, judge their stars by bedroom imagery. But she was in a mess, emotionally and occasionally physically, and stuff like that gets around. At the time, she was carrying a good deal of baggage in that regard.'

She won her first leading role in a movie of little distinction, *No Small Affair*, in 1984 and in the same year was cast as Michael Caine's daughter, one of the lesser roles in *Blame It On Rio*, Stanley Donen's much hyped but ultimately witless comedy. Caine recalls: 'She was a beautiful, young and very skilled actress who impressed me so much that I can remember telling her that I thought she would be a star one day, and how right I was.' That particular movie did little to promote her cause. As Caine admits, it received a tremendous hammering and 'even I was stunned by the vehemence of the critics . . . but I'm glad to say the film went on to make a lot of money all over the world, despite the fuss.'

With her own finances now accummulating, Demi bought a house in Hollywood and provided rooms for her mother Virginia and her younger brother Morgan, then fifteen. She equipped herself with a motorcycle and leathers and became a familiar figure racing, James Dean style, up and down Sunset Boulevard. As her mother would later tell all who were willing to buy her story, both mother and daughter were drinking heavily and into the drugs scene. The partying and the wild times were peaking, for daughter at least, although her mother had several more drink-related sagas ahead.

Professionally, her biggest moment arrived when director Joel Schumacher began assembling the so-called Hollywood Brat Pack for his movie *St Elmo's Fire* whose cast included Rob Lowe and her future lover Emilio Estevez. She had not even been called for an audition when Schumacher saw her; his discovery of her has the qualities of the famous discovery stories of old Hollywood. Schumacher said: 'I was walking along the office corridor at Universal and saw this incredible looking girl coming towards me, like a young Arabian racehorse. I told my assistant to follow her, and find out if she was an actress. She was, and he got the name of her agent. She was wild and reckless, rode a motorcyle, I recall, without a helmet.'

Moore's agent arranged for her to go for a reading and on the strength of that, she won the showy role of a glamorous and rich but desperately unhappy member of the college graduate ensemble, a part for which Schumacher had interviewed more than 500 actresses. When she turned up for a wardrobe fitting, however, she almost blew it. She was staggering. Schumacher called her to his office and told her she looked a wreck and smelled like a brewery. If she didn't clean up her act, she would be fired; for one thing the insurance companies who covered all movies were these days particularly heavy about substance abusers on set. In fact, it was Schumacher who, convinced that she was exactly right for the role, saved her from being ousted there and then. He persuaded the producers to invite her to enter an all-expenses paid residential treatment programme during the period for rehearsals.

She agreed and, as Schumacher puts it, 'within 24 hours turned herself around . . . an extraordinarily mature step in a very fragile life.' With counselling, and her later attendance at meetings of Adult Children of Alcoholics, Moore came out of it with her head cleared, a young woman with positive goals which she proceeded to tick off in an almost clinical fashion. New York writer Leslie Bennetts, who first met Demi Moore soon after her appearance in *St Elmo's Fire*, said she reminded her of a female Gatsby.

She had decided who she wanted to be and proceeded to make herself into that person. At the time, Moore had just completed another movie, *About Last Night*, the slick and cleaned-up version of David Mamet's play *Sexual Perversity in Chicago*, again co-starring Rob Lowe. She was among the cast wheeled in for a series of press interviews. Bennetts recalled: 'Demi sat on the edge of her chair with her hands folded in her lap, hesitating over every word as if she was afraid of saying something wrong . . . her life was all about getting better, every day, in every way. Her determination to move forward was so relentless it is almost scary.'

After the chaos and confusion of her early adult life, Moore clearly sought security. 'I have to move on,' she told Bennetts. 'I don't want to be in a problem. I want to be in a solution. I don't want to wallow. Where did I stash the grief? I processed it, little by little. I realised I could either be trapped by what was going on around me or find a way out.'

As she struggled with her mental transformation, her physical looks altered too. She also seemed to have discovered the stability of a relationship with Emilio Estevez whom she had met on the set of *St Elmo's Fire*, although that in turn became a cause for anguish. They were together for almost three years and the association with the scion of a modern acting dynasty provided something of a safe haven in that volatile city during the crucial formative years of her career.

Because of its Hollywood 'royal' connections, it also attracted much attention among the gossip columnists, if only for its off–on quality which developed during the latter stages of the relationship. Her engagement to him became formal in the winter of 1986 when she blurted it out on a television chat show. Not long afterwards, Emilio was summoned to his father's home to deal with a pressing family problem of a delicate nature. Emilio faced a $2 million paternity suit, and Martin wanted to know if the child was his son's and if so, he should deal with it responsibly. Any Sheen grandchild could not be ignored. When Emilio returned, Moore ended their relationship although they remained friends, close friends. And that was the state of play when she and Bruce Willis were introduced at the screening of Emilio's new movie, in July 1987.

Her decidedly overblown reputation as a recovering wild child, in part leaked by publicists on the movies she had worked on, and her close attachment to the Sheen dynasty ran before her. She certainly wasn't a famous movie star yet but then, neither was Willis. He was 'captivated' by her beauty and intrigued by the off-hand manner in which she dealt with his flirtatious advances, something he was not used to handling. She, a woman of aspiration rather than substance, at that moment, was ready to reject the multi-headlined hellraiser who had but a few weeks ago emerged from the police cells following his rumbustious behaviour.

Willis was where she was at a few years earlier, though in terms of public attention, he was doing it through a megaphone. The word on the streets was still that he was just another television big-timer who would never make it on the silver screen. There was already talk of unease about his behaviour among the television community and Seagrams, the chief financers of his lifestyle. The latter's unhappiness surfaced soon after his arrest in May and the *Wall Street Journal*, in their stocks and shares columns, recorded that executives were discussing their embarrassment over the star's 'flamboyant life style.'

A Seagrams executive was reported as saying that they would seriously re-assess Willis's position when his $2 million a year contract came up for renewal early in 1988, in spite of the 'terrific boost' he had given to the sales of the wine cooler. It was true enough that magazine editors knew well that, with the exception of Princess Diana, there was nothing that would help promote sales more than a picture of Bruce Willis on the front, which was also good business for Seagrams. But it had turned sour, taken a wrong turn. As Willis himself moaned woefully: 'My life has been spread across the scandal sheets.'

Ironically though, by then, Demi Moore was moving firmly and resolutely into his life and during that summer of 1987, when Willis had so much going for him, yet was in danger of scuttling the raft of success, the first tenuous beginnings of what would soon be headlined as the romance of the decade took hold. Changes were already afoot.

6 Out of the Sunset

THE NEW FOURTEEN-WEEK SEASON of *Moonlighting* opened with Episode Forty in October 1987 to a positively unrapturous reception, in spite of a guest appearance by Ray Charles. The plots, written to account for Cybill's pregnancy, had taken the series in a curious direction and the story line of the previous season, which at last had brought viewers up to the point of David and Maddie's intimacy, was suddenly thrown into confusion.

In this batch of shows, Maddie, unsure about her relationship with David, goes off to her parents' home in Chicago. During the ensuing episodes, there is much toing and froing and an apparent mystery over Maddie's state of mind and health, until her father arrives at the Blue Moon Detective Agency and hints that David is the father of her unborn child.

While David tries to prepare for the birth, the earth-shattering blow is delivered to viewers around the world: Maddie is to marry another. Letters from confused viewers continued arriving by the truckload and ABC executives were anxiously watching the ratings as they began budgeting for the next season's series, to be screened in the autumn of 1988.

Later, in the final analysis of what went wrong with *Moonlighting*, the incorporation of Cybill's pregnancy into the plot lines would be regretted. 'It was done in haste,' Willis admitted, 'because they felt they *had* to do something. They *didn't* have to do it. They could have given her time off or shot around her. The characters had been screwed. People tuned in because they were titillating and interesting, to see what these two people said to each other each week. But then it became another story. When they chose to make Cybill's character pregnant, that was a big knife in the heart.'

Tensions were already evident among the cast and crew. Cybill Shepherd had complained bitterly to ABC executives about the way the show, and her role, was developing. Cybill had a heavy falling out with its creator, Glenn Gordon Caron. Behind-the-scenes politics brought the scrap to a head. ABC chose to support her point of view rather than his. 'They put him in an untenable position,' said Willis, 'and he had no alternative but to leave. I'm not going to say who was right or wrong, but suddenly they were talking about Glenn as if he had passed away. I was very angry about that.'

The show that had taken television by storm now seemed to be falling apart.

The hype surrounding the new series, as the PR people struggled to improve the ratings, put Willis back among the *Moonlighting* headlines, yet he made no secret of his own feelings towards the show that had provided him with the entree to Hollywood. In the few public utterances he had given on the subject, he had said he was getting bored with television; it held no future for him. He moaned that signing a five-year contract with ABC was 'worse than joining the army' and he couldn't wait to be free of it. He still had one more season to complete, for the winter of 1988/89, before his contract expired and he could not see himself signing for another series.

Willis was hanging out his sign; he was already heading up the yellow brick road, pursuing what he saw as his route to bigger things, though the future was by no means certain. Few stars so definitively identified with a particular television character have ever come back in that same medium in a new, high-profile role. Some, like Ted Dansen, John Goodman and Michael J. Fox, made a successful transfer to the big screen; equally, many others had fallen by the wayside or, like Henry Winkler and Ron Howard, had been forced to take another direction. Willis's agent, Arnold Rifkin, admitted he had to initiate some serious horse-trading to get him into the movie-star bracket – it didn't happen 'as if by magic' – and this became even more necessary after his second film, *Sunset*, shot in the late summer of 1987 for Blake Edwards.

Willis was still firmly categorised in Hollywood as a television star, as seen in *Moonlighting*, and many would have liked nothing better than to see him remain at that level. The one film he had completed so far had done little to improve that image, presenting him as an actor with a somewhat limited range. Edwards remained staunchly of the opinion that he could make the crossover, but was aware of the need for Willis to be extended professionally, well beyond what he had been able to show to date. He also appreciated his emotional difficulties over the constant barrage of publicity.

On that score, Edwards took him aside and tried some fatherly advice: 'The only thing that will get you through all of this is to find inner peace in yourself. You have got to find out who you are, who you want to be and stick with it.' So the new movie was also a test, and would be closely scrutinised by the critics. 'In *Blind Date*, he did pretty much the same as he did in *Moonlighting*,' said Edwards in a frank assessment. 'Now, he was playing a character with some depth, the brash and cocky Tom Mix, central to the plot lines in *Sunset*, and it was far more difficult because of the nature of the film. I felt that he was at a dangerous point. I loved his demons and his battles with them, but I felt he had to get past them and move his whole persona along. He didn't try to bullshit me, but I had no doubt that he needed to go into the gym, work out and learn his craft – be a better actor as well as a star.'

The screenplay for *Sunset*, like many of Edwards' enterprises of the past, was written by the director himself, based upon the novel by Rod Amateau. It sounded promising, a kind of film within a film, interweaving two legendary names of American history, Marshall Wyatt Earp and the silent movie star Tom Mix, into a murder thriller set in the Hollywood of the late 1920s. The director had also assembled an encouragingly attractive and diverse cast list, including James Garner, Mariel Hemingway, and his trade-mark addition of British actors who, in this case, were Patricia Hodge and Malcolm McDowell.

Willis had a fairly meaty role requiring more than just his stock in trade attributes. As Edwards said, he couldn't rely on the jokes and the leer. In fact, though many thought they were coming to see a comedy, it was not one as such. There were some funny lines and typical Edwards' set pieces, but the script was more akin to the genre of a 1950s detective thriller, with added cowboys. The other immediate problem for Willis was that the character he portrayed – Tom Mix – was still vivid in many memories as being one of America's great showbusiness heroes. Mix starred in over 400 low-budget westerns before his death in a car crash in 1940, although the Tom Mix Radio Show, started in 1933, continued until 1950.

The story for *Sunset* has Wyatt Earp, played by Garner, being hired as a technical adviser on a film about his life, starring Tom Mix in the title role. The two men become good pals and Mix takes Earp for a tour of Hollywood pleasure palaces. They end up at the Kit-Kat Club where one of the hostesses is found murdered. Encouraged by Mariel Hemingway, playing a male-suited, hair-slicked hostess, they set out to solve the crime. Mix falls foul of the underworld elements and is put in jail on a trumped-up rape charge by corrupt lawmen.

Interlude for real-life action, not a million miles from the story line of *Sunset*:

Willis has finished filming early, and takes the night off. He's still wearing his Tom Mix cowboy hat when he and some friends meet up in a Hollywood bar. The place is crowded, jumping, and nearby a large unknown man calls out: 'Hey. Faggot. You with the hat.'

Willis ignores him. He calls again: 'Hey, faggot,' and continues to jibe and sneer. Willis walks over: 'Do I know you?'

'No. Faggot.'

'Why are you doing this? Trying to impress the girls?' Willis turns to the girls surrounding the shouter: 'Are you impressed?'

They giggle. Willis is about to walk away when a fist comes flying past his right ear. One of his friends arrives to rescue him. The guy with the mouth goes down on the floor, and the fight starts around him, tables going over, glasses flying.

Headline: 'WILLIS IN BAR ROOM BRAWL.'

Back on the set, filming *Sunset*, he swears he never landed a punch. Blake Edwards, an understanding man who has seen it all before and struggled with the emotions, for example, of Peter Sellers, continues as normal.

Among the better qualities of the movie is that it is set in Hollywood in the 1920s, and Edwards had gone to great lengths to provide an accurate reconstruction, even down to McDowell's superb mime act at the first Academy Awards. But perhaps therein lay the problem to this film. It was populated with colourful

Hollywood characters, some 1920s-style fun and intriguing sets to match, bolstered here and there by some typically brilliant Edwards vignettes. Beneath that facade hung a gory sex crime and a collection of sordid characters who could have stepped right out of a moody film noir, a comedy thriller that didn't truly hit either mark.

James Garner, the charming old pro for who acting seems so effortless, made Willis look exactly what he was, the new kid on the block instead of the Hollywood veteran he was supposed to be portraying. Evidently, after an initial touch of nerves when Garner told him to 'slow down, take it steady', they got on well. There was an easy carmaraderie on the set and a relaxed atmosphere. Perhaps too much so.

When the film came out the following spring, it was widely panned by the critics and Willis was roundly attacked for what many saw as an uninspired, low-key performance. *Sunset* faded away ungracefully from his life and, for a time it seemed the sun was also setting on his movie career.

To add to his problems, Seagrams were on the verge of confirming their decision to end his lucrative contract 'by mutual agreement', and then he was badly stung by two polls, conducted among the readers and critics of national US magazines, which voted him worst singer, worst comedy actor, worst dramatic actor and worst dressed actor of 1987.

Where did Willis go from here?

The question was on the lips of everyone in the one-industry town which had followed his remarkable rise to fortune with typical back-biting jealousy; there were plenty waiting for the fall. But his momentous year of '87 was not over yet, not by a long way.

He had just completed some gigs with his band, including one before an audience of 22,000 who seemed well pleased with his performance, in spite of another diffident response from the reviewers. The prospect of a second-string career as a warbler, however, was an unlikely option. He wasn't that good.

The gap in his schedule, where he was detained only by his contracted episodes for the next series of *Moonlighting*, was exactly the window Arnold Rifkin needed to secure his client's future. He was tap dancing his way around some delicate negotiations with producer Joel Silver, then emerging as a key figure in the production of Hollywood's big budget, action-adventure movies.

Silver is the New Tycoon born out of the old ones, but with the rasping authority of Money Talking, new money, BIG money. His machine-gun vocabulary speaks MOVIES. He's an imposing man, fleshy, curly-haired and intermittently bearded. It's not the stature that gets his entourage running around like blue-arsed flies but the voice and the powerful, piercing eyes coming from behind the slightly tinted, black-framed spectacles. He wants everything done quickly, not NOW but three seconds before he thought of it. He takes an authoring role in his pictures, not in the writing sense, but in the whole construction of them from beginning to end. He hires yes men, takes risks with untried directors and keeps a foothold in every stage of the production.

He was one of the originators of the art of the spectacular which was well established in 1987. By then, producers were falling over themselves for scripts that would provide their audiences with the next white-knuckle ride in the current popularity of heavy-metal action movies filled with huge, exploding pyrotechnics and often overwhelming violence.

Joel Silver was already bidding for the title of The Most Powerful Man In Hollywood. He'd already chalked up the kind of successes that would earn him that prefix, given that success in Hollywood is based upon the bottom line. At that moment, he still hadn't made it, but in less than a decade hence the combined gross take of his films would be in excess of $2.5 billion – *that's* power. And, though he didn't quite appreciate it at the time, Bruce Willis was to make a substantial contribution to that take.

Silver's list of credits demonstrates that he was in the process of creating a long line of pedigree Nietzschean supermen who were to populate his particularly sturdy collection. Several of them earned a world-wide box office total of more than $100 million apiece: *Demolition Man* (Sylvester Stallone); *Lethal Weapon*, *Lethal Weapon 2* and *Lethal Weapon 3* (Mel Gibson); *Die Hard* and *Die Hard 2* (Willis); *Predator* (Arnold Schwarzenegger); *Commando* (Schwarzenegger) and *The Last Boy Scout* (Willis).

Fortuitously for Bruce Willis, Joel Silver hailed from New Jersey. He was raised in South Orange and studied cinematography at New York University where he produced his first film, a short entitled *Ten Pin Alley*. After completing his degree, he moved almost immediately to Los Angeles where his first job in the film industry was as an assistant to producer Lawrence Gordon, the movie and television producer who originated *Burke's Law* and a string of major television and big screen productions in the 1970s and early 80s.

Silver's first projects with Gordon involved the development, production and marketing of *The Driver*, with Ryan O'Neal, followed by the Burt Reynolds films *Hooper* and *The End*. His first independent production was *Commando*, with Arnold Schwarzenegger, and a year or so later, he produced another Arnie hit, *Predator*. Then came the beginning of the *Lethal Weapon* series in which Mel Gibson provided the other side of the heroic equation, playing a character who actually speaks meaningful dialogue instead of the more common monosyllabic one-liners of these adventures. Though no less violent, it had some very decent acting opportunities, such as when Gibson's slightly unhinged cop attempts to commit suicide.

In between the first and second of the *Lethal Weapon* films, Silver was working on what he believed would be the beginning of another series of movies – *Die Hard*. He had great hopes for it and, though it was planned as another big-impact production, he wanted to keep the adaptation of Roderick Thorp's novel *Nothing Lasts Forever* as close as possible to the original. He had already chosen his leading man – Richard Gere – to play the role of New York City Detective John McClane and the part was written in the screenplay with him specifically in mind.

Gere, whose own career was languishing to the point of near extinction, largely through his own decisions and choices, was in one of his deep soul-searching moods, discussing the meaning of life, and death, with the Dalai Lama in the foothills of the Himalayas. He did not want to play a big, gutsy action-adventure movie and declined Joel Silver's kind offer of $4 million. Another million was added to the offer price, but Gere still said, 'No thanks'. Silver received a similar knock-back from Clint Eastwood and so began casting his net, once again, for his lead actor; time was wasting away. Pre-production schedules were already well advanced. Filming had to start that autumn.

Arnold Rifkin, sitting behind his big desk in a palatial office off Rodeo Drive, in his impeccable pin-striped suit, hand made shirt, silk tie and gleaming black shoes, was monitoring this situation with his renowned eagle eyes. Very soon, the name of Bruce Willis was being whispered in Joel Silver's ear. It seemed an incredible, outlandish idea.

'Bruce Willis? The man's a comedian. Everybody knows that. And he's burning.'

'So he's arrogant,' Rifkin admitted. 'And yes, he thinks he's a star and acts like one. It offends some people, but that's what he walks with. That's Bruce Willis. Behind that, there is talent, a gift.' The agent-speak, from a man who was overseeing the careers of numerous and significant Hollywood inmates was, in this instance, genuinely meant.

They meet. Silver likes what he sees. The guy's a trier, and he could see something of himself in him. He's got no background but, as he keeps saying, 180 million people watched *Moonlighting*. He peers at Willis through his dark spectacles with a look that says: 'You wannabe a star? I'll make you a Star.'

The upshot was that Joel Silver and his director John McTiernan called him for a reading. They were impressed. So much so that Rifkin negotiated one massive fee that was to cause uproar, panic and amazement throughout Hollywood, not to mention considerable unease among the moneymen at 20th Century-Fox who were backing the picture.

Five million dollars.

The deal was personally approved by Rupert Murdoch, who had recently added Fox to his media empire in which, as is well known in Britain with his ownership of the *Sun* and *Times* newspapers, he was always prepared to back shooting stars and promising unknowns.

'$5 million?' cried mogul Alan Ladd junior, then chairman of MGM, in a famous outburst to the *New York Times* which had devoted a lengthy story to the announcement and its effects on star salaries. '$5 million? Who is this guy? This throws the whole business out of whack. Like everyone else in this town, I am stunned.' But then, so was Willis. That a relatively untried actor with so little on his CV could command such a figure was as much of a shock to himself as it was to his friends.

It was Brando money. Even Jack Nicholson, the master of that era, only received $5 million for *Witches of Eastwick* in the same year. Sean Connery, Dustin Hoffman and Matthew Broderick shared less than $10 million for *Family Business*. De Niro was struggling to make $2 million a picture. Even Stallone and Schwarzenegger were only hovering around the fee Willis would get from *Die Hard*. But Ladd was right. The leapfrogging fees syndrome took hold. Hollywood finances, at least in regard to the amount sliced off by the lead actor, would never be the same again.

Silver and McTiernan knew they were gambling. What they saw in Willis was basically what Glenn Caron had seen three years earlier, and what Rifkin pushed as his qualities: a fresh talent who had gained an international reputation through television as an antidote to the New Age male; unrepentant, unabashed and unashamed of his other baggage of being labelled a hot-headed, partying wild man.

Silver was happy with that, although there was some discussion, held with frowning intensity and a crumpled forehead over the heavy specatacles. A short lecture on the meaning of life followed. He wanted Willis's total commitment. He would have to go into the gym for a couple of months during rehearsal period for a crash course to bolster his biceps and pectorals. The partying had to stop. He would indulge in no dangerous activities for the duration of filming, no broken collarbones etc., etc. In short, he was to be on his best behaviour.

Thus, in October 1987, Bruce Willis signed the pledge. He went teetotal, took counselling and attended AA sessions at the Cedars Sinai Medical Centre in Los Angeles. He also had the support of Demi Moore who had her own experience to call on in that regard. Although the gossips would later claim he gave up the drink for her and that she had given him an ultimatum – 'either quit drinking or we're through' – it was never quite like that. Moore encouraged and helped him through it; she did not order it.

The impact of $5 million job security was the overriding factor. His whole future depended upon the success of *Die Hard*. If he blew it, he would be blown out of Hollywood. There was little doubt about that. He buckled down to a training routine which was designed with the help of Demi's fitness instructor, Jackson Sousa.

He needed to tighten up his loose, untoned body and turn it into a taut machine capable of the death-defying activity that lay ahead – although it was never intended that he should become muscle-bound like Stallone and Schwarzenegger, all body-oiled and flexing. The secret of *Die Hard*'s success was that its hero, John McClane, would be portrayed as just an ordinary guy, not some superhuman he-man, who battles on through in the face of adversity.

He began two months of intensive gym work designed, principally to broaden his chest and build-up his biceps. Sousa recommended working with barbells for an hour a day at his home, performing a routine of bicep curls, bench presses and lifts before going into the gym. His reckless diet was vastly revamped. Out went the junk food and chillydogs. Breakfast was, typically, a fibre cereal with fruit. Lunch was a high-energy meal of carbohydrates which included pasta, potatoes or rice with green salad. Dinner was made up of high-protein fish or meat with plenty of vegetables and fruit. Low sodium bottled mineral water was his only drink.

The master plan, to create the New Willis, had one more element to it that took everyone by surprise and would ensure that he remained in the eye of the media hurricane. He and Demi had gone public with their relationship in September when they turned up arm in arm and all lovey-dovey at the Emmy awards. The tabloids said that Moore was just the latest in a chorus line of women and it would never last: 'She'll never tame the bad boy of Hollywood.'

At the end of October, however, a string of Princess Diana style paparazzi pictures of them romping in the surf at Malibu, taken through a long-tom lens from about a quarter of a mile away, were published in a major magazine. They seemed to be heading towards a full-blown romance, the media now conceded, but no one was talking about a wedding.

On 21 November 1987, they surprised them all, including close friends and Demi's mother. They flew off to Las Vegas, ostensibly to see Julio Cesar Chavez win the light-heavyweight boxing crown from Edwin Rosario. That night, apparently on impulse, they registered with the Clark County Marriage Bureau in Las Vegas and, just before midnight, a woman justice of the peace arrived at their room at the Golden Nugget Hotel to marry them.

The news was not long escaping and the rat pack descended upon Las Vegas to inspect the records. There they discovered that Demi had declared herself to be a spinster, thus omitting to state that she had a previous marriage.

An anonymous telephone call from someone stirring up trouble, or a story, sent the police in to investigate the caller's hint of a 'bigamous' marriage, claiming that she was not officially divorced from Freddie Moore. It was totally false, although the tabloids had a field day with (shock-horror) the news that she had failed to mention her previous marriage. And they produced photocopies of her marriage certificate to prove it!

It was all a storm in the hothouse and it mattered not a jot, except to service the gossips and sate the appetites of the readers of scandal sheets who more or less disregarded Demi's explanation that she did not mention it because she did not have the documents to hand to prove that she was divorced – she feared it might delay the marriage.

Three weeks later, they celebrated that quiet Las Vegas ceremony with a spectacular bash more in keeping with their status as the new and fascinating focus of Hollywood matrimony. They hired a studio sound stage for a second wedding, specially chosen so that the media helicopters could not zoom in low and capture still and video pictures. They invited 450 guests. Demi wore a $10,000 wedding gown. Bruce bought her a $60,000 Mercedes as a wedding present. They wrote their marriage vows between them and spoke them clearly and precisely, declaring their undying love, each looking directly into the other's eyes . . .

'I do, I do.'

Willis wrote a song called 'Bruno's Getting Married' which a dozen of his best friends sang as the wedding party came up the aisle with their twelve ushers and twelve bridesmaids. Sixties rock star Little Richard, an ordained minister, conducted the service to the accompaniment by a 30-strong gospel choir. He doubled as a rock 'n' roller for the wedding breakfast that followed, and with a platoon of security guards providing a veritable ring of steel, the paparazzi could not get within a mile of the place.

There was one more mini-party, on the set of *Die Hard*, where Joel Silver had laid on a cake and cracked open a case of mineral water, and then it was back to work on The Big One. What lay before him was an onerous task, not quite appreciated even by the pundits. One of the reasons why Rifkin had been able to negotiate such a bulbous fee was that Willis was up there on the billboard alone – the sole star of a competent but generally little known cast list. The rest put together could barely command a fifth of his fee.

Even the villain, the superb and mysterious Alan Rickman, who was to become so regularly typecast by Hollywood and internationally recognised, was virtually unheard of outside the British theatre. A former graphic artist who did not come into acting until his 20s, Rickman performed with numerous British repertory companies before winning acclaim as the heartless seducer, Le Vicomte de Valmont, in the Royal Shakespeare Company's London and Broadway productions of *Les Liaisons Dangereuses*. It was there that he first came to the attention of the American casters, and Joel Silver and director John McTiernan were responsible for launching him on a villainous career in his first major movie role – the German terrorist in *Die Hard*.

Similarly, modern audiences might have a struggle to put a name to the face of Bonnie Bedelia who was cast to play Bruce Willis's estanged wife. A versatile leading lady, she had racked up a long list of credits on TV and Broadway as a juvenile and danced in four productions of the New York City Ballet. She had appeared in a string of movies in the 1970s (including *They Shoot Horses Don't They?* and *Lovers and Other Strangers*) but in the following decade her big screen appearances were scarce. Thus, the phrase in her biographical notes, that she enjoyed 'renewed attention' after her appearance in *Die Hard*, confirmed her status at the time; she was not selected for her pulling power.

Willis was pretty well on his own, the sole famous face among an inexpensive but brave cast. The one man upon whom similar reliance was placed by the producers – to drag the movie by the scruff of the neck into blockbuster territory – was in the backroom of the movie business: special effects wizard Richard Edlund. If there was another star of this show, it was Edlund himself. He was already a leading figure in the world of visual effects, having made his name on George Lucas's *Star Wars*, which *Time* magazine rightly described as 'a great work of popular art.'

Edlund founded the highly successful Industrial Light and Magic Company for George Lucas in 1975 and worked on *Star*

Wars, which became a historical phenomenon and one of the highest grossers of all time. Thereafter came a succession of massive spectaculars for which he received numerous awards and Oscar nominations, including *Battle Star Galactica*, *The China Syndrome*, *The Empire Strikes Back*, *Raiders of the Lost Ark*, *Return of the Jedi*, *Ghostbusters*, and so on. His role in *Die Hard* was vital, creating the explosive scenario that catapulted Willis, finally, into the big league of movie-making. The question was, though, could he stay there? It wasn't a racing certainty, as his enemies kept reminding him at every opportunity.

7 Moving On

JOEL SILVER ARRIVED bearing gold and gave new shape to Bruce Willis's future. This new beginning, the start of a big blockbuster series probably saved him from becoming the shooting star who had shot his bolt. He was already very rich and internationally famous, of course, but his public focus was kept alive, whether he liked it or not, by notoriety and the David Addison sex appeal, the headlines and publicity that came out of his private life, rather than acclaim for his work. Now, with Demi at his side, the pressure from that quarter doubled.

News item: on New Year's Eve 1987, the Willises turned up for a party at Spago's restaurant on Sunset Boulevard with seven bodyguards. The bodyguards and entourage became a running theme of their lives. The newshounds lapped it up. Anything that showed up the excesses and the self-importance of this pair of unpedigreed people made good copy. It was, though, a total distortion, says Willis. They had one man hired to protect Demi, the rest were people from the restaurant, helping them through the scrum of photographers crowded outside.

The battles with the paparazzi had become a daily occurrence. One night, a few weeks later, they were attending a screening at a Los Angeles theatre. It was for a showing of the remake of Roger Vadim's *And God Created Woman*, starring Rebecca de Mornay, a good friend of the Willises. He was late leaving work and they arranged to meet at the theatre; by then it was dusk. As they walked towards the place, they were surrounded, again, by the blinding flashing lights of photographers snapping the arriving celebrities. Demi was four months pregnant and beginning to show.

It was a picture they all wanted. Thirty or so photographers crowded round and hemmed them in as they made a dash for the theatre. Demi stumbled and fell. Willis lost his cool. For once, he was scared and felt helpless as the cameras clicked away at the sight of Demi stumbling.

'Get the fuck outta here. That's enough!' he yelled, pushing them aside, his face screwed up with rage, pointing his finger and yelling again, 'Leave us the fuck alone.'

That was the picture. The snappers were snapping again, five frames a second angled on his contorted, angry face. It was the one that made all the papers. And it was the photograph that came out, time and time again in the future, whenever he was in the media doghouse.

Stardom or notoriety? For the media, it didn't matter. With *Die Hard*, Willis had performed the showbusiness equivalent of winning the lottery or hitting the jackpot on a Las Vegas slot machine. When Alan Ladd jnr asked, 'Who is this guy?' it was a rhetorical question, not so much about Willis's present identity, more his past achievements. Ladd, and the film community at large, were angry that an actor with such a minuscule pedigree could command fees that not only matched but even exceeded those commanded by current big names like Hoffman, Connery, Stallone and the rest. He had totally eclipsed the earning power of literally dozens of fine actors, many of them household names.

In the long term, it could be argued, actors themselves would benefit by this inflationary trend but, as Ladd predicted, this new largesse would settle largely upon a coterie of big-leaguers whose agents began an unseemly scramble for ever-increasing fees.

Willis's response was simply this: 'I didn't hold a gun to their heads. They agreed to pay me that money. That was their choice. It's jealousy. And if it means that Michael Douglas gets a salary hike for his next picture, that's not my problem.' Nor was it. He just happened to be the flavour of the month at a particular time and was surrounded by handlers who could take advantage of it.

It was, as ever, all about box office number crunching and in this case there was no question that Silver had gambled heavily on Willis's pulling power, derived solely from his television fame, in a movie that had no stars, apart from Willis himself, but lots of action. *Die Hard*, in that respect, was like *Moonlighting* – itself a trend-setter that was copied and mirrored by a dozen action movies that came in its wake.

For a while, it more or less brought to an end the days of packaging a couple of major stars for a movie in order to give it better commercial appeal. From this point on, the one-star syndrome for the high-adventure films became the set form. *Die Hard* proved that one well-known face, heavily promoted and surrounded by explosive special effects and incredible death-defying stunts, could make a fortune.

From a personal standpoint, it also rescued Willis from what was a potentially precarious professional state. The stark reality of his situation has been hidden by later developments. He was on the edge of a real-life precipice. His career was going nowhere. But for Joel Silver's timely intervention, he could just as easily have begun the slide to oblivion that the back-biters were predicting might happen. *Moonlighting* had lost its shine and was dropping in the ratings, and the only two other movies he had appeared in, one of them as yet unseen, offered no great recommendation for his talents.

His closest friends say that, at some point, Willis would have come through it regardless, that he had the talent and the charisma that would, in time, have brought him to the top of the heap. Quietly, Willis admitted that *Die Hard* changed his life, provided him with security and a platform to launch his movie career which the two Blake Edwards movies would clearly not have done. Even before its release, the *Die Hard* sequel was being planned. The series would, in time, go on to become his life-support machine, his pension fund, his multi-million-dollar fall-back position as he tried, often unsuccessfully, to extend his range and scope in other directions.

The movie itself had considerable merit, not in the brilliant category, but eminently watchable. The plot, hatched in Roderick Thorp's novel, centred around a scenario that took it beyond the normal cops and criminals caper and the often far-fetched make-believe of many action adventures. It introduced some measure of interest-retaining undertones and sensible and believable characters who provided the director's acknowledgement that he did not entirely under-estimate the intelligence of his audience – sadly, a lacking feature of so many dumb movies.

Willis, as any of his fans and followers know, was playing New York City Detective John McClane, who ran into trouble while on a private Christmas visit to Los Angeles to visit his wife (Bonnie Bedelia). She had put their marriage in the freezer when she took off to California for a new job. As the festive holiday approached, she asked McClane, in a classic line, 'Why don't you come out to the coast and we'll have some fun?'

It was Willis as never seen before – tough but sensitive, unlovely, hair cropped; the first of his characterisations that did not rely on the standard image. McClane makes his surprise entrance to the office party, which is being held in honour of a party of visiting Japanese businessmen in the high-rise building of the Corporation, a multi-national company of which she is now vice president. Also paying a surprise visit is a crowd of murderous terrorists, led by a superior German named Hans Gruber (Alan Rickman), a bearded intellectual who considers himself a cut above his confederates. Gruber is leading the highly armed and skilful group in a clandestine attack, the object being to take possession of several million dollars in negotiable bonds – a precision-planned heist that unfortunately did not account for the untimely intervention of Detective McClane. Thereupon, the terrorists are forced to take the Nakatomi people hostage, leaving McClane to single-handedly hold the bridgehead, one man against a large, well-equipped gang. He keeps their attention through repeated attacks from his refuge on an upper floor of the building.

But he was not a Stallone-style Rambo. True, the audiences were able to see for themselves the results of his pre-filming workouts in the gym, a more muscular David Addison whose pecs were well displayed through a torn shirt. But this guy McClane was terrified, almost weeping with fear, vulnerable and afraid of what he, a fairly ordinary New York cop, had been thrust into. He was believable. In the typical fashion of American audiences, trained by television to participate, viewers were whooping and cheering.

And now the Richard Edlund special effects come into play as McClane begins his shoot outs. The marvellous stunts and dramatic exploding sequences, as when Willis drops explosives down a lift shaft or crashes through a plate glass window on the end of a rope, are non-stop as he plays his deadly cat and mouse game with Gruber.

It was in the spectacle of the action where the movie was particularly impressive but also noteworthy were the good performances by Willis himself and the excellent Alan Rickman, whose future in such devious roles would now be assured. It was only in the side issues, created as plot diversions, that the film fell away. With McClane in constant contact with an LA policeman on the ground, the interruptions to the action by an idiot police chief who questioned whether this man was a policeman at all, seemed unnecessary and intrusive; filler material.

The Fox marketing people seemed curiously apprehensive about the film as the final cut was delivered for in-house viewing. There was some derisive Hollywood mirth when they produced a pre-opening promotional poster that carried a picture of the building – and not Willis. It was scrapped a week later after the audience reaction to trial screenings had been analysed. The results gave Willis a mighty boost, and a new set of posters were rushed out, blasting his grimy face across the billboards.

Die Hard was given a warm reception by the critics as being one of the better movies of its genre, and the audiences loved it. It entered the blockbuster status almost from the first weekend of its showing, and went on to make everyone large amounts of money, ensuring that there would be a sequel or three.

Filming was completed at the beginning of January 1988, and virtually without a break, Willis returned to his more familiar area of the 20th Century Fox lot to complete his commitments for the current *Moonlighting* series and begin planning the next – and, as it turned out, the final – batch of sixteen shows which would be screened at the end of 1988 and early 1989. The scripts were evidently much improved and back on track, heralding the developments that would capture a better response from viewers in the coming season. Whether the show could ever regain its freshness became a matter of debate and doubt.

The writers were frantically attempting to recapture the original inspiration. Their problem lay in that concept. Perhaps *Moonlighting* had a built-in obsolescence that no one had appreciated. When the newness of it wore off, and David's chauvinism had mellowed, the banter became less surprising and increasingly trite and contorted. Willis was conscious of this fact and, in spite of his now well-known desire to quit the show when his contract expired, was none the less emphatic about quality. Time and time again, he had scenes he was unhappy with reshot until they met his personal criteria.

A similar situation, curiously enough, had occurred in *Cheers*, with Shelley Long and Ted Dansen which was *Moonlighting*'s biggest rival for that kind of television comedy audience. The underlying theme was basically the same – Dansen, the academically challenged former baseball star and recovering alcoholic, was for ever attempting to get the high and flighty Long into bed and finally came to the point where they were to be married.

Shelley Long then upped and left to pursue her ambitions in film which, in the event, did not materialise in the way that she had hoped. Ironically, her departure provided the breakthrough for Kirstie Alley. Against all predictions that she and *Cheers* would flop, she became an instant success as the epitome of the new late-eighties woman, angst-ridden, ambitious and constantly at odds with the sexist Dansen. Whereas *Moonlighting* remained in the danger zone, *Cheers* took off for a new lease of life, establishing itself as the No. 1 television show of the moment and bringing Kirstie Alley to stardom.

That particular development foreshadowed another financially important one for Willis, who was about to be offered the non-appearing voice-over for her baby in *Look Who's Talking*. In fact, his year turned out to be dominated by babies. Cybill Shepherd had returned to the *Moonlighting* fold bearing the sleepless-night hallmarks of a mother of twins and the baby theme was continued in the plot lines. As Maddie, she tells David Addison that the child she is carrying is not his. David refuses to accept it and says, yes, it is his child because he loves her. Maddie will jettison her odd-ball marriage to the anonymous character who intervened during the aberration of last season and there is every indication that she and David will soon be going at each other again in that old familiar way.

The same theme, concerning Willis's personal life, was about to be blasted across the tabloids. It was revealed that Demi was expecting a child in the summer. The story coincided with a flurry of claims, which emerged within minutes of their marriage, that Willis and Moore were splitting up. Though Moore was incandescent with rage about the claims, the publicists of her own latest project were rubbing their hands with glee.

Her new film, about to go on release, was the apocalyptic thriller *The Seventh Sign* in which she is the central character. Just as art and life so often mix and merge in Hollywood, she was playing the role of a pregnant woman. The publicists could not have had a better break if they had manoeuvred it themselves; the Hollywood adage about all publicity being good publicity generally held good. Whatever attention Ms Moore secured, it could only help her new picture, which would apparently need some additional hype to get it noticed.

Demi, meanwhile, was not especially happy about the dubious privilege of being referred to constantly as the new wife of Bruce Willis, rather than her preferred recognition as an actress, as herself. Wherever she went, whoever she spoke to, whatever news or magazine article she picked up, the references to her came only in association with her new husband – and especially now that she was expecting his baby.

For months, when she did interviews, the first question was invariably, 'What's it like being married to Bruce Willis?' or 'How come you managed to tame Hollywood's bad boy?' The more daring might even ask, 'Is it true your marriage is in trouble?' It came to the point where she refused point blank to discuss her husband, and he did likewise in questions about her. They rejected all attempts to get them together, to be photographed as Hollywood's hot couple. Absolutely not. One or other. Not both.

The promotional efforts for *The Seventh Sign* brought home to her for the first time the fact that, in pushing her own cause and her own work, having a more famous partner did have its benefits but, when it came down to it, she had to get past the Willis syndrome in order to establish her own identity.

That fact alone caused more friction among their respective handlers, and between themselves, than anything else. 'I am Demi Moore (pronounced D'-MEE), not Mrs Bruce Willis,' she demanded. To those media spies in the camp, it was further 'evidence' that the marriage was already in trouble, when in fact she was merely attempting to lay down, from the outset, that she was going forward as herself, and not as her husband's wife.

Her new movie was, on that basis, bound to attract attention. She played a neurotic young woman who becomes convinced that the birth of her child will signal the end of the world. Her fears are born out of the discovery that the strange man with staring eyes who has just rented the apartment over the garage in her backyard possesses ancient Hebrew scripts in unidentifiable code. It is a difficult, sometimes silly film, full of supernatural foreboding, with the forces of evil gathering around the lives of fairly ordinary, mundane characters. The seas boil, there are earthquakes that no one seems to notice, odd flashbacks to Roman times and curious figures in frozen deserts and rivers of blood.

It was not an especially good film and Demi Moore held it together with a strong and decisive characterisation that stopped it from total disintegration. Although the movie was generally panned, she at least won that recognition.

Her whisky voice provided the sexiness and contributed to her very obvious charisma. For those interested enough to take note of her talent, *The Seventh Sign* displayed it. She dealt with the part with conviction and strength. Mrs Bruce Willis, on this showing, would emerge through the current media activity as a very determined, exceedingly ambitious Demi Moore.

It was only at this point, when she was actively seeking the limelight of publicity – for the specific reason of promoting her film – and he was positively shunning it, that their relationship went beyond the basic 'Mr and Mrs' scenario. It began to produce some interesting side elements that perhaps neither had really discussed or considered in depth before they married. Moore was on the way up and needed a hook to hang her coat on and, traditionally, that meant giving interviews to talk-up the current movie. She found it virtually impossible in those early days to do this without reference to her husband.

As a couple, they were intriguingly attractive and represented a rare combination in Hollywood. In spite of the open derision they faced from some sections of their profession, the headline-grabbing qualities of their lives – past, present and future – offered a titillating talking point, quite apart from the media interest. There are few couples in Hollywood where both husband and wife are high-profile figures and, as such, they offered up all kinds of possibilities for insight and speculation. Although Demi herself had yet to get anywhere near the A-list of women actors, they commanded microscopic attention in their new goldfish bowl and this situation intensified when it became known that she was pregnant and that the 'Hollywood bad boy' was to become a dad.

The marriage, the forthcoming birth, and the his and her movies brought a fresh blast of media activity. Unlike Willis, she was quite happy to talk to the media in relation to herself and her work. Around the time of the release of *The Seventh Sign*, for example, she gave a frank interview to *Vanity Fair* about her aspirations and was photographed on the beach at Malibu and inside their home. Such attention, at that stage of her career, was not only welcomed, it was a necessary part of the bid for stardom in the movies – and exactly what Willis had been able to disregard because of his instant fame which had come through television.

She was in that classic 1980s upwardly mobile mode. Stardom was undoubtedly close and she needed to achieve it on her own terms. Willis had to adapt to that determination, and she to his desire for no publicity. It would be said that the mere association with Bruce Willis would open a few doors for Demi and, ultimately, further her career. She denied it vehemently and, in any event, it simply wasn't true. At the time, his agent, Arnold Rifkin, was not exactly deluged by offers for Bruce himself, let alone Demi.

The fact that she was now pregnant actually came to their aid. She was able to take herself off the merry-go-round and concentrate on the forthcoming birth; it would be eighteen months before she accepted another movie role. For Willis himself, the options were not overwhelming, partly because he was still tied to his television contract. Arnold Rifkin said that the difficulty he had was in the general perception of Willis first as the smirking playboy and then, with *Die Hard*, the all-action hero. His success as Detective John McClane had been remarkable. But in a way it merely added to Willis's problems. 'He became categorised first as one thing, then as another,' said Rifkin. 'He was positioned by the visionaries of our industry and they would have liked nothing better than to keep him there.'

Positioning has its drawbacks, as every actor knows well and especially two of Willis's contemporaries, Stallone and Schwarzenegger. Typecasting was death. When the character fell out of favour or the genre faded, so did the actor. It also became boring, just as *Moonlighting* had become a chore and, in another age, James Bond had become Sean Connery's detested alter ego. Connery escaped by taking smaller, often risky roles, for vastly less money that he was being paid for Bond. He was prepared to gamble with the vagaries of Hollywood, where nothing was ever a sure fire certainty and where big-budget, much-hyped movies can bomb at the box office and little movies suddenly take off. The only way to break the mould was to take risks, which was always Connery's philosophy. The difference was that directors were queuing up to hire Connery when he ditched Bond.

Willis did not have anywhere near the same clout in that regard, but the strategy he adopted, on Arnold Rifkin's advice, would be much the same: to diversify, to challenge himself. There was also one other lingering problem: directors, who might have taken a chance in ignoring his 'position' as an actor and offered more diverse roles, were now scared of his price. The $5 million tag put on his head by Joel Silver was, in its own a curious way, a burden.

The evidence of past performances was also confusing. *Blind Date* was financially successful but not highly regarded in Hollywood. *Sunset* was roundly panned yet, conversely, *Die Hard* prospered. Even so, serious offers for Willis were actually quite few in real terms. There were plenty of cowboys riding into town with similar scripts to *Die Hard*, all assuring everyone that it was a made-to-measure role for Bruce Willis.

Rifkin advised caution and a policy that they were to use for the years hence: that between big-money roles, if and when they came, he would take much smaller fees – and sometimes no money at all up front – for interesting movies. Rifkin had discussed it with his client often enough. 'When you are in that position, you work a little harder, disregard convention,' Rifkin admitted. He would tell prospective employers: 'Look, you can have Willis and you don't necessarily have to pay him a cent up front . . .'

They would target a particular movie or director when a project was announced and go for it regardless of whether or not Willis was first choice, or even on the short list. They first applied the strategy to his next two projects, Norman Jewison's *In Country*, shot in the autumn of 1988, and, soon afterwards, when he did the voice-over as the baby in *Look Who's Talking*; one provided him with little money but rewarding work, the other paid handsome dividends for ludicrously small effort. But it was only the big money that made the headlines and, as we will see, that presented a wholly distorted view of Willis's earning power – and his choices around Hollywood.

The truth was that, in order to get the diversification that he needed for his career to develop, he took major roles in small movies and small roles in big movies for the scale daily rate. The policy only paid off financially if the movie was a big hit, and some of them weren't.

For the first of these projects, Rifkin set off on his client's behalf to court Norman Jewison, the veteran Canadian director and screenwriter. He is among that band of film-makers most actors enjoy working for; on a good day, he can bring home a smash hit but, equally, quite a few of his projects have fallen by the wayside. His long list of diverse, if patchy, films include a number of classics and Oscar winners, such as *The Cincinatti Kid* with Steve McQueen and Edward G. Robinson, *In the Heat of the Night* which won an Oscar for best film and one for Rod Steiger, the multi-nominated *Fiddler on the Roof* and, more recently, *Moonstruck* which secured an Oscar for Cher. His 1988 film, however, was the indifferent Kevin Kline thriller, *The January Man*.

Now, he had hold of a story that was to provide an updated slant on the American experience in Vietnam. Based upon a moving first novel by Bobby Ann Mason, it would focus on a teenage girl, Samantha, from a nondescript family in Kentucky. On graduation from high school, she is anxious to discover her roots and find out all she can about her father, killed in Vietnam before she was born. Her mother, who has remarried, tells her: 'Honey, I married him when I was nineteen, four weeks before he left for Vietnam. I hardly remember him.' The key to her quest lies with her uncle Emmett Smith, a Vietnam survivor who, suffering from the combined effects of trauma and Agent Orange, has spent his post-war life withdrawing into lethargic and anti-social silence, watching a lot of television.

In a nutshell, it was the rediscovery of Vietnam, told through the lives of ordinary folk in small-town America for the benefit of those who were not around at the time. It was a relatively small movie, low budget and low profile with a cast list which once again included no names that were instantly recognisable on the billboards. The role of Emmett was not the principal character, yet Willis made a bee-line for it. In what was evidently a carefully considered choice, his agent cut a deal with Jewison and the producers to take the scale fee for an actor's daily rate plus a share of the proceeds if the film should go into profit. In other words, given his tax situation, unless the film really took off – and of course, he hoped it would – he was doing it for next to nothing.

The reason is apparent from the movie itself. It was a role so very different to anything he had tackled so far and, in his view, more difficult. It was a distinctly unshowy part, and not at all in the mould of the more common Hollywood portrayal of half-crazy, gun-toting Vietnam veterans who populated so many of the war movies of that era.

In fact, although he had lead billing for audience-drawing purposes, the real star was the then unknown nineteen-year-old British actress Emily Lloyd, chosen by Jewison after an excellent showing in her one and only film to that point, David Leland's *Wish You Were Here*. And so, once again, Willis was the only actor in the cast whose name would be known. In that regard, he carried the burden of the movie itself and, for that reason, Jewison was not easily persuaded that he should hire him. Willis had two meetings with him, and then did a reading – 'which I don't normally do, but I wanted that part' – before the director took him on.

The importance of doing this film, to Willis himself, is perhaps best demonstrated by the arrangements that were made to accommodate developments in his personal life. Demi was in the latter stages of pregnancy and the birth would occur during the time the movie was being filmed on location in Kentucky. They decided that, rather than have her miles away in Los Angeles, they would arrange to have the baby born in Kentucky – in spite of the close medical supervision Demi had received in LA.

Willis rented a country farmhouse at nearby Padacah and was joined for the duration by Demi, surrounded by bodyguards and a wall of security systems large enough to protect a small city. Demi arrived about three weeks before the baby was due. She went immediately to a local doctor, carrying a list of 'things I wanted and didn't want – I had a very clear idea of how I wanted my birth to be.'

She wanted no drugs or pain relief systems; she wanted to feel the whole experience of her 'body opening up to allow a human being to pass through.' She wanted the birth video-taped and would require her husband and several friends present.

'Do you have a problem with that?' she asked the 'sweet' country doctor.

'Not at all,' he replied, and proceeded to book her place at the local hospital.

She went into labour one night while at a local cinema. She went home and prepared herself and Bruce alerted his film crew and the friends who were to attend, and then delivered her to the hospital. The guests who would witness the event included their massage therapist, Demi's personal assistant, Bruce's best friend and aid who had travelled to Kentucky with him, Demi's girlfriend and the video operator.

They set up three cameras at different angles to record the delivery. They gathered during the fifteen hours that Demi was in labour and Willis never left her side except to go to the bathroom. When the time came, and the baby's head was appearing, Moore shouted to Randy, the camera operator: 'Are you getting this?' 'Sure am,' Randy replied.

Willis, in white robes and mask, was actively involved. 'He was so available,' Moore recalled. The doctor was there, of course, but it was Bruce's hands that were in her, pulling the baby out. And they had it all on video: 'I stayed very calm. It was never crazy. When she came slithering out, Bruce and the doctor cleared her mouth and Bruce put her on my chest. Then everyone left us alone for half an hour. We have it all on film, which we've watched over and over again with our friends.'

The baby was a girl. They named her Rumer, after authoress Rumer Godden.

After that very personal performance, Willis returned to the set of *In Country*, where other emotions were in evidence. The author of the novel on which it was based, Bobby Ann Mason, was swept along on the creative tide of seeing her book take shape on film. 'It was hard for me to be objective,' she admitted, 'but to be very honest, I had some reservations about Bruce and how he would transcend being both Bruce Willis and David Addison. But he did. He was terrific. I first met him the day before shooting started. We met with local Vietnam veterans in Kentucky. He seemed pretty overwhelmed by the whole experience. It was very moving the way he expressed himself. He had a real respect for the subject. He spent a lot of time researching and developing the character, and I think it showed in the movie.'

Jewison, also wary of Willis's reputation of being an arrogant

loudmouth, found a man totally opposite to the popular carica-
ture. 'I think it was because I got him at a particular time in his
life,' said Jewison. 'There was something about him becoming a
father and, at the same time, playing this role had an effect on him
personally. I saw him maturing as a person before my very eyes.
He was a joy to work with.'

Willis drew on his own blue-collar background for the role and
explained that he based his portrayal on the wan, expressionless
way ordinary people in small towns get on with their lives.
Unfortunately, such lives, when translated to film, can also be
incredibly dull and Jewison clearly had problems in overcoming
that difficulty. *In Country* had to be a performance-led movie, in
which the story and the characters are revealed through the
mundane happenings of daily life. It was not about conflicts, but
about people discovering themselves. It is here that the film almost
stifles itself with the snail-pace unfolding of events that do not
conform to conventional onscreen storytelling, occurring through
a rambling array of interlinked subplots.

Only in the final scenes did Jewison show where they were
leading with an incredible, tear-jerking finish in which he releases
all the pent-up emotion and misery. The trouble is, of course, that
when words like misery, mundane and snail-pace can be contained
in one paragraph, it does not augur well for any movie. There were
strong and powerful scenes, but they were overtaken by others
that were slight and ordinary, almost meaningless. *In Country* was
acclaimed by the critics but only for the performances of Willis
and Emily Lloyd, otherwise it drifted quietly into oblivion.

From Willis's point of view, it was put down to experience.
That he needed to work with directors like Jewison and take roles
that might be considered eccentric, even career threatening, was
beyond doubt; he needed the challenge and the restraint that such
roles brought to his more aggressive talents. Above all, as he
admitted himself, he had to throw away the crutches on which he
had relied so heavily – 'no shtick, no funny lines, no smirking
faces.'

What he did next was neither a gamble nor a challenge. It was
strictly for the money, even though the bountiful result was not
initially expected. The movie was *Look Who's Talking*, the one
that provided the first revival of John Travolta's flagging career –

before it flagged again – and made Kirstie Alley a movie star. It is based upon the idea of having a baby boy narrate the events, from his delivery to his infancy. As he grows, he is commenting on the relationship between his unmarried mother (Alley) and a taxi driver (Travolta). It was a cheaply produced movie for which Rifkin negotiated a remarkable deal for Willis. He would receive an upfront fee and ten per cent of the profits. TriStar, the studio responsible for the movie, agreed. No one, other than producer Jonathan Krane and writer-director Amy Heckerling, really had great faith in its box office appeal and they judged that, at best, they would have to pay Willis a few hundred thousand dollars when the time came to settle up.

The story was pretty weak, more like a television sitcom. The chemistry between Travolta and Kirstie Alley, in the depths of her now typical anxiety complex, was nothing to write home about. Derek Malcolm's review in the *Guardian* was fairly typical of critical reaction: 'Carelessly put together, ugly to look at and mawkish and stupid in turn.' But it took off – and that was largely down to Willis.

The novelty of having a sharp-talking, David Addison-style, adult voice with streetwise attitudes issuing forth from the mouth of Mikey, the babe in arms, was in itself very funny and caught on. The film was an unexpected success around the world and a sequel, *Looking Who's Talking Too*, was rapidly cobbled together and released within the year, although did not do as well. Willis, through the deal struck at the front-end, was suddenly richer by around $10 million – for voice-over tasks that took him little more than a month to complete.

Was Hollywood green with envy? 'It certainly was,' recalls producer Trevor Wallace. 'Everyone, and I mean everyone, was talking about it. Not about the movie – just Willis's expected take when they cashed up. You know in this town, everything is exaggerated beyond belief. But this was precedential in every way. They were paraphrasing Churchill's famous line and coming up with things like, "Never in the field of human endeavour has so much been earned for so little." It was true, and the realisation was beginning to dawn that when you put Willis in a movie, you never quite know what you are going to get.'

8 Goodbye, Maddie

H E WAS BACK ON THE SET of *Moonlighting* to complete the last few shows of the final series. The afterglow he had experienced from the first series had now been replaced by that from the international success of *Die Hard*. Willis, announced *Vanity Fair*, was bigger than ever. Until then, he was only bigger than *Moonlighting*. That was about to change. Hollywood was suddenly paying attention. *Die Hard* had secured his future. He was being courted by a jostling queue of potential employers, egged on by Arnold Rifkin and his deal-making. There was some interesting material around. But first, *Moonlighting* . . . the last take.

The new season opened on 6 December 1988 with Episode 54, entitled *Womb With a View*, in which an angel visits Maddie's baby to inform the child of the relationship of its parents: Maddie and David are battling to put this on a new footing. They are back in the old routine, sparring like an old married couple, yet still not married. Time is running out and viewer interest is flagging. There are twelve shows to go before *Lunar Eclipse*, on 14 May 1989, brings the series to a close. Willis is ticking off the weeks like a man in a prison cell.

He's back in the gloomy trailer on the Fox lot where he hides away from the outside world, retiring there at every opportunity during the fourteen-hour days of filming. There he has his cellular phone, ringing constantly, his stereo, his books, his poster of the Three Stooges and the signed photo of Frank Sinatra, just like it's been these past four years. Currently, he's absorbed in a book about parenting. Cybill arrives on the set after feeding her babies.

'So nice to see you,' she purrs.

'So nice to be seen by you,' he replies, grinning in a sophisticated manner. Then they begin.

Later, Lawrence Grobel arrives to tape some more of his thoughts for his *Playboy* interview and Willis tells him that television is over for him. 'I never considered TV a medium in which to achieve what I thought was my idea of success . . . enough time has gone by that I've been able to get some objectivity on what was happening to me since my success first occurred. It's tempting to lose sight of that, to become the person they want me to be – some big pompous asshole who stomps around Hollywood, shoves baby carriages out of the way, smokes cigars, kicks ass and talks loud. People want me to become that person. I have no desire to be that person.'

Grobel, eyebrows raised, puts on an air of grinning mystification, tempting him to pontificate further: 'Wait a minute Bruce – you've been known to kick some ass, talk loud and stomp around Hollywood. Are you trying to tell us that you're not really a BIG POMPOUS ASSHOLE?'

'No . . . what I'm saying,' Willis replies, 'is I'm at a totally different place than I've ever been in my life now. I'm a lot more comfortable with myself. I'm taking life with a lot more humour . . . not taking all this shit so seriously . . . Demi helped by teaching me the philosophy of letting go. The more I hung on to my anger the more I gave those people power over me.'

The flamboyance was diminishing, perhaps, and hadn't a gossip columnist remarked recently that he'd become boring since he was married? He was heading towards his goal, to be in the mainstream of Hollywood: that oft-discussed, publicly analysed career was not yet in full flight and he was trying to push it higher. Like so many other stars who reach a certain level of financial security, he had formed his own production company, Hudson Hawk Films, and was laying plans for a movie that would take that title. It was still in the early planning stages but Joel Silver had agreed to produce it and a script was being prepared which would, hopefully, rouse interest among potential backers.

In the meantime, Silver was moving ahead on the sequel to *Die Hard* and Willis was negotiating terms: $8 million this time, and Alan Ladd jnr was forced to take another deep breath. Willis was also popping in and out of the recording studio, taping tracks for a second album with an autobiographical title song, 'If It Don't Kill You It Just Makes You Stronger' – inspired, he said, by the catharsis he had gone through in the past five years. And Arnold Rifkin was tap dancing again, this time with Brian de Palma who had been hired to direct the movie of the book of the moment, Tom Wolfe's *The Bonfire of the Vanities*.

Demi had other offers too – 'Not because I'm married to Bruce Willis. That has nothing to do with it.'

Apart from behind-the-scenes efforts to produce her own movie, she was on the road to making her tentative re-emergence on film after an eighteen month gap – since she completed *The Seventh Sign*. Her new role arrived courtesy of Bruce's good friend Sean Penn, and it had an interesting background.

Penn's own career was in the doldrums, and had been for some time. He had been shunned and rejected for anything of note; his own hellraiser tag and a couple of police busts had done him more harm than similar escapades had for Willis. Now, another of his good friends, Robert De Niro, who was in the throes of setting up his own production company, called TriBeca Films, had stepped in to launch a rescue operation.

He promised Penn he would find a movie in which they could work together. He mentioned that possibility to Art Linson, producer of *The Untouchables*, a massive box office hit with Sean Connery and Kevin Costner and in which De Niro played the cameo role of Al Capone. Linson liked the idea of De Niro and Penn together and, from the pigeon holes of his brain, produced the thought of a remake of *We're No Angels*, the 1955 black comedy which had starred Humphrey Bogart, Peter Ustinov and Aldo Ray. Even back then, Bogart had regarded it as no more than a potboiler.

The producer telephoned the famed Broadway dramatist, director and writer David Mamet, who had scripted *The Untouchables*. Coincidentally, his long list of credits included the compelling adaptation of *The Verdict*, in which Willis had appeared as an uncredited extra, *Sexual Perversity in Chicago* and the play *Son*, in which Demi's film *About Last Night* was based. Mamet wasn't too keen, but proceeded to produce a script loosely based on the original.

So the wheels within wheels were turning and, on the face of it, things looked promising: instigated by a major star (De Niro, who was also listed as executive producer), scripted by an award winning author (Mamet), backed by a leading producer (Linson) and financed with a generous $20 million budget from a top studio (Paramount). The screenplay had De Niro and Penn as a couple of convicts who escape to Canada and take refuge in a monastery, being helped on their way by Moore. Linson approved, at a cost of $3 million, the construction of a mock border town with almost two dozen buildings, the largest film set ever constructed in Canada. That was one of the more interesting statistics of this picture. As Hollywood has proved so many times, and goes on proving, a recipe of choice ingredients doesn't necessarily produce a fine dish.

The film was an utter let-down. De Niro mugged his way through a sleep-inducing plot and the critics gave it a mauling. Penn did actually liven up the proceedings and the film did get him started again. 'Bobby De Niro saved me from despair,' he said later, 'and he saved my career.'

Demi Moore, with third billing and a fee of less than $300,000, came out of it best of all. After being tipped-off by Sean Penn, she fought tooth and nail for the part of the single mother who helps the two convicts to do some religious thinking, and she justified her selection with a very decent performance in a relatively modest role. That more or less summed up her position at the time. But Demi, too, was on the move. A movie called *Ghost*, with Whoopi Goldberg and Patrick Swayze, was coming up, and she called her agent: 'I want it.'

The New Year of 1989 was full of promise for both of them. *Moonlighting* was history. The last show was in the can and the cast had stood around looking into their champagne glasses – filled with Evian water in Willis's case – wondering, just as they had in the final episode, why the Blue Moon Detective Agency had to close. But they all knew it had run out of steam.

Willis didn't look back. His trailer home on the Fox lot was emptied and gone for ever. Cybill breathed a sigh of relief and took her babies home for a few weeks of relative calm. She too had a couple of movies in the offing but, unlike Willis, there was no big future ahead in that direction. She had already completed *Chances Are* with Robert Downey jnr and Ryan O'Neal which didn't create much of a stir. As soon as *Moonlighting* finished, she revived her long-ago relationship with Peter Bogdanovich – this time on a purely professional basis – as he attempted to recreate the magic of *The Last Picture Show*.

The sequel was a little late: it was called *Texasville*, adapted from the novel by Larry McMurty who also wrote the original screenplay that turned Cybill into an overnight sensation exactly twenty years earlier. It was a moody, downbeat work, but well worth watching in spite of its patchy reviews; the audiences, most of whom were too young to remember the original, stayed away in droves.

After that, Shepherd did a couple more forgettable movies, then called it quits, went back into television and eventually saw a revival of fortunes with her own show, called *Cybill* – occasionally breathing curses towards the rise and rise of the man who had been her mythical pain in the side for four hard years.

Willis came out of *Moonlighting* with determined aspirations for his own movie, *Hudson Hawk*. There was a long history to the project which was tied to his original dreams and ambitions when he was a struggling actor in New York. According to legend, he used to answer his telephone with the words, 'Hudson Hawk Films.' Then, he began writing, toying with a screenplay for a movie of the same name. Eight years later, the dream was coming true, although the script wasn't right even yet. It had been pored over for months and then went on the backburner again while he filmed *Die Hard 2* for Joel Silver who, since their last encounter, had dashed off *Lethal Weapon 2* with Mel Gibson, the exploitational comedy *Road House* with Patrick Swayze, a dreary flop entitled *The Adventures of Ford Fairlane* and the frenetic, gore-filled *Predator 2*.

Die Hard 2 would be better than any of them, and also a veritable milestone in Willis's chequered future. Silver had placed the *Die Hard* sequel in the hands of the young Finnish director Renny Harlin who had burst on to the Hollywood scene a couple a years earlier at the age of 27. He cut his teeth on *A Nightmare on Elm Street 4: The Dream Master* which turned out to be one of the more imaginative of the slasher series, and the most profitable.

Showing he could make a decent movie on a low budget, he thus became a hot number and was being talked of as the new Polanski without the hang-ups – offers and scripts came flooding in. It was Joel Silver, a modern day Roger Corman with money and a keen eye for fresh talent, who gathered him up and drew him with a lucrative deal, just as he had done with Willis. He gave him *The Adventures of Ford Fairlane* as his first film for Silver Pictures, a vehicle designed specifically for the controversial comedian Andrew Dice Clay. It was a disaster that even the new young genius could not rescue.

Undeterred and amid gasps of surprise around the Hollywood village – just as there had been when he hired Willis first time round – Silver handed Harlin the script of *Die Hard 2* and said: 'It's all yours. Let's do it!' The backbiters said he wasn't up to it, that Silver had gone mad, risking a $40 million budget on an untried director with one slasher picture and a hefty flop to his name, much the same as they'd said about Willis.

It turned out to be an inspired choice. The difficulty, as always, with a sequel is to keep up the standard and expectations overhanging from the original. In this case, the sequel was bigger and better in almost every way. For one thing, Silver had virtually double the original budget but the easy working relationship between Willis and Harlin, four years his junior, was evident. They hit it off from the moment they met. 'I had heard he could be truculent and difficult,' said Harlin, 'but it wasn't so, at least not as far as I was concerned. There is always tension on a movie set, especially with an unknown director like me but Bruce was very easygoing. He likes to get his co-actors laughing and I was pleasantly surprised. It was my first experience of working with a movie star and he made it special. He brought me into his own life too. Demi would come and visit the set very frequently and he would walk around holding the baby between takes.'

They picked up the action a year after the terrorist high-rise take-over in the first *Die Hard*. This time, the scene is Dulles International Airport, Washington, D.C. It is Christmas again and the airport is bustling with the extra holiday traffic just at the point when Federal agents, aboard a military aircraft, are bringing home a South American dictator named Esperanza (played by Franco Nero) who is being put on trial in the US for his involvement with drug cartels. It ought to be a routine arrival, except a murderous group of highly skilled terrorists have been hired to free the dictator.

The terrorists, led by a psychopathic former US intelligence operative (William Saddler), have set up their headquarters in an old church near the airport. There they intercept control tower communications and put a skyfull of circling aircraft in jeopardy. Only the safe landing of the plane carrying the dictator and his immediate freedom aboard another 747, fuelled and ready to go, will save all other aircraft from crashing.

Of course, you don't have to look too closely at the technical details of these plots and you must have an open mind about remarkable coincidences. It just so happens that the hero of the Nakatomi terrorist attack in Los Angeles a year earlier, Detective John McClane, is already in Dulles airport heading for a vacation. He is waiting to be reunited with his wife who is aboard one of the incoming planes. He's already been recognised by waiting photographers as being the LA hero cop, and then finds himself in the middle of a shoot-out after he recognises one of the terrorists. He winds up killing one man, but no one listens to his warnings until it is too late.

By then, the mad colonel has shown his determination to free the dictator by crashing a plane full of people . . . and now it's over to Willis, once again portraying the reluctant, fear-ridden hero, to rescue the remainder of the circling planes, including the one carrying his wife, before they run out of fuel.

Harlin's message, as director, is clear: you don't have to believe it, just sit back and enjoy the spectacle. And that's just what he provided. His direction on this well-crafted movie was exceptional, each frame carefully constructed so that the audiences didn't even have to bother about reality. It is mindless, mind-boggling, edge-of-your-seat stuff; hugely spectacular entertainment.

Willis is thrown into even more hair-raising exploits and brilliant pyrotechnics: careering around on a snowmobile, hanging from the wing of a moving 747 and, in one sensational stunt, catapulted away from an exploding plane in an ejector seat. Where the film disappointed was in its virtual exact coping of the original in terms of introducing dumb and dumber figures of authority whose sole reason for being in the film seemed to be to enhance Willis; cretinous subplots which disturbed an otherwise first-rate example of action movies.

Willis, noticeably less of a wise guy without upsetting some of the humorous moments that relieve the tension, gave his best showing to date. His appeal is his personal believability which overrides some of the aspects of the plot that do not bear too great a scrutiny. He still has none of the bulging muscle of Stallone and Schwarzenegger, just the reasonably athletic appearance of an average cop. The subtitle of the movie, *Die Harder*, is the key. He portrays a man who will not give in even in the face of incredible odds because, as he says, 'My wife is on that plane.'

When filming was done, Silver was one of the hosts for Willis's 35th birthday party: a mass bash staged on 24 March 1990 at the San Fernando Sports Centre Bowl. The 250 guests were all sent bowling shirts in advance, printed with the legend 'Bruno's Birthday Bowlerama', and no one would be admitted unless they were wearing one. Some didn't. Eddie Murphy arrived with an aide carrying his shirt on a hanger. Sylvester Stallone was also there, but big Hollywood names were few. Willis played and sang with the band. Then it was back to work: three movies in the immediate future and the promotional efforts for *Die Hard 2*.

Of all the over-the-top and over-hyped movies around in that summer of 1990, *Die Hard 2* had a style of its own, although there was a good deal of competition about from the plethora of high-profile action movies rushing into the cinemas: there was Arnie's new blockbuster, *Total Recall*, which opened in June with its gruesomely spectacular special effects and which took $260 million; Frank Marshall's cunningly scary shocker, *Arachnophobia*, with Willis's pal John Goodman in the riotous cameo role of the termite exterminator, came out in the same month but didn't do very well; Warren Beatty's long awaited, hugely promoted, but ultimately bland comedy strip adventure, *Dick Tracy*, with a host of stars including Madonna and Dustin Hoffman, was another major attraction and, coming up on the rails, was Martin Scorsese's violent masterpiece, *Goodfellas*, with Robert De Niro and Joe Pesci. Stallone, too, entered the fray again, pulling out the final entrails of his punchy boxer series in *Rocky V*.

Willis's own blockbuster was premiered in Los Angeles on 2 July 1990 and Joel Silver, now bigger than ever, was going to make it a Hollywood opening to remember. It was also Bruce Willis's Big Night Out. Silver had booked two screens at the

Westwood Cineplex, one for the A-list guests and one for minor mortals, each status being discernible by the colour-coded invitations.

At 7.30 that evening, the scene was typical of opening nights of old: searchlights lit up the skies, television arc lights glared and the flashbulbs of the paparazzi exploded every half second. Two dozen police and security guards manned the barricades. Interviewers with microphones were ready to get a glancing comment from the stars as they began arriving, purring up Sunset Boulevard in a fleet of truck-length limousines with smoked glass windows which hid the identities of the occupants until they were disgorged onto the pavement in front of the theatre.

Star-watching crowds and photographers shouted the names of the recognisable among them; well-known faces beamed, turned momentarily to face the cameras, flashed their gleaming shark-likes and hurried on, some deeming to stop for a brief 'Great-to-be-here – terrific-movie'-aside into the microphones.

Lesser known and unknown faces lingered longer, soaking up the atmosphere of Fame: old men, grey haired and tuxedoed; young men, gregarious and in hip gear competing for the ultra-cool award, top-heavy young ladies in micro-skirts and perched on six-inch heels trotted precariously along the red carpet and matronly women, in their glittering gowns and dramatic $300 hairdos, made a more sedate entrance giving Queen-Mother-waves to the hoi polloi.

Willis and Demi arrived to a great whooping cheer which was repeated inside the theatre. There were more applause and cheers when the titles rolled, and then throughout the movie, especially in the big scenes when Willis's all-action bravado was greeted with whoops of encouragement more akin to a crowd watching ice hockey.

And when it was over, and the credits were rolling, there was a standing ovation through a shower of popcorn. The big names marched forward in unison to congratulate Silver and Willis. Stallone and Schwarzenegger took it in turns to squeeze the living daylights out of them with big, big hugs. As he moved on, Willis's right arm was actively responding to the gimme-fives accompanied by assurances that the movie was going to be mega, to which he replied confidently, 'You betcha!'

Outside in the now cooler late-evening air, the limos were already lining up, engines purring, surrounded by guards with darting eyes waiting for the famous departees to be transported to the premiere party. Those with colour-coded A-list invitations would move on to the New Tycoon's humble crib, a huge property at the transvestite-free end of Hollywood Boulevard. The place, one of his several abodes, had cost millions in restoration and was now lavish and spectacular, like a set from a Billy Wilder movie.

There, another small army of white-gloved security guards, dashing around and speaking into walkie-talkies, checked invitations and faces against the guest list. Inside, the house was mouth-opening magnificence, eliciting envious ooohs and aaahs from those among them for whom it was a first visit to this monument to Mammon. Among the architectural splendour, the bejewelled, the bewigged and the befamous mingled and talked about their favourite subjects – themselves, dollars, and who-else-is-doing-what in this single-topic town.

An armada of swirling flunkies filtered through the crowds, dispensing champagne, cocktails, mineral water and oriental canapes. The star of the show was Silver himself, followed closely by his man of the moment, Willis, swaggering through the melee with lots more gimme-fives and hugs and kisses. These extraordinary scenes, commonplace among those present, were witnessed for the first time by virtually the whole of Willis's family, drawn en masse into Silver's extravagant world.

Willis's father, Dave, had a bit part in *Die Hard 2*, as a tow-truck driver. Now Willis Senior could have his fifteen minutes, and proudly told all that only five years ago, his son was dead broke. It was one of the occasional sorties he made into his son's Hollywood life, preferring the anonymity of Carney's Point. He had turned down Bruce's offers to buy him a house on the west coast. He preferred to fly back to New Jersey with his second wife Alma to their modest trailer home, where Bruce himself stayed whenever he went back alone to his home town.

Marlene, Bruce's mother, was also at the party, resplendent in Rodeo Drive glitterama and chatting fearlessly to her son's new friends and associates as if they were a gang of schoolmates, just in for a Saturday night party. His younger brothers Dave and Robert were also there. Dave would be working as a production assistant on the next Big One, *Hudson Hawk*, and had his own personal attachment to the Silver empire. He was partnering the producer's young fast-talking walking-computer assistant Susan Forristal who exuded all the confidence needed to run around ahead of the great man.

And so *Die Hard 2* was launched upon the world. The anxiously awaited reviews were pretty favourable across the board, and Willis won particular acclaim. The first weekend, when it opened in 1,800 theatres across the nation, business was rapid and on target for the magical $100 million that declares it a winner for all concerned. He was out and about promoting the movie but very soon found himself in direct competition for business from a surprising source.

While he had been filming *Die Hard 2*, Demi Moore had been quietly working on her own new movie called *Ghost*, an altogether more modest affair costing less than $15 million, with Whoopi Goldberg and Patrick Swayze. It arrived in the cinemas virtually unheralded, opening one week after her husband's new one. There had been little publicity about it, certainly nothing in terms of the hype that surrounded that summer's crop of action movies.

No one, not even Demi in her wildest moments of expectation, had predicted it would take off the way it did. Reviewers were pretty offhand, generally dismissing it as pleasant and rather soppy entertainment although conceding that the performances of the three principals were quite engaging. Some even sought to argue its fundamentalist view of heaven and hell which were clearly depicted as the souls of the good and evil characters were gathered up and directed to their assigned destinations in the afterlife. There was even discussion about the inner motives of revenge being good for the soul.

It is doubtful that director Jerry Zucker and writer Bruce Joel Rubin ever intended any serious undertones. The movie was what it was – an amiable and sentimental piece of frippery that just happened to catch the imagination of the mass public, ever eager for answers to the eternal question and, perhaps, a little intimidated by the blood and gore and Joe Pesci's 312th use of the word 'fuck' that summer.

In *Ghost*, Patrick Swayze plays an investment broker who has a very large loft apartment where he and Demi, a pottery sculptress, perform some rather sexy operations over a potter's wheel. But Swayze is quickly disposed of, seemingly murdered by a mugger but, having discovered the truth that it was a planned hit by a crooked colleague, he hangs around in spirit form to protect his lover, Demi Moore. In order to get this important information through to her, he searches for a medium who will act as his voice.

Enter Whoopi Goldberg, playing a previously fraudulent seance practitioner who is shocked to discover that she does indeed possess the power of communication to the spirit world – or at least with this particular ghost. Swayze eventually persuades her to contact Moore, and passes on a lot of 'only-you-will-know-this' information. It takes an inordinately long time for the penny to drop and, in the meantime, the mourning lover trusts the villain instead. But, of course, eventually she sees the error of her ways and there is a particularly touching scene when Swayze takes over Goldberg's body; you wonder what is going to happen next.

It was all good, clean fun and Goldberg, in need of a hit after being adrift for too long on poor material, provided roustabout humour that kept the sometimes languishing plot on the move. By August, *Ghost* had assumed the proportions of a Hollywood miracle. It zoomed up the charts, eventually overtaking *Die Hard 2* and some of the other big guns. It went on to take $217 million at the box office in the US alone, considerably more than Willis's film, and, come the Academy Awards, it secured Oscar nominations for best actress (Goldberg), best original script (Rubin), best picture and editing. Goldberg and Rubin converted their nominations and the movie went down in history as the biggest ever earner of its kind, taking $450 million world-wide.

Although Demi Moore was competent enough, it was Goldberg's and Swayze's picture. But that didn't matter. As far as Demi was concerned, she was just as much the star. She fought director Jerry Zucker all the way to the cutting room. She argued that her character should be stronger, less passive. 'Demi obviously wanted to be more assertive in the role,' said Zucker. 'She isn't attracted to soft characters and doesn't like to smile a lot on screen.'

She lost that battle, but the rolling success of *Ghost* gathered her up and carried her with it. She came to fame as an actress, not in an aggressive role, as she would have preferred, but as a rather nondescript character with no waist, short cropped hair, elfin looks and doey eyes. It was the moment, however, when she began to grasp the power, such as it was, and she was making demands even before the movie took off. 'She learned from a master demander,' said an unnamed studio executive quoted by the *Guardian*. 'Only, unlike Bruce, she didn't earn it. Demi has always been impatient while waiting for things to come to her. She says she doesn't ride on her husband's coat-tails but when she hired a bodyguard after *Ghost*, that was fame by association.'

By the time she hit France on the European press and promotion tour, she was, according to writer Jennet Conant, 'in the throes of a fully fledged star trip.' She would travel only in private aircraft, she was being attended by an assistant who had an assistant, along with three other people who did her hair, make-up and wardrobe, plus the masseuse. 'Of all the female stars in France that week promoting movies, including Whoopi Goldberg and Goldie Hawn, Moore was the only one who felt in need of a bodyguard.'

That particular aspect of her claim to fame seemed to attract the writers' imagination more than any other. What really threatened to cause grief among the local media was her insistence that she should have approval of any photographs taken of her *before* they were published.

Uproar.

'Who the fuck does she think she is?' (in French), came the cry. Nobody asks for photo approval, not even Diana. In the end, after a hasty head to head with worried studio execs, Demi conceded, although she didn't let it drop. When she came to London a couple of years later, to promote *Indecent Proposal*, she made an even more unusual suggestion to the 60 Fleet Street veterans who gathered to attend her road show. When asked to pose for photographs, she provided a list of 'approved photographers' for whom she would sit. Most commanded fees somewhere around her own, in proportionate terms. She said she could not allow herself to be the 'object of someone else's choice; that doesn't seem right, because this is about me. I must retain control of what image of me is published. It is essential.'

After a few mutterings, roughly translating to 'get lost', she once again pulled back and, with great reluctance, agreed to pose for one or two photographs – but 'only the serious newspapers. No tabloids.'

That summer, the combined impact of *Die Hard 2* and *Ghost* had a remarkable effect on the standing of Bruce Willis and Demi Moore. Into that one household poured the millions that each derived from fees and profit-participation. Just as Willis had become a virtual overnight sensation, now they were a successful double act and, as such, became the focus of renewed attention: the most talked about, most written about, most admired, most *hated* couple in Hollywood.

Comparisons had to be made and, as ever, it was all about money; they were beating all previous Hollywood pairings by miles. Successful couples of the past could be counted on one hand: Clark Gable and Carol Lombard, Spencer Tracy and Katharine Hepburn, Humphrey Bogart and Lauren Bacall, Paul Newman and Joanne Woodward, Elizabeth Taylor and Richard Burton are among the few who come readily to mind. But never mind the talent, look at the size of their incoming cheques. That month, the magazines were soon chanting in unison: 'Hollywood's Hottest Couple.'

It was still a presumptuous thought but as such, they were sitting ducks, on the brink of a long-running tirade that was often inspired from within the industry itself, and by so called colleagues, branding them a pair of prima donnas with so little pedigree that they might be called movie mongrels. The reaction that began then, in a steamy hot Los Angeles summer, would build into an ongoing stream of vitriol to which was added the voice of Demi's tell-all mother, Virginia.

As soon as Demi hit the jackpot in *Ghost*, the tabloids began tearing into her past and soon uncovered the details of Virginia's drink problems and Demi's wild-child existence. A posse of scandal scribes, chequebooks in hand, discovered the whereabouts of Virginia Guynes, an intermittently recovering alcoholic who still slipped back on occasions into her old ways. She'd recently had several brushes with the law from which Demi had bailed her out on a couple of occasions. Now, realising the value of her knowledge, she was ready to tell all, for the right consideration of course.

Headline: 'MUM JOINED DEMI IN DRUGS PARTY: GHOST BEAUTY'S COCAINE SHAME.'

Beneath it, they ran the story: *Ghost* star Demi Moore went on a wild-drink-and-drugs binge with her mother! And now wayward mum Virginia Guynes has taken the lid off the amazing story. 'Life was one long, sick party,' she said. Virginia treated her daughter's fame as her own ticket to ride. She had received several large cash donations from Demi – reportedly $45,000 in stage payments – to help her recovery from alcoholism. But unlike daughter, the mother couldn't get straight. In one of her several brushes with the law, Virginia was arrested for drunken driving in New Mexico and spent three days in jail. Demi refused to bail her out because she believed it would help shock her mother into getting her act cleaned up.

Eager supermarket 'journos', as Rupert Murdoch liked to call them, targeted Virginia and gathered up the more lurid aspects of Moore's past, about which she herself had been quite open. They used it for months ahead to entice their readers as Demi now became serious competition among the select band of women actresses in Hollywood, all jostling for position.

Notoriety was just part of it.

9 Flare Up

THERE WERE STILL detractors aplenty ready to dismiss Bruce Willis as a flash in the pan, a one-act wonder who wouldn't last. There was, it was true, little or no tangible proof that he had the ability to tackle roles outside of his personal bag of tricks. Where was the evidence of any kind of acting technique that could sustain him through big-screen diversity? It was all still a bit of a mirage.

Disregarding the television series, *In Country* and *Die Hard* were the only movies in which he had shown real promise. But then, who could argue with the judgement of Joel Silver? When the New Tycoon signed him for *Die Hard 2*, at even bigger money than the first, there was a veritable stampede behind him, both from directors wanting to cast him and backers ready to support his own projects, although it must be said also that Arnold Rifkin's policy of 'work now, pay him later' had also attracted some.

By the early months of 1990, Willis had an incredible seven movies lined up for completion and release by the end of the following year. It was an unprecedented total in modern times which harped back to the production-line tactics of the movie moguls during the Golden Age, when stars like Kirk Douglas and Henry Fonda were making three pictures a year. On paper, Willis's calendar looked very impressive: three movies to go on the circuit in 1990 (*Die Hard 2*, *The Bonfire of the Vanities* and *Look Who's Talking Too*); four in 1991 (*Hudson Hawk*, *Billy Bathgate*, *The Last Boy Scout* and *Mortal Thoughts*). Only Robert De Niro, who had a particular flurry of activity around that time (to finance his own freshly built New York film production centre), could match it.

It was true that two of the movies, *The Bonfire of the Vanities* and *Look Who's Talking Too*, would require minimal time and effort (but paid handsomely). Others, including his own upcoming *Hudson Hawk*, would be a considerable strain on his resources as an actor as he stepped on to the conveyor belt to cash in while the going was good. As he repeatedly told his friends: 'It could all end tomorrow.'

Apart from the work put up by Silver and other producers, Willis and Moore were also intent on making their own his-and-hers movies. As is the want of freshly made Hollywood talent, the desire to be the masters of their own destiny remained a goal that went well beyond the realm of personal satisfaction. Recent history showed that Warren Beatty made $30 million as producer and star of just three pictures, *Bonny and Clyde*, *Shampoo* and *Heaven Can Wait*. Since then, every actor who made it big eyed the greener grass with ambitious envy. Many were provided with their own production offices within the major studios, to explore possible production opportunities.

A few, like Michael Douglas, secured major deals. Douglas, that year, had just 'got into bed', as he termed it, with Columbia. His production company, Stonebridge, was contracted to produce two pictures a year for the next five years. De Niro, as we have seen, had set up TriBeca in 1990 and soon had half a dozen movies in production there. Robert Redford had long ago created the Sundance Institute in Utah from which he was lately producing his own movies, like *The Milagro Beanfield War*. Clint Eastwood was doing the same, skipping to both sides of the camera as producer/director/actor in movies such as *Heartbreak Ridge*, *Bird* and *Unforgiven*. Women actresses too, had turned to producing: Goldie Hawn, Bette Midler, Sally Field and Barbra Streisand all produced their own projects, although the female activity was perhaps more to do with the competitiveness of modern Hollywood for women than with a search for artistic satisfaction.

When the Willises turned towards that direction, however, it was viewed among the Hollywood establishment as merely another sign of their joint and several arrogance in that they, the newcomers, should deem it both feasible and desirable to take a behind-the-camera involvement in their movie making at such an early stage in their respective careers.

How could they possibly have anything to contribute, apart

from their wealth and notoriety? As one who was close to their hub at the time remembers, 'Bruce had been talking about making his own movie for years. He bought up a couple of projects, scripts and books, that never came to anything. He also had his script for the movie *Hudson Hawk*, such as it was, that he had dreamed up years ago in New York. It was basically no more than a scribbled outline, pretty amateurish, but he became determined to try to get it made. Joel Silver encouraged him and gave him a scriptwriter and the whole thing just moved on from there. Hudson Hawk Films suddenly became a reality and Bruce was jumping at the prospect of getting his movie made, with him involved in both production and as its star. Now, while that was going on, Demi said, "Me too"; she wanted to become a producer as well. She formed her own company, linked up with another independent company in New York which was touting a screen-play for *Mortal Thoughts*. So now, they both had a project and it was the talk of the town, especially as they both found willing backers without great effort. It's not uncommon for well-known actors to spend years trying to get something off the ground; the big deal is always over the next Hollywood hill. Then the Willises come along and fix it in one. Everyone was asking: "How the fuck did they do that?" They were on a roll. Nothing was stopping them.'

Demi's movie, which beat Bruce's into production, was backed by Columbia Tristar and her company was one of three independents involved. She would be the star; Willis was naturally cast as her screen male interest. As co-producer, she had nailed down a tough contract that gave her cast approval, script approval and hire and fire rights. She negotiated pre-production finance through bankers and then dealt personally with the studio moneymen, marketing and promotion. She drew up the filming schedule which was, in part, to accommodate the commitments of her husband. 'I started cautiously,' she admitted, 'tiptoeing and learning as I went along, but suddenly I was in deep and involved in decisions that went right down the line. It was a good experience, but Bette Davis was right. When a man gives his opinion, he's a man. When a woman gives hers, she's a bitch.'

The latter opinion emerged in week one of filming, when she fired the director Claude Kerven over 'creative differences'. Demi said she 'didn't like what we were getting.' She replaced him with the quirky but highly competent Alan Rudolph who had won some excellent reviews on his last two movies, which he also wrote – *The Moderns*, an excellent film with Keith Carradine and Linda Fiorentino, and *Love At Large* with Tom Berenger.

Coming in at a late hour to *Mortal Thoughts* gave him little time to prepare; Demi's influence was also firmly established and although Rudolph was not a man to take liberties with, she pretty well got her way. Rudolph speaks of her demanding nature not in a derogatory sense, but regarding it as her strength: 'She has an opinion on everything and she lets you know it. She's very, very smart, like a beautiful ballerina who can also kick a box. But there's an honesty about her; she's absolutely straight. She and Bruce both. They come from some place that has a real truth about it. You go to their house and the warmth between them is totally genuine. I reckon that's their ultimate protection.'

It was a woman's picture in terms of lead roles. Moore was the star, along with Glenne Headly (fresh from *Dirty Rotten Scoundrels* and *Dick Tracy*). Willis took third billing and there was a strong support team that included the ever-staunch Harvey Keitel, the Willis's neighbour and close friend. *Mortal Thoughts* is a suspense thriller about two friends who work in a New Jersey beauty salon. The owner, Joyce Urbanski (Glenne Headly), is married to Jim, played by Bruce Willis. He is a drunken despot of a husband who beats her, lies to her and steals her money. Joyce's friend and business partner, Cynthia (Moore), watches, with growing concern, the violence in her friend's marriage. They are to be seen discussing the question whether Jim ought to be murdered. Once, she had even put rat poison in the sugar bowl, but retrieved it at the last minute. Then, when the two women go to a carnival, Jim is found dead. Thus, the story unfolds, framed through a series of flashbacks during Keitel's interrogation of Moore.

In spite of the offscreen pressure, Moore was clearly growing in strength as an actress. It was certainly one of her better performances to date. Equally, Rudolph eased Willis through his scenes as the unpalatable Jim, an especially unglamorous role, with few hints of his usual trademarks. Overall, it was a courageous offering of a downbeat story, racked with banal language and pathetic lies. Rudolph conducts the whole thing with style and wit, aided by an ingenious plot construction. It was, however, never a contender in terms of being a box office hit. It was competent but not compelling enough to attract big box office success, but it was a financial success for Moore. With herself and Willis taking fees from the end result, the movie was made for $12 million and earned three times that in receipts.

The experience for Demi Moore was strong enough to add some more grist to the tabloid mill. As lady boss of the movie, she acquired additional status and before long, there were stories filtering through that this event merely increased her proclivity towards prima donna instincts.

Word had it that, as a busy producer and actress, she wanted private planes, a suitable entourage of aides (from secretaries to bodyguards) and limos at every point of her journeys to and from the west coast. The words of Douglas Thompson, a British writer resident in LA, were not taken kindly when he posed the question about her: 'Where does assertiveness begin and megalomania end? Where's the fine line between Sunset Boulevard and peel-me-a-grape indulgence?'

In reply, Demi admitted she wanted it all: 'Yes, all those youthful, hopeful ambitions of childhood. Who doesn't? A lot of people want things but not everyone is willing to go out and get them. I am. It's hard walking away from opportunities now, chances I've been waiting for all my life. There are too many good actresses around to fill the roles for women. So you have to go out there and fight, pay attention, know what's going on. The reality is you have to generate roles for yourself. That's right, and nobody will stop me now.'

That was fighting talk. The more virulent writers took up the call and were soon headlining her autocratic stance, her petulant ways, her 'Gimme more' attitude. In a trice, she was sharing top billing with her husband as the tabloid's patsy.

It was, then, ironic that at the height of this minor war between them and the media, Willis should be offered the very role in which, through his portrayal, he supposed he might be able to score a few points back – although in reality it would never work out as he hoped.

* * *

The yuppies had already gone belly-up. Margaret Thatcher, the queen of avarice, and her chief cohort in that era of monetarism, Ronald Reagan, were being assigned to history. Oliver Stone had pierced the facade with *Wall Street* in 1987, berating not so much the greed-is-good philosophy of the financial operators who flouted the law (as epitomised by Michael Douglas playing the slimy Gekko), but the system itself that put wealth and profit above all other considerations. He could easily have been directing his message at Hollywood itself, and a moving target was soon in view.

Tom Wolfe's bestselling novel, *The Bonfire of the Vanities*, dealt with the same theme, the corrupt eighties, in a brutally sardonic, highly entertaining way. He set out to delve deeper into the social parallels rather than the financial shenanigans and his satirical saga of Sherman McCoy quickly became America's favourite tale of its time. The author set up a series of characters based, it was said, on real life prototypes whom he then clinically dissected and demolished with brilliant wit and style.

McCoy typified the so-called masters of the universe who earned millions from their shifty manoeuvrings on Wall Street and for whom the bottom line, cash at the bank, was just a way of keeping score. They had stunning lifestyles – flash motors, antique and art collections, beautiful wives at home and younger models as mistresses, tucked away in lavish apartments somewhere close to the office.

McCoy had all those things but put them in total jeopardy through one silly mistake: he took a wrong turning into a bad district of the Bronx while driving his mistress from the airport. As a result of that one error, his world falls apart: while searching for a way out, they are confronted by possible muggers and the mistress unwittingly backs the car over a black youth. They speed away, apparently leaving the youth dying. The story is sniffed out by an alcoholic tabloid journalist.

Desperate for a big story, he blows this one into the headlines with the aid of a black minister and soon, a whole circle of religious leaders, black activists, white politicians and opportunist lawyers are all using the story for their own particular causes. Sherman is finally tracked down and ends up in jail, disgraced and discarded by his friends.

What makes Wolfe's book so compelling is the way he gets into the heads of the characters he has created. His story is filled with well-crafted nuances about their attitudes, ambitions, their relationships and lifestyles. Nothing is left to the imagination.

The tome went straight into the *New York Times* bestseller lists and was bought at proof stage by Brian de Palma with the backing of the Warner studio. It then became what *Variety* termed 'a misfire of inanities.'

That well-aimed missile came later. In the beginning, there were high hopes and lots of big talk. The movie of the book of the moment? How could it fail, especially as de Palma was, at the time, a hot director in the aftermath of *The Untouchables*, his biggest ever success in an otherwise infuriatingly inconsistent collection of movies. As he went into a huddle with screenwriter Michael Cristofer, there was much speculation over the identity of the real-life characters who had provided Wolfe with his inspiration – especially concerning the narrator, Peter Fallow, who was supposedly British.

The *New York Post*'s gossip page related the tale of one British journalist, proudly boasting that the character was based upon himself – a curious admission since it put him immediately in the low-life bracket of lax morals, even worse ethics, perpetual drunkenness and a nasty habit of leaving his guests at the dinner table before the bill arrived. Yet another claimed the same and said he was contemplating issuing a writ against Wolfe for libel, although he did not pursue it.

After the who's who? speculation came the trade press discussion of who's playing who? A number of possibilities were being mentioned but, as it turned out, none of the suggestions matched the actors de Palma eventually hired. Bruce Willis, for example, was hardly a name to be associated with the British tabloid journalist, other than as a subject of one of his stories – or the fact that he loathed the whole species. Willis admits that he wanted the part as soon as he read about it, for exactly that reason. He thought it ironic and amusing that he might play a hack and twist the knife a little.

He wasn't de Palma's first choice though. For a start, his fast, New York wise guy voice had no hint of British intonation and he was nothing like the character Tom Wolfe had laid out. But, once again, Arnold Rifkin cut a deal for which de Palma was prepared to ignore the accent and any other discrepancies. Willis was hired and placed on standby, to perform as soon as he had finished *Die Hard 2*.

Eyebrows were also raised as de Palma named his other star players: Tom Hanks and Melanie Griffith. It was now clear that commerce and box office would take precedence over all other considerations. He was going for young actors currently enjoying success at the box office: Griffith had just appeared in her own best-ever movie, *Working Girl*, for which she received an Oscar nomination, a success she found difficulty in repeating. Hanks had also scored hits with *Big* and then *Turner and Hooch*. But neither could be compared to the task now at hand. Two years down the line, when Hanks was beginning to show greater maturity, he might have been better equipped to deal with Tom Wolfe's creation. At the time, he was a fairly lightweight actor although that, as it happened, was more or less in line with the screen adaptation presented by de Palma and Cristofer.

They came up with a script that might just have stood a chance of being accepted as half decent if it had been an original idea. That, in a nutshell, was the problem with de Palma's movie. There had been so much hype and such great expectations for the film version that he was on a hiding to nothing from the start. He compounded his difficulties with a lacklustre conversion in which Wolfe's subtle undertones and character insights were largely lost. This was partly due to the quality of the performances of the lead actors but perhaps, as with the F. Scott Fitzgerald novels which have never been successful on the big screen, these subtleties were always beyond transfer from the written word.

The film, which cost $40 million and suffered various production delays, wasn't all bad. There were many entertaining moments and some strong secondary performances by a supporting cast of fine actors including Morgan Freeman, F. Murray Abraham, Donald Moffat, Robert Stephens, and Andre Gregory.

The three principals, however, all seemed to miss the mark. Hanks was flat and showed little real emotion as he ploughed through Sherman McCoy's troubling adventures. Griffith, whose normal monotone delivery did not suit the Southern accent required by the part, was perhaps the least impressive. Willis, as the journalist Peter Fallow and thus the subject of particular interest from the media, ambled through the story in typical conversational style but provided little in the way of verbal elegance or insight.

In the cold light of day, when the history of it had subsided, the film could be watched again with a less jaundiced eye. It was an entertaining movie, but it could also have been so much better.

Willis, whose role as the narrator detained him for little more than a month, pocketed his $3 million and moved on. The release of *The Bonfire of the Vanities* was months away when he returned to pressing matters of his own creation – *Hudson Hawk*, his self-inspired, self-motivated, self-starring and semi-self-produced mega-movie was ready to go into production.

And so The Big One finally lumbered towards fruition. It was Willis's dream. He had been working on it for years, since he had scribbled the outline in long hand during his bartending days in New York. Joel Silver had read it, and found the money.

It was to be a big budget movie and the trade newspapers, who had been giving a running commentary on its development, were talking about 'a spend' in excess of $35 million. Willis would be the star, co-writer and co-producer although the bulk of the latter department was in the hands of the New Tycoon. Willis, though, was also putting a large chunk of his personal fortune behind *Hudson Hawk*, just to get it made. Having confidence in yourself is one thing but backing it up with your own money might be considered unwise – something many luminaries greater than himself had already done, and ended up losing their shirts. But *Hawk* was going to be a winner. Joel Silver said so.

He had made the prediction to his assembled admirers at the premiere party of *Die Hard 2*: 'We'll be bringing home a great movie – bigger than *Die Harder*.' How could anyone disbelieve the great man?

The screenplay had already been the subject of much tinkering and delay but now filming was scheduled to begin in the first week of August at the Cinecitta studios in Rome, where much of the movie is set.

The movie is a contorted caper-cum-adventure tale which owes more to *Indiana Jones* or Michael Douglas's *Romancing The*

Stone than anything Willis had been involved in previously. The story evolves around Willis's character, a famous catburglar who is released from prison having done his time. The sympathy card is played early on, with Hawk being blackmailed back into the business to save the life of his best pal. There is a CIA connection, an assortment of curious and miscellaneous villains, priceless Leonardo da Vinci treasures and three crystals which, when put together correctly, are supposed to bring great wealth and gold: on the whole, a string of sequences and subplots that are supposedly filled with jokes and humour that would have the audiences carried away by good feelings of mirth and excitement. At least, that was the plan.

Willis and Silver, plus entourage (which included two large bodyguards for Willis), flew out of LA at the end of July, ready for the first day's rehearsals on 1 August. The film people were the only people arriving. Didn't they know that all Romans who could do so got out of the place in August to escape the horrendous heat? Soaring temperatures and hot passions lay ahead. The shoot was going to be expensive, with hefty travelling costs to Italy and a lot of toing and froing between Rome, New York, LA and various other venues.

The bulk of filming was to be at Cinecitta where the taxi ride from the airport is expensive enough to launch a battleship. However, a fleet of hire cars were standing by to meet the incoming first-class passengers. Among the wheels specially flown in was a deep-purple 1955 Chrysler, customised and stretched for interiors in the movie and equipped with telephones, fax and shredder so that the star would never be too far from his communications system.

The cast was assembling for what was supposed to be a three-month shoot, maximum. It was an impressive array of talent that checked into Rome's expensive hotels: Marushka Detmers, then famous for her appearance in the X-rated *Devil in the Flesh*, and booked to play Willis's love interest; James Coburn, accompanied by partner Paula who was constantly on hand wherever and whatever he was doing; Willis's onscreen sidekick, Italian Danny Aiello, whose wife also popped over now and again and Sandra Bernhard and Richard E. Grant, who made up a comedy double act both on and offscreen.

Above left The boy Willis, an ugly duckling, spotty and stammering, emerges into a handsome teenager *(Yardley Collection)*

Above right Top row, far right – the life of every party and born leader of the youthful revelries at school *(Yardley Collection)*

Above A young Demi Moore, in search of icons, focuses on Marilyn Monroe *(Yardley Collection)*

Right Demi with her first husband – small-time rock musician Freddie Moore, who later spoke bitterly about their time together *(Yardley Collection)*

Above Willis's only
television appearance of
note was in an episode of
Miami Vice in which he
met his future friend and
good-time accompanist
Don Johnson (*ABC
Television*)

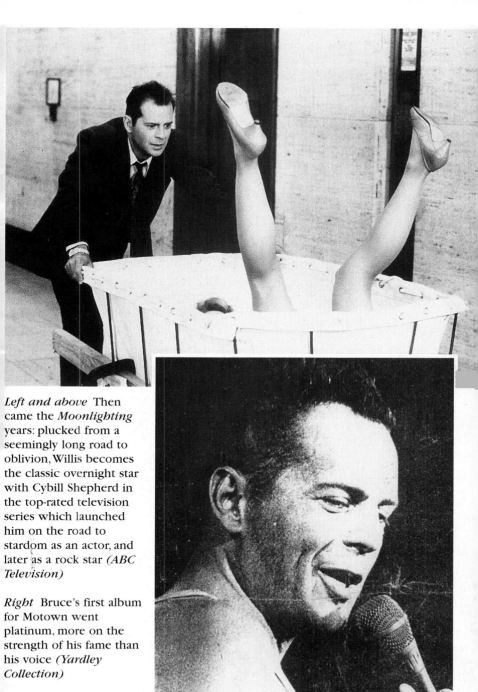

Left and above Then
came the *Moonlighting*
years: plucked from a
seemingly long road to
oblivion, Willis becomes
the classic overnight star
with Cybill Shepherd in
the top-rated television
series which launched
him on the road to
stardom as an actor, and
later as a rock star *(ABC
Television)*

Right Bruce's first album
for Motown went
platinum, more on the
strength of his fame than
his voice *(Yardley
Collection)*

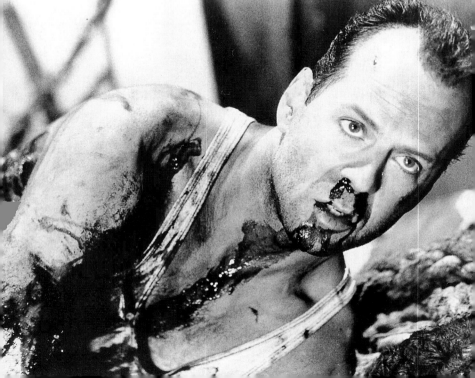

Into the mainstream of Hollywood, and after two low-key movies for Blake Edwards, Willis hits the big screen with a bang in what has become a classic series in the action adventure genre: *Die Hard* ... then *Harder* ... and *With a Vengeance*. Unlike the body-oiled, muscle-bound supermen of Stallone and Schwarzenegger vintage, Willis presents his hero as just an ordinary, vulnerable guy *(Fox)*

Left With Damon Wayans in *Last Boy Scout (Warner Bros)*

Below With Sarah Jessica Parker in *Striking Distance (Columbia Pictures)*

Bottom With British actress Jane March in *Color of Night*, in which he gave a full frontal performance *(Hollywood Pictures)*

Above As Butch Coolidge, the role that gave Bruce his fading career a much-needed boost in Tarantino's brilliant *Pulp Fiction (Miramax Films)*

Below Willis consolidated his revival in Terry Gilliam's highly rated *Twelve Monkeys (Yardley Collection)*

Above Back on top as one of Hollywood's highest earners, Willis is matched by his wife Demi Moore in on-screen and off-screen dollar activity *(Yardley Collection)*

Left Demi's career is bolstered, perhaps, by a propensity towards taking her kit off, as in *Striptease (Columbia Pictures)*

Director Michael Lehmann, then 30 years old, was supposedly in charge. He was another of Joel Silver's 'I'm-gonna-make-you-a-star' young bloods, and had absolutely no previous experience of a multi-million dollar movie populated by strong actors with a star who set the whole thing up and a producer whose moods swung from charming can't-do-enough-for-you persuasiveness to total Atilla.

At that time, Lehmann's claim to fame comprised only two movies. The first was *Heathers*, the black comedy starring Chris Slater and Winona Ryder who had waded through the foul-mouthed dialogue to become macabre cultist heroes. He followed that with *Meet The Applegates*, another cult hit which had Stockard Channing and Ed Begley jnr leading a xenophobic parody of the average American family. Neither equipped him for what he was about to experience in Rome where, apart from the fact that Cinecitta has a particularly *Italian* way of doing things, the New Tycoon was in charge and it was Willis's picture in every other way: 'Mikey . . . don't you think we should do it this way . . .'

There was a three-way split, with each having a different view of things. Willis, as the instigator of the piece, also had cast and script approval built into his contract and so had the right to alter the script, add and subtract jokes, watch the daily rushes, order retakes of scenes he was not happy with etc., etc., etc., etc. Slow progress (with Silver looking at his watch and his aides hollering their concern over missed deadlines) was exacerbated when Marushka Detmers threw in the towel one week into filming. There was much rumour and gossip, and very soon American and British tabloids were running the story under such headlines as: 'DEMI TELLS BRUCE IT'S HER OR ME.'

The parable according to the gossips was that Willis had taken his love interest too far, was having a fair old fling with Marushka and that Mrs W. had become exceedingly angry, demanding that she should be fired immediately or he could say goodbye to their marriage. The truth was far less sensational. Detmers wanted out and, according to her managers, had been suffering fainting fits because of a back problem. Goodbye Marushka.

The Silver-Willis-Lehmann triumverate went into a panicky huddle, scouring an imaginary *Who's Who in the Movies* and thinking up names who might replace her. Silver faxed Madonna with an offer she couldn't refuse, but did. Joanne Whaley-Kilmer also turned them down. The search went on.

Richard E. Grant's account of the tempestuous, combustible atmosphere of the *Hudson Hawk* set, as recorded in his diaries, sums it all up in a few legendary sentences. Grant describes Silver's frustration at the time difference with Los Angeles and his attempts to make a deal with an agent: 'What the fuck is fucking wrong with this country that it should be eight fucking hours ahead of everywhere else? Answer me, you fuck! . . .'

Someone, somewhere, picks up the phone, and Silver continues: 'You tell that fucking dickbrain to stick her up his ageing asshole you fuck-faced wasp. That if he had any decency he would have returned my call instead of acting like his shrivelled old dick was already in the Metropolitan Museum of Fucking . . . We could have done the fucking deal . . .' And so on.

Eventually, a friendly face came to the rescue in the shape of Andie MacDowell, who brought her husband Paul and two children along for the ride. Filming resumed and continued for weeks and months, event upon event. A saga superbly set out and highly recommended for further reading in Richard E. Grant's book, *With Nails*, in which one memorable phrase perhaps best typifies the scenario: 'Standing in "Vargas-girl" high heels, crotchless leather panties, brassiere, stockings and lipstick, like a lost member of some touring *Rocky Horror Show* is the *exact* moment that I know – beyond reasonable doubt – THAT THIS MOVIE IS A ONE-WAY TICKET OUT OF MY MIND.'

The icily taciturn James Coburn (seen it all, been there a thousand times and definitely won't wear the T-shirt), calmly surveyed the hysteria. He smiled that great toothy smile and told Grant to cool it: 'This is a big budget movie, with big budget egos. Enjoy.'

In September, Demi Moore flew in with baby Rumer. It was her first visit and she chatted merrily to Andie MacDowell as they compared notes about their children. Demi's visit coincided with the appearance of a spread of photographs featuring Bruce and Andie, taken with a long-distance lens by an Italian paparazzo hidden in some Roman ruin, or perhaps a passing helicopter. They were published in the *Sunday Mirror* and elsewhere.

Headline: 'A TOUCH OF MOONLIGHTING,' and the story began: 'These sensational pictures are likely to land actor Bruce Willis in hot water' – alleging, by implication, that Willis had taken MacDowell off on a secret trist somewhere in Rome to explore an unscripted romantic liaison. They even printed an assessment by a 'leading psychologist' who claimed that the body language displayed in the photographs revealed a 'warm and tender bond between Andie and Bruce.'

Once again, the truth was less enticing than the fiction. The pictures were close-up shots of MacDowell and Willis, arm in arm, arm around shoulder, her head on his chest – fully clothed. Nothing particularly sensational, even if the implication of an affair had some basis – which it didn't. If the photographer's lens had been widened to its full setting, the scene would have also shown about four dozen actors, crew and technicians in the foreground.

Upon such a slender thread hung what amounted to a disparaging attack on two marriages, Andie MacDowell's and Bruce Willis's. In this instance, it could be dismissed as so much garbage, but the public never sees the denials. In a way, the creative journalism and outright lies published by some of the more virulent scandal sheets has the effect of nullifying the truth, even when it is learned.

Denials are disregarded by the mass public with, 'Well, they daren't print it if it isn't the truth . . .' And then, when something really sensational happens, and it is true, there is no way of discerning its validity. Here truth and fiction, with the cruelty and the crassness of modern publicity, was becoming a tangled web of idiosyncrasies that only time could unravel.

These interludes apart, the progress of *Hudson Hawk* was beginning to gather a few rather more serious undertones in the more responsible sections of the media. The arrival of first-class suits on a flight from Los Angeles signalled problems on another front. Money.

According to the usually impeccable source of the showbiz bible, *Variety*, by the end of October, *Hudson Hawk* had a financial commitment of $61 million, which was rather a lot over budget. It was still not beyond salvation, provided the movie was brilliant. The jinx-like attachments to its progress, however, seemed to get worse rather than better. The lead cinematographer was fired or quit, depending on which version you believe, during continued delays in filming. Several members of the cast were suffering from what Richard Grant described as 'industrial fatigue.' Director Michael Lehmann collapsed with a bout of pneumonia and Willis himself injured his hand during one of the many stunts he performed himself.

The dog-eared script had so many multi-coloured revisions that it was becoming indecipherable. As co-producer, Michael Dryhurst recalls: 'It sounds like a nightmare and it was, believe me.' Another observer, however, went further and was quoted by the trade press back in LA, cruelly citing some of the movie's non-technical setbacks as 'overwhelming ambition' and, in the case of Willis, 'setting new standards for the misappropriation of star power.'

By then, filming had moved to a vast and remote studio near Budapest for the last month of filming where, for some inexplicable reason, they were shooting against mocked-up *Italian* sets. They also moved out into the countryside which provided scenic values which might pass for Russia, as required by the screenplay. Willis returned after another brief disappearance to New York and demanded: 'Let's get this fucking show on the road . . . I don't want to spend the rest of my life eating goulash.'

And so it went on until the third week in November when they called it a wrap. Willis and Silver made a fast exit, back to LA to prepare a trailer and try to put three and a half months of film into a presentable two-hour blockbuster.

Willis refused to concede that he was sitting on a potential disaster. 'It is every movie you ever wanted to make,' he declared. 'It fun and thrilling – action, adventure and lots of jokes. People will love it.' Only time would tell if he was right.

10 More Naked Ambition

A N AIR OF FOREBODING! The atmosphere was thick with it when Willis returned from Europe. Gleeful chuckles up and down Sunset Boulevard said it all: Willis was in trouble. Four of his movies would be released into the cinemas in the coming twelve months. There was shuddering apprehension about three of them, already being dissected, even trashed, long before they were on view in the cinemas. *The Bonfire of the Vanities* was getting a hugely bad press ahead of its release. *Hudson Hawk* was hidden by dark clouds and being spoken of with derision. No amount of hypery could disguise it. There was also strife on the set of the much-heralded $40 million gangster epic *Billy Bathgate* starring Dustin Hoffman and Nicole Kidman and in which Willis played one of the lesser roles.

Director Brian Benton was reportedly on the verge of being fired by Disney during the latter stages of production. Willis had filmed his scenes in the movie before he left for Rome. Completion was delayed several months to reshoot some sections, including the ending. Willis had been recalled in November while still at work on the *Hawk*. The rumoured discontent on the set was confirmed later when Hoffman went public to accuse Benton of shutting him out of the creative process. Benton, the quiet-spoken former screenwriter who directed Hoffman in *Kramer vs Kramer*, responded by saying he never felt a lack of studio support and was 'dismayed' by Hoffman's comments.

As far as Willis was concerned, Benton was full of praise: 'An immensely gifted actor who in his quieter movies is also very powerful.' Once again, Willis had worked for a scale fee of $1,685 a week and a back-end deal. 'You can count on one hand the number of actors who are prepared to do that,' said Benton. 'If the material interests him, he doesn't care about the money.'

The public's chance to view the outcome was still months away. The premiere of *Billy* was put back indefinitely and would eventually get into the schedules for November 1991; it was one more ticking time-bomb in Willis's future. A more immediate one was waiting to explode as his plane touched down in Los Angeles. Brian de Palma's film *The Bonfire of the Vanities* hit the cinemas just as Willis got back.

It was pounded into the ground by the critics, and that was no surprise. In Willis's view, it was a stillborn movie: 'It was born dead, already reviewed, critiqued, shat on and discarded before anyone saw a frame of it.' This was true to a degree, but the reaction was not wholly undeserved, either. As already noted, *Bonfire* had its moments but generally missed its targets by a mile.

Critic after critic kicked the limp body and phrases like 'laughing stock' and 'miscast and banal' were amply applied. As the fictional journalist among the cast, and the character which had attracted so much speculation from Wolfe's novel, Willis was a particular target for their acidity. Worse was to follow.

Way back, as filming began, Brian de Palma had allowed author Julie Salamon total access to the set for a book on the making of the movie, presumably on the assumption that it was going to be a major hit – as in *The Making of Gone With The Wind*. In her eventual tome, *The Devil's Candy*, Salamon was brutally frank in her observations, quoting everybody's high hopes and then their excuses. She spared nothing in her assessment of Willis's portrayal, along with disparaging references to his bodyguards, salary and other excesses. Even his hair rates a mention in the index.

Willis's personal hairdresser, Jose Norman, was instructed to be on set at all times, according to Salamon. 'Whenever the lights shone so that his scalp peeked through his thinning hair, she would complain to Zsigmond (the cinematographer): "Back lights, take out!" The bald spot obsessed her.'

Salamon saved her most savage invective for Willis's acting which she observed firsthand throughout filming. 'He was trapped by the limitations of his range,' she wrote. 'He simply couldn't turn off the smirk.'

Willis's response was potent. He fantasised with stuttering sarcasm: 'I wish her the best. What I had hoped for her was that she would become so famous that she had to start worrying about her life, that she had to start feeling that she was threatened and then had to sleep with a gun by the bed every night because she thought that she was so famous someone was going to attack her ... And then one night, she finally realised the sick life she was living and she just put a gun to her mouth AND BLEW HER FUCKIN' BRAINS OUT.'

It was the smirk that did it.

It helped launch him and now it was his curse. Once, it had been the hook to hang his success story on; by 1990, it had been turned against him and was being used in the most negative sense. *Whipping boy. No fuckin' pleasing them.* He moaned and talked of malice aforethought, but he ain't seen nothin' yet!

Sweetness and light did not prevail in the Willis household that Christmas, for Demi was gloomy, too. While Willis was away in Rome, she had taken on two more movies. The first was for Dan Aykroyd, making his debut as director in a movie he also wrote and starred in entitled *Nothing But Trouble*. Along for the ride were his old friends Chevy Chase and John Candy, plus Moore in a fourth-billing role. It was a collection of old jokes and abysmal, often grotesque 'humour' applied to an improbable plot about a New York couple stranded in a village where some old fogy of a judge has absolute rule.

Her other movie at that time began rather more promisingly. In *The Butcher's Wife*, directed by Terry Hughes, she plays a clairvoyant who marries a New York butcher and then falls in love with a local psychiatrist. Along the way, she is telling her husband's customers about her premonitions concerning their lives. It is a whimsical tale, a folksy, romantic comedy with supernatural leanings – thus at least aligning it to the hugely successful *Ghost*.

The film had originally been developed for Meg Ryan, but she had dropped out at the last minute. Demi came in at a late stage and was able to negotiate some favourable terms. Although she badly needed another hit, her personal attitude was one which gave no ground, no indication that she was anything but a Star, regardless of the fact that she had not yet really become one.

She was a tough lady who set her own agenda and the producers of *The Butcher's Wife* pandered to her every need, desire and whim – they, too, aware that her success in *Ghost* and the vague association of plots could help carry their own movie. They provided a dialogue coach, a masseuse in daily attendance and a psychic consultant who would be her guide in her clairvoyance, along with the usual entourage of personal aide, make-up artist, hairdresser and stand-in.

She was given a personal limo to take her to the studio and had a private plane to deliver her to and from locations. 'She's a very focused woman,' said movie screenwriter Ezra Litwak. 'She is also very much a movie star and everything revolves around that fact. As far as the movie was concerned, she had a strong conception of the role and it wasn't up for discussion. Period.'

This resolute stance clearly caused dissension during filming and first-time director Terry Hughes didn't stand a chance. Having seen the producers give her all she wanted, he could be forgiven for feeling intimidated by her. At the beginning of filming, she suddenly turned up in a blonde wig and announced she would wear it for the movie. She wanted her character to be quite different, physically, from the one she had played in *Ghost*. It altered her looks totally, from the elfin style to a harsher appearance. One set observer claimed, 'Terry Hughes knew if he upset her, he might be sacked. He did get very angry, though, when she started handing out notes to other actors with hints on how they should play a particular scene.'

Hughes later accused her in print of being unable to take direction, refusing his suggestions. She responded: 'Very offensive. I was fighting to make a good movie, not crying for an orange juice on set.' The hints of bitterness did not auger well. The movie was due into the cinemas in the summer, soon after Willis's *Hudson Hawk* premiere, just as *Ghost* followed *Die Hard 2*.

As for *Nothing But Trouble*, it would provide exactly what the title forecast. Why she ever became mixed up in it is a mystery. She knew when she had done it that it was a vile clinker, deservedly sent packing, though her set-backs on these two films were nothing like the desperate hours facing her husband during the coming months. She, incidentally, also took herself off the rota for the whole of 1991, having discovered she was expecting their second child.

Willis went straight back to work with the stinging reviews of *Bonfire* still rebounding off the walls. Joel Silver told him to forget it; it was a blip he had no control over. He was just one actor. How could he affect the outcome of the movie? Blame de Palma. Or studio boss Peter Guber who personally chose Tom Hanks. It was a stigma they all shared. Nor was Silver apprehensive in paying Willis $8 million in his next major project, ready for immediate production – *The Last Boy Scout*, for which great expectations were also stirring.

Silver had already hit the headlines when he coughed up a reported record $1.75 million for the screenplay and, doubtless, the author, Shane Black could not believe his luck. There was, however, an emerging pattern to Mr Silver's largesse and loyalty to his employees and friends: Black also wrote the screenplays for *Lethal Weapon* and *Lethal Weapon 2*, both Silver productions, of course, which had done well.

A large budget had been secured for this one with the backing of Warners although it was clear from the outset that the money would be spent on big action scenarios and special effects. Willis was the only star in an otherwise fairly anonymous cast list, another of Silver's previously observed tactics in these movies: one star, lots of action, big bucks, high profit. The same was happening in another production running parallel to the Willis movies: the New Tycoon was also producing the Denzel Washington action-thriller, the ultimately disappointing *Ricochet*. The greenbacks must have been floating around the Silver organisation like confetti at a wedding.

Tony Scott, now fed up with being described as the younger brother of British film-maker Ridley (but its always worth recording), was hired to direct *The Last Boy Scout*. Doubtless Silver remembered those scenes from Scott's first feature film *The Hunger* (1983), which provided us with the romantic passions of ageing roué David Bowie and vampire Catherine Deneuve, along with a few lesbian clinches between Deneuve and Susan Sarandon. Latterly, his most successful film was *Top Gun*, with Tom Cruise.

Scott is a skilful director, and this movie offered a new challenge which he handled with exceptional aplomb, turning exceedingly cynical material into a slick if mindless (and certainly mind-boggling) movie. Why, exactly, the story was judged to be worth such a large fortune is not so obvious. One can only assume that it had something to do with Black's ability to conjure up from his imaginings the savage content or, possibly, it was linked to the word-count of 'fuck' and 'motherfucker', both of which were used incessantly in the supposedly modern locker-room dialogue that passed for scripts at the beginning of the 1990s. Or, on the other hand, the writer may have been taking copious notes while listening to an angry Joel Silver speaking on the telephone.

It was, none the less, sharp and witty and provided the kind of lines that bring the best out of Willis – although, taking account of his then current situation, it seemed that some had been written by a prophetic hand.

Playing the role of private eye Joe Hallenbeck, there is a scene where his buddy Jimmy Dix tells him:

'Hi, you're nobody!'

Hallenbeck: 'Shhh, don't tell anyone.'

The jokes come thick and fast, *Moonlighting* dialogue spiced with expletives, as in his encounter with a gun-toting thug in an alley:

Thug: 'Wrong place, wrong time. Nothing personal.'

Hallenbeck: 'That's what you think. Last night I fucked your wife.'

Thug: 'Oh? How'd you know it was my wife?'

Hallenbeck: 'She said her husband was a big pimp-lookin' motherfucker with a hat.'

Thug: 'You're real cool but you've got to take a bullet.'

Hallenbeck: 'After fucking your wife I'll take two.'

And later, in more verbals with a baddie:

'You think you are so fucking cool, don't you? You think you are so fucking cool. But just once, I would like to hear you scream in pain.'

Hallenbeck: 'Play some rap music.'

Otherwise, it is a standard formula plot which has Willis cast as a too-honest former secret service agent, now retired after stopping several bullets intended for President Jimmy Carter and running a seedy private eye agency. He is hired by a disgraced former football star who was kicked out of the game for gambling. He wants him to protect his girlfriend, a stripper by profession, who is being threatened.

The connection leads to a wider involvement with a corrupt football team owner. At this point, the sleaze balls and heavies are rolled in. This basic one-sentence storyline explodes from its opening with a scene of stomach-churning violence, and then Silver's trademark pyrotechnics take over: big bangs, edge-of-the-seat car chases, machine gun battles and blood and guts in a rolling crescendo of non-stop violence.

Rough treatment of women is not an uncommon feature of Silver's movies, and this one expands the theme. They are whores and bitches and get their usual comeuppance, but this time he pushes the boundaries even further, towards children. Willis's character is accompanied by a 13-year-old daughter, as foul-mouthed as the rest of the characters in this film, who is hauled around by baddies threatening to blow her brains out.

Somehow, and awful though it was, it all hung together. Perhaps not too surprising given that the genre was in vogue: indiscriminate, gratuitous, mindless violence and extra-strong language was spreading from the confines of cult movies and across the spectrum of Hollywood output.

So, *The Last Boy Scout* took its place in the Willis movie queue, scheduled for general release in December. *Billy Bathgate* now had a date: premiering October, general release November. But the big showdown was already on the horizon. His very own Big Picture, *Hudson Hawk* would premiere on 17 May 1991, and hyperventilation set in.

The movie had already undergone open-heart surgery following poor reaction from test audiences. Director Michael Lehmann came back for the final cut but unhappiness still abounded. Around the opening, Columbia-TriStar Pictures 'proudly announce' a press conference to launch the Michael Lehmann film, *Hudson Hawk*. A two day junket was laid on, culminating in the showing of the film.

On the morning of the 16th, the stars of the show were herded into the ballroom of a plush Hollywood hotel, filled with tables for individual chats with the assembled media corps, as is the way of such occasions when super-hype is necessary. The stars were given a short lecture on tactics before they went in: talk up the movie, tell 'em it was terrific, inspired, everybody had so much fun and Bruce Willis was terrific, too.

The media, well briefed on the foregoing story, came armed with pencils honed to a perfect stabbing point and dipped in poison. Hostility lay across the proceedings like a wet blanket. It was rumoured that someone had a barrel of tar and a bag of feathers in the boot of his car.

They didn't want to hear Bruce telling them that this was it, the movie he had always wanted to make, a James Bond spoof caper that is action packed and full of jokes and moronic wit and teeming with excitement. They wanted to know about the money, the overspend, actors' salaries, the reported 80 drafts of the script, the departure of Marushka Detmers and all the other things that went wrong.

One of them even managed to elicit a bitter quote from Michael Lehmann who was reported as saying: 'That's what happens when a box office star is surrounded by yes-men and who let him put on his own show without question.'

On the second day of the junket, reports from the first day were already filtering through; the news was all bad and the shredding machines were overheating, ripping up photocopies of the nasty clippings. Willis and Silver continued to speak in grandiose terms and wouldn't let go. 'Fuck 'em,' said Silver that day over lunch with Bruce and Richard Grant. 'They have it in for us, they always have. That's all. We're gonna open massive across the nation next weekend – MASSIVE!'

'You betcha!'

On to the premiere: the venue was the same Westwood Cineplex where *Die Hard 2* had opened to a rapturous reception barely a year earlier. The scenario was the same: long lines of limos ferrying the stars; search lights and television cameras, lots of paparazzi and crowds lining the pavements. Bruce and Demi got a cheer, she wearing a stunning new gown, glittering and shimmery in the lights and he in best bib and tucker, black tie and winged collar. Inside, the lights went down, the TriStar logo and the white horse galloped forth and a loud cheer greeted the rolling credits.

Thereafter, there was subdued reaction building to a crescendo of silence. Richard E. Grant, among the audience to witness the reception, recorded his own feelings thus: 'I remember how the cinema erupted at the end of *Die Hard 2* and engulfed Bruce ... while tonight you would swear some miraculous special effects crew had been in to make a thousand people disappear. By the time the house lights are up, the stalls are bare. Like that old Emperor's balls.'

The premiere party turned into a wake. It was not, this time, at the Silver mansion but an ill-chosen club called The Asylum where, according to Grant, the cast waited like inmates for the VIPs who never arrived – or precious few. 'The waiters finally outnumber the guests. I flee,' wrote Grant. 'Absolutely certain that I will never work in this town again. THE SHAME . . .'

The reviews were universally bad, and invariably went well beyond a pure assessment of the movie. Attacks on Willis and Silver were rolled up into one vitriolic package. Willis was devastated by them. Criticism was one thing, but this was a wholesale attack against everything he stood for – professionally and privately; his work, his lifestyle, the golden money-grabbing couple image, the entourage, even his past misdemeanours – everything was dredged up and smelled of pent-up press emotions.

Could this be it? The crash and burn?

As to the film, when readers got past the elongated poison pen letters, they discovered this was a perfect example of vanity film-making, overblown and incoherent. There were some good action scenes, some nice set pieces, even some very funny interludes – but nothing to hang them on except Willis's steady output of wise-cracks which in the end became tiresome. 'A whopping blooper,' said the *New York Post*. 'A fractured flick that easily qualifies as one of the worst films ever made.'

The hawk that became a turkey; the caper that was a capon. The jibes were all there, and frankly quite deserved. It was a dead cert for the Turkey of the Decade Award by the Alternative Academy. Nor was *Hudson Hawk* anything like Joel Silver's predicted 'massive' opening in 2,000 cinemas across the nation. It bombed in all of them. The first weekend, when box office returns indicate festivities or failure, *Hawk* took measly money and registered only 3 on the Richter scale, behind two other not very good movies, Ron Howard's *Backdraft* and the Bill Murray vehicle, *What About Bob?*

Willis's ambitions as a film-maker were on the floor, along with his $65 million flop that barely covered costs when the international returns came in. There was unrestrained glee in some quarters, and the whispers on everyone's lips at the double-A parties, which Willis doesn't get to, was: 'He's had it. Finito. No more . . . and no Moore.'

The last point was a reference to new and, incidentally, unfounded rumours of a split. Demi, it was said, wanted out because Bruce was a loser and it was pulling her down with him. It was impossible for the marriage to survive. 'So much crap,' she said. There was, however, no doubt that she was suffering too.

She was caught in the backwash from Willis's bad press and a huge question mark hung over her own movie, *The Butcher's Wife*, due for release in August. Reports from the front were not encouraging. It was a nice, decent, pleasant picture but quite lacking in that quality that makes a movie a hit. The marketing people were already saying it would need a substantial kick of adrenaline to get it noticed.

And they got it.

Demi's masterplan began as she toyed around with ideas for promotion; something special. She couldn't go on the talk circuit because her second baby was due around the time of the release and anyhow, the movie was probably beyond being talked up. What transpired went beyond the movie and on to a more focused level: with a clinical analysis of her current situation, she decided that the promotional effort would be for Demi Moore.

The movie would be merely a hook and an aside; she knew by then that *The Butcher's Wife* would do nothing for the star status temporarily granted by *Ghost*. It was a small movie; small appeal and totally uncontroversial. She was nine years into her career, and should have followed *Ghost* with something that at least did good business. Instead, she had slammed herself into reverse. With the pregnancy keeping her off the screen for at least another year, she knew well that, unlike most leading men, a woman in Hollywood can fade to oblivion in that time.

She needed a sensation. And she achieved it in one.

Moore was a great storer of 'things to do or try' in the area of her ambitions, and one of those was to get on to the front cover of one of the major glossies like *Life* or *Vanity Fair*. She had tried it once before, when she was sixteen and had agreed to pose for a titillating spread of pictures that were published in *Oui*. The 'Cindy Crawford Story' was also current: how Richard Gere's good pal Herb Ritz virtually launched her into the heavens with a terrific set of topless photographs commissioned by *Playboy*. She quickly rose to be the highest paid model in the business, and was soon competing with Princess Diana for glossy front covers around the world.

Months before her second child was due, Demi had agreed to be interviewed by *Vanity Fair* for a story about herself. Later, out of conversations with *VF* photographer Annie Leibovitz, came the idea for a set of photographs of her in her heavily pregnant state, to accompany the article which was to be published at the time of the release of her new movie.

Nothing seedy, of course. Glamorous and stylish. During the planning of the shoot with Leibovitz, Demi had the thought of wearing something sexy. 'Wouldn't it be kind of quirky to put a pregnant woman in black lingerie?' she pondered. They agreed that this set-up would be ideal for one of the photographs – she would wear just a black lace bra and scanty, matching panties.

Then, they decided to go for the 'more natural state' – i.e. nude – that seemed in keeping with her condition. 'I did feel glamorous and beautiful and more free about my body,' she told the *VF* writers. 'Bruce had a lot to do with that. He told me often that I was beautiful in pregnancy – and of course I wouldn't have done it at all if I'd felt it was morally questionable.'

Willis gave apprehensive approval and even agreed to give a rare interview about his wife for the article. The whole idea was snatched up by the editors of *Vanity Fair*. A posse of writers, photographers, make-up artists, hairdressers, haute couturiers and jewellers descended upon the Willis household at Malibu and stayed for eight days. They dolled her up in high fashion and beach wear, adorned her in jewels lent by Laykin et Cie and robes supplied by Neiman Marcus of Beverly Hills and photographed her in various poses, at the house and elsewhere.

The Superpic was Demi, eight months pregnant, looking a model of glowing motherhood and wearing nothing but diamonds and a beatific smile.

It's publication on the front cover of *Vanity Fair* did indeed cause a sensation, even in this age of nudity on film and in the media. No one had ever been photographed nude *and* pregnant for anything other than a medical journal. Here, Demi Moore was presented in an iconic style that combined her Hollywood image with that certain chic in which pregnancy was regarded at the time.

As a PR stunt it was a classic – and it was also a fake. Few women have the ability, or the means, to put such a gloss on pregnancy by surrounding themselves with a small army of assistants, dressers and make-up artists. Demi tried to build up the 'natural' way of pregnancy; she was 'very comfortable' with it, and nakedness was part of basic motherhood.

Nature, in this case, had nothing to do with it and what really showed through was not naked motherhood, but naked ambition. Both she and *Vanity Fair* editors were expecting a big reaction; they discussed all the possibilities before hand; it was, after all, a double-headed promotional exercise – for them and for her. But even they were surprised.

The cover brought international reaction and was reproduced by virtually every major newspaper in the major cities across the world. There were many, many protests, too, from groups complaining about the exploitation of 'this most precious gift' and in some Bible Belt towns across America, news-stands were ordered to put a white wrapper across the cover, to hide her naked and bulbous belly.

Yes, as a PR exercise, it had stunning results. *Vanity Fair* kept a check. In the US alone, there were mentions in 95 television stories, 64 radio shows, 1,500 newspaper articles and a dozen cartoons. Who used whom? Moore was quite frank about the commercial intent: 'I think we used each other,' she said. 'I would say in the usage of each other we were equal.'

The article that went with the photographs opened with a quote from Demi which seemed as if it was placed at the beginning in order to give a clear perspective of her intent: 'I don't think I'm a big-time movie star. My career's been very slow. I've certainly not jumped into the [superstar] crowd, the flavour of the month. I don't know that it will ever happen . . . I want to have enough going on in my life – the real stuff – so I can roll with the ups and downs.'

Later on, she conceded that many people viewed her as a bitch. That was because she asked for what she wanted, or believed should happen. 'I'm strong and opinionated, but not difficult in the sense that "My motor home isn't big enough." It doesn't bother me. Besides if you're a woman and ask for what you want you are treated differently than if you're a man . . . it's a lot more interesting to write about me being a bitch than being a nice woman.'

Interestingly, Moore also seemed ready – if not eager – to distance herself from her husband's recent troubles. 'The reviews [of *Hudson Hawk*] have been incredibly malicious,' she said. 'But in truth it hasn't absorbed into anything going on for me. Obviously I have compassion for my partner and would prefer the response . . . to be more positive. Other than that, I'M NOT INVOLVED WITH IT.'

In spite of all this, the promotional activity did little for her movie, *The Butcher's Wife*, which had little impact upon its release in August and it vanished quickly from the circuits. On the other hand, it had blasted Moore to international notoriety as the Nude Madonna Expecting Child; the child, a second, was born in August and they named her Scout, not after Willis's latest flick, but a character in *To Kill A Mockingbird*. The name was chosen by Demi. One of the immediate effects was that she was 'among the finalists' of women actresses who had read for the forthcoming Jack Nicholson/Tom Cruise film, *A Few Good Men*.

As for her husband, the year continued to offer no respite to the mass of bad press he had received from *Hudson Hawk*. The media focus and even greater scrutiny and assessment of his work was revived in late autumn. First came the critical appraisal of Robert Benton's gangster epic *Billy Bathgate*, receiving a tepid response upon its release in November.

It was another of those movies for which so much was, rightly perhaps, expected: Disney had donated $40 million to the cause; Robert Benton was directing; British writer Tom Stoppard wrote the screenplay from a successful novel by E. L. Doctorow; famed cinematographer Nestor Almendros was running the shoot, and Dustin Hoffman, Nicole Kidman and Bruce Willis led a competent cast. It was also popular, if now familiar, gangster territory enjoyed by American audiences – with hoods in fedoras, big black sedans, night-clubs and broads, all set in the moody rain-swept streets of grimy tenements. It was similar in plot, though nowhere near as good, to Martin Scorsese's recent hit, *Goodfellas*. Yet, once more, the acting, directing and writing talents, the money and the historical colour merged unconvincingly into a dry and unappetising dish:

Willis's role, though small, is pivotal to the opening of the movie. Billy Bathgate, played by the miscast screen newcomer Loren Dean, is the rising gangland apprentice of Dutch Schultz (Hoffman). He has witnessed the gangland killing of the Willis character, Bo Weinberg, who is ditched from a tugboat wearing concrete boots. This fitting retribution for an earlier act of betrayal is explained by flashbacks which is more or less the extent of Willis's involvement. Thereafter, the story moves on to portray the rise of Billy Bathgate – from the street kid who charms his way out of the Depression-era New York slums to the high ranking aide of Dutch Schultz. Nicole Kidman, meanwhile, is Willis's former girlfriend who takes up with Schultz. Billy, with shades of Richard Gere in *The Cotton Club*, is ordered to look after her while Schultz conducts his battles with rival Lucky Luciano and the federal tax authorities.

Robert Benton's film was stylish, even graceful, and dealt intelligently with the multi-plotted novel but surprisingly lacked the elements of impact which give life to these gangster stories as with, for example, *Goodfellas*. It was, then, a failure at the box office and Willis himself did not fare well in the reviews – 'an embarrassment,' according to one acerbic critic. The movie took a mere $16 million in domestic gross, a disaster in anybody's book, and Willis suffered again in the collective indictment of the movie's failure.

Whether or not he could redeem himself, and extricate himself from a seemingly endless bashing, now rested on *The Last Boy Scout*, which was set for general release in December. It was premiered with another big opening by Joel Silver who spoke in typical ebullient fashion of its high-action, high-drama content. Yet, ultimately, it too was something of a disappointment. It took less than $60 million in domestic gross, although with overseas sales it went over the $100 million mark.

Most of the reviews, while recognising the movie's entertainment value, had a sting in the tail. 'The boy scouts' "Be Prepared" motto could be taken as a warning to check one's brain at the door,' said *Variety*. The reviewers faced a dilemma best summed up by one of America's leading critics, Roger Ebert. 'To give it a negative review,' he said, 'would be dishonest. To be positive is to seem to approve its sickness.'

Willis, at the end of 1991, may well have been reminded of the line he spoke as Joe Hallenbeck in *The Last Boy Scout* where he wakes up in his car, looks at himself in the mirror, and mutters:

'Nobody likes you. Everybody hates you. You're gonna lose. Smile, you fuck.'

11 Unbecoming Death

REWIND: WE ARE BACK at the BIG premiere of *Hudson Hawk*, 17 May 1991. A few rows from the galaxy of VIP celebrities, sitting almost anonymously and nodding occasionally to familiar faces, is the formidable figure of Robert Altman. He is, of course, the director of M*A*S*H and many other fine movies that carried his individualistic stamp but whose talents had lately been ignored by Hollywood because he refused to kowtow to commerce. Regarded as a maverick and with a reputation as being difficult, he has never accepted formula work and always tried to present a different view of life through each of his movies.

In 1980, he commented bitterly: 'Hollywood is afraid of me, I guess. I can't make the kind of films they want to make, and the kind of films I make they just don't want to make.' Since then, he had come through some lean times.

An acquaintance sitting in front of him at the Willis premiere spotted him and, surprised to find him there, inquired: 'Robert, dearest . . . what *on earth* are you doing here?'

'Researching,' Altman replied.

'Researching? Researching what . . . ?'

Altman tapped the side of his nose with his finger and said, 'All will be revealed in due course.'

Indeed it would be. Altman was not there specifically to see Willis, and certainly not the film itself, although he would invite the actor to appear in his upcoming, but as yet unannounced, movie. Willis's role would be minuscule, but a brief diversion into the making of that film is worthwhile, especially as it slots effortlessly and ironically into his own tale of woe.

Altman was getting the lowdown on a high-budget, modern movie, predicted by its producer as 'massive' but which was already getting bad-mouthed in the press. He was there to get the colour, to observe the occasion and all its particular peculiarities: the utterly false kiss-kiss, bear-hugging, gimme-five atmosphere, the largesse, the hopes, the ambitions, the back-biting, the back-stabbing and, eventually, the disappointments on view at a big Hollywood opening that all goes wrong – and he couldn't have chosen better.

At that moment, he was plotting what many would see as his revenge on all the years of resentment and rejection that he had suffered because he wouldn't play the game their way. He was working towards a triumphant return with a savagely satirical movie on Hollywood itself. It was also a courageous act on his part because, although renowned for his cunning virtuosity, especially with his 1970s output, Altman had himself directed some pretty poor movies, and many commercial failures. Stones and glass houses immediately spring to mind.

But he strode on, and his attendance at the *Hudson Hawk* premiere was merely part of his observation process as he gave birth to his movie, *The Player*. Out of it came a wickedly mordant exposé of the film industry in which he launched an across-the-board attack on its institutions, its studio bosses, the overpaid and precious stars, the hustlers, the deal-makers, the gold digging agents and casting directors – pretty well everyone, in fact, who is involved in the daily process of movie-making.

In a perhaps not-so-coincidental way, *The Player* provided an instant 1990s insight into Willis's World: a hothouse of egos and power play, where vogue rules in a follow-my-leader merry-go-round of corporate wheeler-dealing. One false move and you might fall off; three false moves and you're flung off.

And the director, of course, had a wealth of other material to draw on, quite apart from the modern acridity. Hollywood has always been overtly critical of itself and its own, portrayed on film and in books as Sodom-by-the-sea, driven by a moneymad, power crazy, amour-propre society. The movie reflections began to appear with Billy Wilder's brilliantly sardonic *Sunset Boulevard* which was followed by the finest performance of Jack Palance's career in *The Big Knife*. Then came Kirk Douglas in *The Bad and The Beautiful*, and other, more bitter exposés in *Hollywood Boulevard*, *Inside Daisy Clover*, *Whatever Happened to Baby Jane*, *Myra Breckenridge* and Christopher Guest's *The Big Picture*.

Even in the early days, its luminaries were bemoaning their fate. Sir Cedric Hardwicke, the distinguished British actor who settled in Hollywood in the 1930s, said of the place: 'God felt sorry for actors so he gave them a place in the sun and a swimming pool. The price they paid was to surrender their talent.'

Charlton Heston once gave me a similar description: 'They are ignorant of talent today. In this town, talent is in the eye of a curious beholder. If it has big tits, so much the better.' Maureen Stapleton recalled for me the words of her dear friend Marlon Brando, as she headed west for her first movie: 'Don't come, darling, don't come. Stay in New York and be happy. Hollywood is not a dream, it's a fucking nightmare – a cultural boneyard.'

Marilyn Monroe saw it as 'a place where they pay you $50,000 for a kiss and 50 cents for your soul.' Likewise, Carrie Fisher abandoned her quest for true affection 'because here everyone does fake affection too well.' Lauren Bacall's long list of credited quips include: 'The only place on earth where an amicable divorce means you get fifty per cent of the publicity.' And, on leaving, she said: 'Of the twenty friends I thought I had, I'll miss the six I really had.' Errol Flynn made much the same point: 'The only time people wish you well in Hollywood is when you are dying.'

And in 1990s Hollywood, nothing had changed. 'The only way to be a success,' said Sylvester Stallone, 'is to be as obnoxious as the next guy.'

So there was a wealth of material for Willis to ponder in the wake of his disaster, and for Altman to research for his movie in which the characters were invariably drawn from the actual, portraying situations that have an everyday quality. He blends cynicism with compassion, dreams with setbacks. *The Player* would pull together many of his better themes of the past and turn them in on the movie so that, as Altman said, it became a satire of itself. Meantime, there was a story, a screenplay to which his carve-up of Hollywood was attached and yet was in itself incisive; a thriller plot going off on so many detours that it would draw in the audience and keep it riveted.

If there was to be a distraction, it would come from trying to spot famous faces in the background – Willis among them. It was a measure of the respect in which Altman was held by actors that he persuaded a large number of Hollywood stars to appear in the film as themselves. According to a count by *Variety*, there were 65 famous names appearing in cameos threaded through the movie, thus giving it a totally modern and believable pitch.

They included contemporary and former big-names like Burt Reynolds, Anjelica Huston, Jack Lemmon, Harry Belafonte, James Coburn, Richard E. Grant, Nick Nolte, Julia Roberts, Rod Steiger and Bruce Willis, a diverse list of names that in itself gives a clear indication of the frailty of celebrity. Apart from bringing to the movie an atmosphere of believable realism, Altman used the device to puncture the culture of hype, where creativity and the art of movies is subservient to marketing and where individual fame is ultimately just another dispensable commodity. Altman's Hollywood is mysterious yet, at once, hollow.

The hall of mirrors analogy has been used often enough in descriptions of the place but it was no better applicable than here, as Altman delves into the deal-making and power breakfasts, the writers' pitches, the agents pleading and threatening and the casting director's influence in order to demonstrate that Holly-wood output is, for the most part, controlled by the hype-driven culture that surrounds it – totally immersed in the scent of mega-bucks which occasionally have traces of white powder.

The scenario is set in an opening sequence lasting six minutes. His camera casually eavesdrops on a dozen random conversations between stars who meet in the studio car park, and then moves to a first floor window and into a room where a writer is making his pitch for *The Graduate, Part II*.

Now, we meet the central character of the movie, a sharp, go-getting studio executive named Griffin Mill, played by Tim Robbins. There were plenty of role models around at the time and his character must be a composite of those who populated Willis's own environment: a cool, aggressive character whose sole object is to make big-hit movies, but not necessarily good ones. Once again, never mind the quality, feel the greenbacks.

Through Griffin, Altman begins to pull back the curtain on Hollywood, revealing its worst kept secrets as he moves, fawning and fornicating, through parties, clubs, watering holes and big-bucks openings, talking deals throughout and listening to three-minute pitches for a movie that will cost $50 million. The dialogue is sharp and cutting. To sexy seductress Greta Scaachi, he says, 'It lacked certain elements that we need to market a film success-fully.'

Scaachi: 'What elements?'

Griffin Mill: 'Suspense, laughter, violence. Hope, heart, nudity, sex. Happy endings. But mainly happy endings.'

Scaachi: 'What about reality?'

Then there is the exchange between Griffin Mill and the even more viscid executive Peter Gallagher, who says: 'I'll be there right after my AA meeting.'

Griffin Mill: 'Oh . . . I didn't realise you had a drink problem.'

Gallagher: 'I don't, but that's where all the deals are being made these days.'

Then comes the rumours of the crash and burn. The grapevine says he is about to be fired and replaced by a close 'friend'. He has also been receiving threatening postcards which he believes are being sent by a disgruntled screenwriter he has upset – so Griffin kills him. A dastardly deed, of course, but no less than is required in his mind. And thus, Altman's tale moves to another ingenious level, where there is sympathy, almost, as he becomes the key figure in a story far more intriguing than any of the movies he produces.

Life matching art, and even beating it, is one more well-versed aspect that abounds in the continuing saga of Hollywood Babylon and one which, in the 1990s, arrived in plenty, ranging through O. J. Simpson, the desperate troubles of Robert Downey jnr and the various marital dramas of Elizabeth Taylor, Melanie Griffith et al., with subplots courtesy of Michael Jackson. In this instance, *The Player* provides a happy ending of sorts: ironic, really.

And the irony continued. Whilst Willis's personal involvement in the above was of a peripheral nature, a walk-on cameo, it came into his life at a time when he was getting first-hand experience of some of the darker aspects of Altman's commentary.

What would be next?

He was looking for a safe haven. Something good and big. Never mind the money. *Get me a gig with plenty of pzazz and cred!*

Arnold Rifkin was working on it. There was a deal in the offing. Zemeckis. Big budget. Forty mill.

That's got to be good, hasn't it? He'd already signed Streep and Hawn. *How about that?*

Yeah . . . Yeah!

Robert Zemeckis, three years older than Willis, had a star-studded recent past and was a highly regarded young director who came to fame as a protégé of Steven Spielberg. He was one of the so-called 'movie brats' from the University of Southern California Film School. He wrote and directed one of Spielberg's early modest works, *I Wanna Hold Your Hand* and in 1980 won some excellent reviews for his small but neglected screwball comedy *Used Cars*, with Kurt Russell. After that, he faded for a while, doing some screenwriting for Spielberg. That was until Michael Douglas asked him to direct *Romancing The Stone* which he owned and was producing himself because no studio would take it on – at least, not with him in the starring role. Douglas made no secret of the fact that he was hiring Zemeckis only because he was personally averse to working with big-name directors.

The movie was the sleeper of 1984, an instant hit, and made Zemeckis a much-sought-after star of the Guild of Directors. He went on to direct the ultra-successful *Back To The Future* trilogy. In between, he scored a massive hit with *Who Framed Roger Rabbit?* with Bob Hoskins, which won an Oscar for visual effects. In short, there was not a movie he had directed in the past decade that hadn't struck gold, and in 1991, he headed the league of highest-grossing directors for the previous ten years.

Now, he was extending his scope further by producing, as well as directing, his own movie and found a willing backer in Universal Studios. The project was *Death Becomes Her*, a black comedy which was altogether a different kettle of fish. It was deeper and more complex than his past movies. The subject matter also required delicate handling, especially since he planned to incorporate his now established trademark of visual effects. He had some startling shock-tactic features on the drawing board.

He made a bee-line for Goldie Hawn, one of the few natural comediennes in Hollywood and then took a chance on the second co-starring role, signing the accomplished but usually downbeat Meryl Streep for her first-ever comedy assignment. It was basically a two-hander but with strong support from the third central character, the nerdish plastic surgeon who was romantically involved with the former, then the latter, and then the former again.

Willis went after the male lead which would take him, yet again, well away from his usual fare, as he continued his attempt to break out of the flash-bang mode. It had become an ongoing theme as he struggled for prestige roles as an actor, not as an all-action hero.

Respect. That was his desire. The Zemeckis movie seemed to offer at least some of the criteria he was seeking: a change of pace and style, at the very least. But, as Arnold Rifkin explained, he had to go into battle to secure it: 'Bob Zemeckis didn't wake up one morning and say, "I've got to get Bruce Willis for this movie." He certainly wasn't Bob's first choice.' Rifkin once more employed the strategy of a back-end deal with little money upfront. So Willis was off and running again. Big budget. Flash director. Top-line co-stars. Lavish sets. An ace crew. Hugely expensive computer-generated special effects.

How could it fail?

The screenplay aimed itself towards a combination of New Age satire and slapstick horror. It had the potential for social commentary, with insight into the lengths the rich and famous go to push back the advancing years. And the opportunity was there for some very funny set pieces. Sadly, Zemeckis piled his concentration into the stunts and left the rest of the movie floundering.

It was Hollywood's most expensive movie of its kind and the first to attempt a computer-aided reconstruction of actors' physical appearances: such as a large and bloody shotgun hole through Goldie Hawn's torso and the spinning head of Meryl Streep. Zemeckis, widely applauded for his experimental animation in *Who Framed Roger Rabbit?* was once again treading fresh ground, and many would follow. He employed the wizards of his old employers, the Lucas Industrial Light and Magic Company, to create these effects which, in turn, attracted the most attention in the movie.

Willis again plays a pivotal character around whom the plot develops. He is the quite unattractive and bespectacled Ernest Menville, a noted plastic surgeon whose partner Helen Sharp (Goldie Hawn) has a long-running feud with fading actress Madeline Ashton (Meryl Streep). She steals Ernest away for no other reason than to hurt her own 'friend' and to have him on hand, of course, to administer the occasional nip and tuck operations on her sagging body.

Goldie's character goes off into a manic depression which leads to a doubling of her size through over-eating and an enforced stay in a mental hospital. A few years later, she reappears on the scene, all svelte and beautiful, intent on destroying the relationship between Willis and Streep.

Henpecked Willis is, by then, reduced to a drunken wreck who earns extra money beautifying Hollywood corpses before they are laid to rest – thus he is well equipped to deal with the later twists in the plot. Hawn persuades Willis to murder Streep so that they can resume their own relationship, unaware that Streep, by then, has already discovered Hawn's secret – that she has been given the elixir of life by an occult lady, superbly played by Isabella Rossellini.

In spite of a broken neck and dangling limbs, Streep does not die after her spectacular tumbling down the magnificent staircase, in which she was aided by a gentle push from Willis. And Hawn is equally unkillable when she takes a shotgun blast to the stomach. So we have two immortal bodies, slowly degenerating and in need of Willis's skills as a mortician to keep them looking presentable – a new twist on the eternal triangle.

The movie was seriously flawed and many blamed the script, though much chopping and changing in the editing suite probably disturbed the flow even more. It was lightweight and exceedingly unfunny in parts as the joke quickly began to wear thin. Any attempts at satire were abandoned after the first few scenes, and if there was to have been a theme, it vanished on the cutting room floor. It was impossible to take it seriously as a movie; in fact, there was no point in thinking about the movie at all. It was so unbelievable that it was simply one to sit back and watch the computer-aided stunts that rescued it from oblivion.

Even so, there was evidence of some drastic surgery before its release. Trailers featured a sequence (where Willis was wrestling Streep's body out of their freezer) that was nowhere to be seen in the released version. The original ending also had Willis eloping to Europe with Tracey Ullman who had a small role. She does not appear at all in the final cut. In the new ending, Willis had died and the two disintegrating bodies of Streep and Hawn fall down some steps and break apart, with their heads still arguing.

As to performances, Willis, in a smirk-free role, was funny and quite competent within the limitations of a script that gave him the burden of physical dullness while Hawn and Streep camped it up unmercifully. It was no mould-breaking appearance for him, though, and one more chance to show his mettle evaporated through no real fault of his own.

He wasn't alone. Streep fans despaired at what was done to her in this movie. She, the seven times Academy-Award-nominated actress of fine sophistication, the winner of two Oscars and the veteran of memorable performances in *Kramer vs Kramer*, *Sophie's Choice* and *Ironweed*, became a living cartoon character created by computer. Only Hawn, of whom wackiness is expected, looked comfortable.

In spite of the advance hype, the movie was one of the big disappointments of that year of 1992. Reviews were lukewarm and were attracted only by the special effects. The movie took $58 million in domestic box office receipts – not bad, but well below anticipated projections. It served, above all, to point up the caution needed by directors as Hollywood set off down the road of serious experiments with computer imagery.

It was also one more caution for Willis: he did not have many lives left. Still, if all else should fail, he could always go off and sell hamburgers and T-shirts!

In the autumn of 1991, two go-getting entrepreneurs, Keith Barish and Robert Earl, formed a company called Planet Hollywood. They planned to open a series of showbiz orientated eateries not a million miles from the concept of Hard Rock Cafe, with which Earl had been involved, and aimed at 'capitalising on the universal appeal of movies, sports and other entertainment-based themes.'

Earl had the bright idea of offering share options to a small band of famous movie stars in exchange for their participation in the company, promoting its openings and products. The original five approached were Arnold Schwarzenegger, Sylvester Stallone, Bruce Willis, Demi Moore and Whoopi Goldberg. They all joined in.

The deal was that they would take a slice of the equity and, in due course, the profits in exchange for lending their names to the company and, according to its prospectus:

> frequently attending the grand openings of new Planet Hollywood units as well as other special events at the units, thereby generating significant media attention and publicity for the PH brand. Moreover, as a result of the popularity and high visibility of the Planet Hollywood units, the motion picture community [would] frequently use the units as sites for well-publicised movie promotions and other celebrity-sponsored events.

The first Planet Hollywood was opened in New York with the aforementioned celebrities in attendance, mixing with guests, signing autographs and T-shirts and with Willis singing. It was the beginning of an international bonanza for the stars, not to mention the original founders of the company, as it proceeded to expand to major cities throughout the world and at which, as will have been very evident from the resultant publicity, the Schwarzenegger-Stallone-Willis triumvirate would be especially active. Not an opportunity to promote their business was missed. Again, reverting to the corporate-speak of the Planet Hollywood prospectus:

> the Company has promoted its brands primarily through the operation of theme restaurants, which provide a unique dining and entertainment experience in a high-energy environment, and their integrated retail stores, offering a broad selection of premium-quality merchandise displaying the Company's logos.

By the end of 1996, the company expected to have a total of 51 restaurant-merchandise stores set up in 16 countries. They are typically located at high-profile sites in major tourist areas such as Walt Disney World in Orlando, Caesar's World Forum Shops in Las Vegas, Piccadilly Circus in London and the Champs Elysees in Paris.

While the restaurants are the main attraction, the sales from its merchandising stores produce the highest profits from goods such as jackets, T-shirts, sweatshirts and hats. The future was in the stars, literally: the famous shareholders were pushing the business for all its worth.

A typical opening of a Planet Hollywood resembles a promo for one of their movies, and the media invariably falls for it. When they opened up in their homebase of Hollywood, for example, the crush was akin to a royal visit or a presidential address to the nation. The new 'unit' opening its doors that day was on the corner of Wilshire Boulevard and the swank Rodeo Drive. Arnie, Sly, Bruce and Demi turned up en masse to give a press conference in the elegant Regent Beverly Wilshire Hotel.

Beverly Hills cops had the place surrounded and had blocked off the area for the occasion. Three hundred journalists and photographers from around the world waited patiently for the stars' arrival, which came one hour late. They were delivered, as ever, in a fleet of white stretch limos. Finally, they marched in, accompanied by PH executives and surrounded by a ring of bodyguards, to take their seats on the platform like high-powered leaders of a business conglomerate about to report on their company's performance.

Demi Moore had a new piece of skin art – the Planet Holly-wood blue and red logo temporarily emblazoned upon her left shoulder, which was an obvious attraction for the paparazzi. Neat touch. As they ascended, the flashes from 100 cameras went off in unison. 'I'm about to go blind,' Willis said. 'I'll sue every one of you.'

But, far from any significant revelations about the business or themselves for that matter, the press conference descended into a bizarre and banal Q and A about matters of no importance that were curiously lapped up by the less cynical among the gathered throng of scribes. Willis told a story about shearing sheep in Australia, where he had gone to reconnoitre the new PH site. 'Cute little sheep,' he said. 'But they turned nasty when they smelled my dinner, mutton pie, on my breath. They started to kick me. I had to give the sheep some vodka.'

Demi, embarrassed by his banality, virtually told him to shut up and asked if they could get another question. She wanted to talk about her dress. She was wearing a black, tight sheath at the time but was looking forward to a change when they would go down to the new PH place on Rodeo Drive later. 'They've loaned me the dress that Rita Hayworth wore in *Gilda*, for the dance scene,' she said in an oh-gosh way.

Her husband chipped in: 'I'm wearing Dorothy's dress from *The Wizard of Oz*.' She glared at him as if to say, 'Don't be so bloody stupid.' One reporter, attempting to raise the level of the meeting, raised questions about the business and inquired as to the extent of the stars' participation in shareholders' meetings. 'We smoke cigars,' Demi replied. Bruce was still being silly: 'We wear various women's dresses.'

Arnie tried to bring a more serious tone to the proceedings. 'We are proud to finally open in Los Angeles,' he said, actually sounding businesslike. 'We tried fiercely to find a location because we only select sites among major properties and real estate.' Stallone, not to be outdone, stated seriously that 'wherever there are tourists, there'll be a Planet Hollywood.'

Schwarzenegger went on to explain how the company located the 'memorabilia' for their restaurant displays. They trawled the studios – not them personally, of course – to buy up unwanted props and costumes. 'We pick movies that were successful. It doesn't mean anything if the movie went into the toilet.' Makes sense. They all nodded and smiled, though Willis was looking a touch sickly at the mention of movies going to the toilet. Planet Hollywood was booming.

Willis's day job remained more volatile.

12 Demi's Turn

THE SPOTLIGHT MOVES.

After the years in which Willis's own work, good, bad or indifferent, had dominated their lives and the headlines, the focus switched to Demi. It happened when director Rob Reiner called to say that she had been selected from a shortlist of five to co-star in his new movie, *A Few Good Men*. It was the nearest she'd come yet to a pre-determined Hollywood main-stream movie, given that *Ghost* was an almost accidental happening. The salary hardly mattered, but it was good anyway: $3 million and a slice of the action. It would be a showy, powerful drama, with a strong and true story, creatively cast with all eyes firmly fixed on marketing.

The line-up was Tom Cruise, the young male lead of the moment and charging $12 million a picture, Jack Nicholson, the pro supreme whose middle-aged leer and sixties spit-in-your-eye irreverence still arouses every generation, and Demi Moore, straight from her sensational, show-stopping appearance on the front cover of *Vanity Fair*.

'This is IT,' she screamed to Bruce.

'YOU BETCHA!' said Willis, who would have liked very much to have something similar in his own life to shout about; he'd have given anything to work with Rob Reiner 'even if it was just reading the phone book'. They cracked open a bottle of Evian to celebrate. Good news for her; nothing for him. Willis, for the first time in seven years, was staring at a blank calendar.

When he completed his work on *Death Becomes Her* he had nothing definite scheduled. His production line ground to a halt just as Demi's career swung on to a higher plane. Work had evaporated. Seven movies in two years had earned him upwards of $40 million. But the poor critical reaction to several of them, regardless of profit and loss, had severely dented his ego and his standing in Hollywood.

He was bemoaning his plight: 'If a film comes in, I'm the hero. If not, I'm the dog. It's easy to say it's Bruce Willis's fault. But I've worked with guys who shouldn't have been at the wheel. I've always taken the high road and not said, "Don't blame me." I just hang my head and say "Look, I'm sorry, it didn't work." ' Ahead lay his leanest period since he came to Hollywood: one movie and a couple of cameo roles in the next two and a half years; the downhill run looked steep.

If there was ever a points-scoring chart within the Willis household with a his-and-hers league table chalked on the kitchen wall, you would see that Demi was beginning to catch up. She received the news of what amounted to her elevation to the bottom rung of the A-list just before she gave birth to Scout. Now, if she could continue the momentum, she could put a finger up to all those who had accused her of blatant exhibitionism in going nude while pregnant the previous August.

Although she was criticised, derided and nicknamed 'Gimme', she was not without sympathy, grudging though it may have been, among the women of her profession. *If that's what it takes, so be it.*

What was going on in Hollywood, all around her, had much to do with the shaping of her attitude – it played as big a part as the motivation of ambition. Apart from having ability, women actors had to be of a certain age, shape and height (never taller than the male lead), have the right looks, wide-eyes and innocence, usually be blonde (but occasionally brunettes will do), not be too pushy but smart, compassionate or funny, depending on the moment.

Offscreen, they had to be as tough as nails to withstand the pain of rejection – 30 actresses might be called to audition for one major role. The competition was FIERCE. It was ironic that Demi should begin her climb to the summit just as a major debate was opening up on the role of women in Hollywood (in the face of rampant chauvinism) and at the same time that her husband, the man who put macho back into television, had suddenly gone into decline.

Female groups, unions and guilds were planning a co-ordinated attack which would culminate in gaining the support of the

Academy of Motion Pictures, which nominated 1993 to be the Year of the Woman. Susan Lyne, publications director of *Premiere* magazine, which brought out the special issue *Women in Hollywood*, said that far from benefiting from the upsurge of women's rights in the previous decade, Hollywood remained a bastion of male-domination.

'Getting in has never been easy,' she wrote in her editorial to run with the campaign. 'For decades, Hollywood was the most self-satisfied of the old boys' clubs, a network of exclusive relationships, handshake deals and autocratic decision making.' The dilemma for women in movies had become intense. How did they break into the business, get noticed and build a power base? What track did they follow to get to the top? And once there, how could they sustain it?

A mass of interesting statistics was produced to prove the point, the most poignant being that, of the $1 billion a year earned by performers in the Screen Actors Guild in 1992, women took less than 34 per cent. Top earning male actors at the time were Schwarzenegger ($15 million a picture), Cruise ($12 million), Kevin Costner ($12 million), Eddie Murphy ($12 million) and Mel Gibson ($10 million). Top women earners were Julia Roberts ($7 million), Michelle Pfeiffer ($6 million) and Barbra Stresiand ($6 million), with Jodie Foster and Sharon Stone both on $5 million. Five years down the road, most of the men would still be up there; the women would be replaced by the next generation.

As the debate took off, some high-profile stars came in with their thoughts:

Bette Midler: 'Are there any decent roles for women? No. You have to dig and scrape and claw and meet and greet and schmooze . . . It's the bottom line mentality and the blockbuster mentality. There are more people willing to gamble big sums in the hope that they are going to have a big payday than there are people looking to the long-term. In my life, I have been treated really badly . . . really horrible treatment.'

Glenn Close: 'After the feminist movement, everyone was supposed to treat each other fairly and with understanding. In *Fatal Attraction*, they did a lot of work on the script to make Michael Douglas's character more sympathetic . . . so [my character] got the shaft. And I deeply resented that because I had invested a great deal of emotion and work into that movie.'

Whoopi Goldberg, Moore's friend and advice-giver who also has a reputation for being demanding: 'There's good reason for being difficult . . . you don't get that many opportunities and when you do, you want to do it right. I've learned to say, "No, I disagree. These are the things I want." And to throw up my middle finger at those people who are wishing me ill.'

Women actors were at their earning pinnacle between the ages of twenty-five and thirty-five. Then, decline set in. Forty is a difficult age; fifty and beyond brings the character roles, and the work gets scarcer. Sean Connery, Robert Redford and Clint Eastwood could make love to twenty- and thirty-year-olds, but when the reverse happened and a sixty-year-old woman had a young boy in bed, it had to be the subject of the plot.

As Jessica Lange pointed out: 'Actresses have to assume that once they're past a certain age, they'll just do character roles – which are few and highly competitive. They won't be doing romantic leads like men in their forties, fifties and sixties are still doing . . . it's become impossible. I see lots of women my age who have had extensive [surgical] work done. Because they have this fear of aging . . . that they'll never work again.'

All of the above was vital to Demi Moore, who was twenty-nine years old when she got the call-back for *A Few Good Men*. It was the veritable 'window of opportunity' and she couldn't afford to blow it, especially as her last three movies had hardly set the world alight. She was by no means alone in that dilemma: Sharon Stone, then thirty-three and 'fed up to the teeth with years of mediocre crap and directors ogling my tits,' was seriously thinking of giving up acting and taking a law degree when she was cast, that same year in *Basic Instinct*. She still had to show her tits – and more – but at least she was getting real money and a crack at the big time.

Demi, after the birth of Scout, had two months to get back into shape before going to work. She hired fitness guru Rob Parr, who had been Madonna's trainer as she began her Blonde Ambition world tour. During the last stages of pregnancy, he put her through a programme of pool exercises. Straight after the birth, he started her on a schedule of sheer sweat and toil for three hours a day, seven days a week, which continued during the making of the movie.

Every day, before she was called for work, she would be up at four in the morning, running, biking, hiking, weight-training, swimming – the whole body-honing routine. There were also rumours, on which Moore refused to comment, that she had a breast implant and some work done on her face.

Studio filming coincided with the last stages of Willis's work on *Death Becomes Her* which was being shot in a nearby sound stage – so they were able to meet a lot and go off on after-hours jaunts, or take the kids to see wild tigers on the set of Billy Crystal's new movie, *Mr Saturday Night*. In fact, the place was crawling with children and the producers of Demi's movie had set up a creche to accommodate them. There were Demi's two, each with their own nanny, Jack Nicholson's two children by Rebecca Broussard, Rob Reiner's baby son and co-star Kevin Bacon's son, who was also in the movie.

There were also some studio politics going on and Demi was once again fighting her corner. Tom Cruise, as the headline star, had it written into his contract that he should have the trailer nearest the set. In Hollywood, these small details matter. Nicholson was next. Moore was third in line. First, she asked for, and got, a double-sized trailer because she had to have her children with her at all times, and the children's nannies, plus her friend and employee for the past six years, the formidable figure of Daneen Conroy. She was her personal assistant, bodyguard, telephone answering service, rebutter of unwanted approaches from media, photographers and fans, plus general factotum, on call 24 hours a day. Daneen herself also had an assistant. Moore also wanted her trailer to be closest to the set, so that she could dash back to see the children during the long days of filming. Nicholson said he didn't give a fuck where he was located, and even Tom Cruise, the nice-guy who had been known to call journalists 'Sir', was no match. So Demi moved to the front of the line.

As to Rob Reiner's movie, it had actually been around for some time. When the script was originally submitted to the decision-makers in the previous administration of Columbia TriStar, the first notes back to screenwriter Aaron Sorkin read: 'Why is Jo [Moore's role] female? SHE DOESN'T TAKE HER CLOTHES OFF! And there's no love scenes.'

Reiner fought on in his role as both director and co-producer. He didn't want love scenes. No kissing or squelchy bedroom wrestling – just a straightforward drama, for once, that only hinted at a developing relationship between the Moore and Cruise characters. Reiner admits he was apprehensive about Moore, having heard 'she was trouble'. But he experienced no problems. 'She had all the qualities I was looking for, strength and sexuality which was crucial. She was sharp and intelligent.'

On the set, she took his directions and ran with the show. Reiner, once an actor himself, formed the view that Moore was a better actress than most of the movies she had been in so far suggested, and he remained a defender against the back-biters: 'I know from personal experience, what actors go through when they are as intelligent as the powers that be. What comes out is a person who is being difficult, when all they are trying to do is make a decent movie.'

Nicholson, whose brilliance can be intimidating for his fellow actors, liked her too.

The story is based on fact and had an earlier life as a Broadway play. A Marine at the Guantanamo Naval Air Station in Cuba, where Nicholson as the commanding officer rules with a rod of iron, dies in a barrack room fight. There is a cover up; to speak out will go against the so-called code of honour. Two young Marines are charged with the death. Only when Moore, playing a young naval executive in Washington, goads the lazy lawyer, Cruise, into a full investigation is the truth discovered. After a long and laborious investigation, Nicholson is finally trapped into a dramatic courtroom admission over what happened.

The movie had a number of flaws, and critical reaction was far from wholehearted. Cruise was seen as lightweight for the role, though Moore came out of it well. Regardless of the critics, it took major money in the cinemas, grossing $158 million in the US alone. That, incidentally, was around $100 million more than Willis's then latest film, *Death Becomes Her*. Moore's future now seemed assured, although she confessed: 'I'm not quite in the place I want to be although I'm in a better position than I've ever been. Better offers are beginning to come in.'

One of them came along while she was making *A Few Good Men*. British director Adrian Lyne, of *Fatal Attraction* fame, called her to do a reading for his new one, *Indecent Proposal*. Demi had auditioned for roles in every one of his past movies and had not been cast in any of them. Lyne was not sure he wanted her for this one either and was still looking at other actresses.

The Willises dropped out of Hollywood for a while, until the dust settled. They had other projects in hand that were far away from the phoney, smog-ridden, earthquake-threatening atmosphere of LA, or the mad whirl of New York where they had an $8 million four-level penthouse off Central Park. They had found themselves a hideaway on the edge of the 'home town' they had adopted in Idaho, 900 miles from the swank of Beverly Hills. This was the place they were making their own – almost literally.

The town is called Hailey, a sleepy former gold-rush community which nestles in the valley of the snowcapped Sawtooth Mountain. It is a typical American town of its kind, one main street with stores serving a population of 3,687. They first came across the place eight years earlier when they visited Sun Valley, the celebrity-favoured winter resort area – star of the old Glen Miller movie *Sun Valley Serenade* – about twelve miles away. The valley had been attracting the stars since the 1930s but somehow the little town of Hailey, which started life in the 1880s around a clutch of gold and silver mines, was overlooked. It was like a fifties town – unhurried and largely unaffected by the pressures of the outside world.

The Willises found a rambling six-bedroom ranch mansion set in 25 acres on the outskirts of town which they decided would be their home base – somewhere to escape to and where they could give their children a home life away from the crazy horrors of suburban Los Angeles. They restored the property and made a comfortable home, with indoor swimming pool, guest annexe and a massive garage where Willis still houses his increasing collection of vintage cars and motorcycles. They put horses in the stables, completed the renovations and then turned their attentions to the town itself, where the main street was looking a touch jaded, with properties falling into decline.

At the time of their visit in the early months of 1992, they were at the beginning of a real-estate shopping spree which would extend on through the next three years. They invested more than $13 million, every so often purchasing a piece of the main street, restoring it to its former glory and installing new businesses. Willis was first attracted by a bar called the Mint, an old miners hang-out on Main Street which still attracted Hailey's rougher elements.

He brought his band there once, for a concert on a Saturday night, and the place erupted in a brawl. When he bought the freehold, he closed the bar down, gutted the inside and set about building a smart 160-seat bistro, trimmed with Peruvian mahogany and had the walls covered with vintage movie stills and posters. There was also a pool room, sauna and steam room. Demi designed the upstairs, which featured a quiet, relaxing lounge with deep sofas and soft decor.

It was all very swish but, as the local newspaper editor Dan Gorham said, it seemed a pretty lavish place for their small town with not much hope of making money. But the Willises didn't seem to care about that. Next, they were negotiating to buy four more properties on Main Street. One was the Liberty Cinema for which they had great ideas. Another was a parcel of land opposite, where Demi planned to build a museum to house her own collection of 2,000 dolls. Then, there was a large office building which Bruce would, in due course, convert to professional rooms with a diner below. They also talked of building a 65-room hotel.

Editor Gorham said the townspeople left the Willises pretty much alone – 'they're just ordinary folk with money' – and were generally supportive of their property buying spree, although some feared it would bring unwanted tourist elements. Willis admitted to the locals that they did not expect to make any money out of the redevelopment (it might even be a tax write-off) – they were doing it for the town, and to provide work for locals.

The stay in Hailey was not long enough. By the summer of 1992, they were both preparing to go back at work. Willis had finally concluded a new picture deal which again looked good *on paper*. It was a project for producer Arnon Milchan, with a working title of *Three Rivers*. Filming was not due to begin until the autumn of 1992 for release in September 1993 – which would mean a sixteen-month gap since Willis's last appearance in the cinemas.

His wife, on the other hand, would have two big movies out long before then. *A Few Good Men* was due for release in December 1992; and she had now received confirmation from director Adrian Lyne that she had won the role in *Indecent Proposal*, for which she would receive her largest ever fee of $5 million – and, more importantly, the key of the door to superstardom, with second billing to Robert Redford. It would be out in April, 1993.

In the meantime, she decided that her public profile would benefit from a timely boost, to signal her forthcoming rise to eminence and let the world know, too, that Bruce Willis was alive and well and about to start work on a new movie. Once again, she went into a huddle with photographer Annie Leibovitz who had produced her pregnancy pictures almost a year earlier. Seemingly prepared to forgive *Vanity Fair* the 'horrible' article that accompanied that bodily exposure – she had objected to a raking over of her past and some bitchy quotes from industry insiders – they were plotting another big hit.

The philosophy of that old Hollywood adage about all publicity being good publicity still held firm. Indeed, Demi had made a clinical study of the publicity machine that operated during the Hollywood Golden Age and would wax lyrical on how the studios and the stars worked together to achieve maximum impact for whatever movie they were promoting at the time – or to massage the image of a star.

She had worked out her own technique of media manipulation, attempting a measure of control over the presentation of herself to the public and, as we have seen, seeking photographic approval in exchange for her co-operation. It didn't always work and she could certainly never control the editorial matter in a magazine like *Vanity Fair*; she had to accept what they wrote. Some, like *Hello*!, were willing to be uncontroversial just to get an interview.

In the summer of 92, Demi Moore was plotting another newsstand special for the cover of *VF*. She was going naked again, to demonstrate how she had transformed herself 'from nude madonna to sleek siren'. She wanted it done, as ever, with style and sophistication – but different. Body painting was all the rage at the time, and so they consulted one of the most prominent exponents of that art, Joanne Gair, for ideas. She pondered for a while and then produced her masterplan: Demi's entire body should be painted in the style of a man's suit.

And so, just ahead of the release of *A Few Good Men*, her

publicity coup, which a thousand professional publicists in Hollywood could only dream of, was set in motion. Once again, a posse of aides descended upon her, courtesy of *Vanity Fair*. The body painting, by Joanne Gair, took a mammoth fifteen hours to complete and then a further two hours to photograph. 'The time consuming part,' said Gair, 'was building up the density of paint and maintaining the pattern of the cloth before it melted through the body heat. But Demi was really into it.'

The photographs completed, she then co-operated for another article to accompany them, which would run over five pages of the August 1992 issue of the magazine. For this, Demi agreed to be observed and interviewed in her home, at work, over lunch and so on, for the verbal picture of her lifestyle. She seemed unperturbed by the incisiveness of the interviewers and did not temper her style. However, in the event, she didn't care for that article, either.

Vanity Fair carried the usual sting in the tail to make the point that 'This *isn't* a promo piece'. They quoted studio executives who complained that she had caught her husband's worst habits in making demands. They recorded that during a two-hour interview at home, a parade of household staff had passed by – thus, once again, re-emphasising the 'entourage'. It was no secret by then, anyhow. Willis himself had said they had 27 people working for them, including staff at their joint offices in Beverly Hills and their home in Hailey. *Vanity Fair* quoted an unnamed friend who said: 'They are never alone. If you ask me, it's a pretty weird marriage and a pretty weird way to live, surrounded by people all the time.'

The last line of the piece pointed up Moore's single-minded ambition, which may also have jarred: [she wanted] 'good work, things to be the best they can be ... I want greatness.'

Afterwards, she moaned bitterly about the tone of the article. 'It took eight days of my life including another body shooting which they didn't use. It's not that I need to have a sugar-coated story. It's just a matter of attitude.' But she was also honest enough to acknowledge the motives for doing it in the first place, and could see a value in what many regarded as another typical piece of Moore exhibitionism: 'When I walked away from it, I discovered the advantage to me was that people only remember the photograph – not the words.'

Notoriety, again.

It was her continuing theme, and she was unaware then, that within a few months, she would be deluged by it: first from the reaction to her movie with Tom Cruise and Jack Nicholson, but then even more so as the focus of an international controversy spawned by the film-making combination of producer Sherry Lansing and director Adrian Lyne (who had last shook the world in 1987 with *Fatal Attraction*).

What followed for Demi Moore was not about 'greatness' or even fine acting, and certainly not about an especially good film. She, D. Moore, actress and wife of the famed Bruce Willis, was the tangible focus of the hype that surrounded *Indecent Proposal* and the exploitation of its one basic, titillating, intriguing ingredient that was suddenly being asked of married couples around the globe: 'What would you do if someone offered $1 million to spend a night with your partner?'

Fantastic idea . . . for a movie, anyhow.

All was not as it seemed, and before going on to the effects of *Indecent Proposal* it is worth recalling a piece of cinema history that has some bearing on the way Moore was finally rocket-launched on to the world stage:

Sherry Lansing, one of Hollywood's women of power, originally achieved fame as the first woman president in a Hollywood studio when she became head of production at 20th Century-Fox in 1980. Her partner, Stanley Jaffe, had a similar role, having become the youngest studio boss since *The Last Tycoon* when he became head of Paramount production at 29.

In 1987, they were both back producing their own movies as independents. *Fatal Attraction* was among them; it was Lansing's baby. Her follow-up was *The Accused* starring Kelly McGillis and Jodie Foster, which explored the issues of rape. They were both supposedly designed to be supportive to the cause of feminism and social concerns but came close to exploitation: *Fatal Attraction* is about a woman who seeks revenge against a married man who dumps her after a brief affair. In a dramatic climax, she is killed.

The movie became a massive talking point, inspiring acres of newspaper and magazine coverage and hours of television debate. Audience identification was aroused on an unprecedented scale, especially in America where vocal reaction is common. Michael Douglas, who played the husband and became the number one bastard to the female population, got scared. He called his father, Kirk, and told him: 'They're going nuts in the theatres. People are screaming and getting hysterical.'

Feminist groups began protesting outside cinemas, holding up placards describing the ending. Critics, aware that three endings had been filmed, complained that the film's executives, producer Lansing and director Lyne, had fiddled with the emphasis to turn Glenn Close's character into a raving monster for the sake of commercialism. Even Close, as we have seen, repeatedly complained that her character had been 'shafted' in the interests of the greenback.

Lansing was forced on the defensive, insisting that the movie had been conceived in support of the feminist cause and that she herself was a campaigner for women's rights and was 'shocked and hurt' by the reaction. The hurt was soon soothed away as she was deluged by enough dollar bills to wallpaper the north face of the Eiger.

How do you beat that?

Fast forward to 1992: Sherry Lansing and Adrian Lyne were together again and poring over a project which had a plot, such as it was, that could be pitched in a single sentence without leaving anything out: struggling newlyweds go to Las Vegas with all the money they possess, try to double it, lose the lot, agree to a wealthy businessman's offer of $1 million for a night with the young wife then split up in the anguished aftermath.

This, incidentally, was a movie to be released during Hollywood's Year of the Woman, a celebration in which Lansing would be a prominent figure. It was not, they insisted, an exploitational movie – she would be 'shocked and hurt' at the very suggestion – but one which explored the reactions of a woman faced with the consequences of the situation, being torn between the reactions of the two men.

Lansing and Lyne (the British director who made his name with television commercials), knew all about making pictures that make fortunes and they had track records which proved they had a nose for knowing what would strike a nerve with the cinema-going public. Critics of the movie would later allege that it was exactly that – the desire to find another blockbuster like *Fatal Attraction* – which inspired the movie.

It was, said some, a cynical Hollywood packaging exercise

carved up by the deal-makers who delivered three names, a director and a script into a studio and to which, in the pre-production hype, was added the sure-fire attraction of Demi Moore going naked again on the front cover of *Vanity Fair*.

Lyne denied it. 'Horseshit!' he said. He never worked like that. He went for Robert Redford because it was the kind of role the audiences did not expect to see him in. He chose Woody Harrelson, largely famous then for his role in *Cheers*, because he had innocence and was 'the kind of guy that audiences can forgive'. The main character, the wife at the centre of Redford's indecent proposal, took longer to choose. Lyne auditioned many actresses for the role, including Nicole Kidman, Annabelle Sciorra and Lisa Stansfield, the British singer who, he said, will one day be 'a wonderful actress'.

Then he saw Demi Moore who came in to read. He saw her at the point when he had already made up his mind to offer the part to another actress. He admits he had never really liked her. She had read for every one of his past movies and he had never called her back. This time, something clicked as she and an actor who was standing in for the Harrelson role played the scene where they are in bed discussing the $1 million offer, and whether or not they should take it.

Lyne was enthralled by her relaxed performance. He also liked the way she looked – kind of Rubenesque, he said, after having her baby. He played back the film of her audition and decided he would offer her the role.

Filming began at the end of August 1992, on the Paramount lot and on location in Las Vegas. Lyne, like other directors before him, had heard Moore was difficult and soon found personal confirmation of those claims. He said she saw her character as being strong, like her role in *A Few Good Men*. Lyne saw her as being vulnerable. 'We pulled and pushed and tugged, which was perhaps not a bad thing. At the time, I thought, "God, is anything worth this pain." Half the time . . . I could have murdered her.'

When *Indecent Proposal* was released, in April 1993, with another big opening in Hollywood, it was met with a barrage of bitchy reviews: 'So unintentionally silly, so thoroughly implausible, all you can do is bow your head in astonishment,' said the *Los Angeles Times*; 'Unredeemingly awful,' grumbled Philip

French in Britain. Judged purely on the basis of its qualities as a movie, the criticisms were pretty well deserved: the idea was intriguing, the delivery of it was weak.

Adrian Lyne, admitting a wounding crucifixion by the critics, complained that they hadn't seen the point; it was intended as pure escapism. The theme, rather than the quality of the movie, however, caught public imagination. As with *Fatal Attraction*, it inspired an international media reaction with thousands of headlines and articles on the rights and wrongs of 'What would you do if . . . ?' Countless television chat shows took up the same idea, and Oprah Winfrey managed to find enough real-life people who had had similar proposals to devote an hour-long special to the subject. It did very well at the box office, and on video, grossing over $200 million world-wide.

Demi, the central figure in all the hype, travelled across the globe in April and May 1993 to promote the movie, accompanied by a phalanx of studio executives and PR people all led by one of the toughest of Hollywood's ring-of-steel publicists, Pat Kingsley, whose job was not so much to get publicity as guard against the unwanted kind. Moore was warned to expect a rough ride, especially in London where, unlike Europe, they showed 'no respect for celebrity'.

She faced a tough reception from almost 70 journalists who crowded her press conference. But she fielded the questions with quiet confidence, batting back the ones she didn't want to answer with aplomb:

'How do you feel about your husband's villification by the media?' asked one.

'That probably affects you more than me,' she replied.

Those journalists who requested a one-on-one interview first had to sign an undertaking that they would not ask questions of a personal nature. Why, if she was so guarded, was she subjecting herself to this world tour of interrogation? In that respect, she was as candid and honest as ever. She was doing it for herself, pushing towards her ultimate goal. If, by her efforts, more people came to see the movie, it would help her own career. She would have a greater choice of roles, and could choose the ones she wanted to do. It was about control.

Above all, the Demi Moore roadshow was about her. She had

edged her way into the superstar zone, coincidentally at the very moment her husband faced the possibility of dropping out of it.

13 Deeper in the Mire

WILLIS WAS HEADING TOWARDS his darkest hours. While Demi Moore remained the main attraction as the momentum of publicity grew and grew from her travelling road-show in the early summer of 1993, his own troubles went from bad to worse. Before long, the name Norman Maine was creeping into party conversation around Hollywood. He, of course, was Judy Garland's husband in the 1954 version of *A Star Is Born*: a famous actor on the slide while the wife he helped into the limelight is streaking ahead. Snide gossip suggested that the Willises were perfectly placed to do a remake, a thought not entirely without foundation.

A side issue to his career was also evolving in a way that matched the disturbing trend in Hollywood itself. Over the past few years, high-powered producers and deal-makers – rather than directors – had become the key figures in getting movies made. Director-led movies had largely become a thing of the past, certainly in the arena that Willis was operating in.

With so much money riding on the mass-market movies, the whole packaging operation was done in advance through agents and independent production companies. It goes like this: get a script, find a star or two, do the pitch, connect with a backer, agree a budget and off you go. The director, once that intriguing, enigmatic figure whose name could sell a movie on its own, was becoming an afterthought in the scheme of things. Unless he (and they are mostly men) was one of the decreasing number on the A-list in the directory of directors, he was seldom a key figure in the preliminaries unless he was also personally involved with the production set-up – and so Hollywood became awash with directors for hire.

Willis, throughout his career, had largely been dealing at the front-end – producers first, directors second – because he was in that kind of marketplace. Since he and Demi formed their own production companies, they were also increasingly seeking to initiate their own movies which, again, led them towards a production-led environment, rather than involvement at director level.

It can also be seen that both, as they passed through their various films, were never backward in challenging their director's judgement; they were always quite forceful in making their opinions known on whatever film they were working on at the time. Some directors were willing to accept it, others stood up and occasionally went in for a major battle. Both Willis and Moore have been highly critical of some of the directors they have worked with. Now, as a matter of course, they dealt with The Producers, but even that could never ensure a successful outcome, as Willis discovered on his latest project.

The trade grapevine brought word that all was not well with *Striking Distance*, completed at the beginning of the year and due for release in September 1993. Willis had high expectations that the film would restore some of the credibility lost on his string of critical flops and he had a lot of personal status riding on the outcome.

It ought to have been good, if only for the reason that it was in the hands of Arnon Milchan, the Israeli born producer who was known for some high quality, if occasionally off-the-wall, output. These included two of Robert De Niro's best movies, *The King of Comedy* and *Once Upon A Time in America*. Neither were commercially successful, but that was not the point; he was admired by directors and actors alike for his willingness to allow creativity and the art of cinema to take precedence over money. Or, at least, that had been his yardstick in earlier days, working with directors like Martin Scorsese, Sergio Leone and Terry Gilliam who directed his *Brazil*, another De Niro movie.

Lately, with the pressure of the Hollywood moneymen and packagers piling in from all directions, Milchan had moved firmly into potential blockbuster territory. He produced the successful *The War of the Roses* which he gave to Danny DeVito to direct and which starred Michael Douglas and Kathleen Turner. Then he brought Richard Gere back to life in what became one of the largest grossers of all time – *Pretty Woman* – which took $450 million world-wide.

Milchan was now producing what was billed as a high-action thriller. The screenplay was originally entitled *Three Rivers*, which was familiar to its Pittsburgh location, but this was changed later to what was considered a more apt *Striking Distance* – although it could have been Die Hard on a Police Boat. This genre of movie was already sagging; there had been a plethora of films inspired by the *Die Hard* movies, and several still in the pipeline. The most successful were *Speed* (Die Hard on a bus), *Passenger 57* (Die Hard on a plane) and *Under Siege* (Die Hard on a ship) which starred Steven Seagal and was produced by Arnon Milchan. There were also a batch of low-budget rip-offs which began to fill the remaining gaps in audience desire for this kind of action.

However, Willis persevered. He had agreed terms of $8 million and filming would take him out on location to Pittsburgh and then back to Los Angeles for completion. The director was Rowdy Harrington who also co-wrote the screenplay. Harrington was a rare bird. He came up through the crew ranks, from the lowly starting point of 'best boy, electrics' in 1984. He was 'gaffer' on two films in 1986 and was elevated to director of a small movie in 1987. Joel Silver picked him up to direct *Road House*, the 1989 kung fu roustabout starring Patrick Swayze which the *Monthly Film Bulletin* described as 'the nearly perfect exploitation movie.'

And now, Milchan was giving Harrington the chance to direct his own screenplay. Why, exactly, remains something of a mystery and it also pointed up Willis's own weakness in script reading. This was one he should certainly have returned to sender, regardless of the money, at such a crucial time in his career. There was one other major drawback. He was once again on his own, the only star above a casting-agency package of character players, competent but of little note, save for his love-interest Sarah Jessica Parker who was just coming to big screen fame after *LA Story* and *Honeymoon in Las Vegas*.

He would be the only moving target of whatever critical onslaught might follow. This is fine if the end result is anywhere near decent but this supposed thriller was a mishmash of a story, with elements of lots of other familiar themes which had been done much better in a dozen other movies.

The 'plot' is so convoluted and implausible as to almost defy a brief description. In a nutshell: he is the honest, ordinary cop caught up in an internal affairs investigation; there is a serial killer on the loose and, in the investigation, he runs foul of his superiors; he is demoted, takes to drink and then is assigned a new partner, played by Parker, who is really an internal investigator sent to keep an eye on him; they fall in love, etc., etc., and on the way the movie delivers all the now tired clichés that go with this genre – rough language, cut-to-the-chase scenes by land and by water, explosions and blood-splattered corpses. Only some first-class stunts liven up the gloomy proceedings.

Willis made the best of a bad job but was let down by a dire script. The movie itself took a critical pounding, though the reviewers did acknowledge that Willis had done his best to pull it together. The only consolation was that it went rapidly to number one in the charts – demonstrating that Willis still had remarkable pulling power – although it quickly slid away and took only $38 million in domestic gross.

At the time of its release, he was clearly fed up with life and the continued bludgeoning of his work. He bemoaned his fate in a surprisingly frank interview with the *New York Times*, which he gave to help promote the film: 'Look, I am simply an actor. I am not a devious man. I don't cheat, lie or go out of my way to mess people over but I'm still amazed at the venal garbage that goes on [in Hollywood]. People lie about you. People want to see you fail. It's so competitive here. you can see how much people want to see you go down . . . FAIL.'

He'd already moved on to other things by the time *Striking Distance* came out. Once again, he had taken the initiative and joined in the production of his next movie, *Color of Night*, a project he had been involved with since its conception. Director Rob Reiner also called to say he wanted Willis for his next movie, *North*, which he was also producing. As we will see, neither would do much for his fading reputation.

Elsewhere, however, other developments were stirring that would have a more profound effect on his future. Months earlier, in the summer of 1992, Quentin Tarantino, bolstered by the international accolades and enjoyable controversy from *Reservoir Dogs* (which he wrote and directed), gave a pitch to Danny

DeVito and his partner Michael Shamberg on his next script, still to be written.

On the strength of that verbal outline, DeVito's production company, Jersey Films, secured an incredible $900,000 from TriStar for Tarantino to write the screenplay and direct the movie, entitled *Pulp Fiction*, based upon an idea he had been toying with for years. Tarantino, then 29 years old, could not believe his luck. That kind money is usually only seen by top-notch directors on big-budget movies whereas he had directed only one small-budget film. He pocketed the first instalment, kissed his mother Connie goodbye, and took himself off to Amsterdam where, in the pungent, heady atmosphere of the 'smoking' cafes, he began to commit his idea to paper. He found himself a small apartment to rent, bought some cheap yellow notepaper and on the first page, like an instruction to himself, he wrote: 'This is the notebook I am going to write *Pulp Fiction* in.'

His idea was to create a movie based upon intertwining crime stories, containing dark humour and broadening the appeal he had established in *Reservoir Dogs* while retaining its offbeat flavour.

The title was perfect: a homage trip linking back to the pulp fiction and the characters of old crime magazines like *Thrilling Wonder Stories*, *Official Detective* and *Black Mask*. He researched the wonderfully lurid tales of that forgotten genre, where Dashiell Hammett served his literary apprenticeship writing hard-as-nails thrillers littered with bodies and blood – before he wrote *The Dain Curse* and *The Maltese Falcon*. Raymond Chandler, too, began his career writing short stories for pulp magazines, including *Black Mask*, and used them as the basis for his early novels like *The Big Sleep* and *Farewell My Lovely*.

Tarantino had copies of the old magazines flown over to Amsterdam and settled down to begin writing his screenplay. It would be set in modern times, with characters moving in and out of the plot, doubling back and then reappearing. As he extended his research among the sharp, breathless prose of the past, the screenplay bulged to a massive 500 pages, four times the length of a normal script. He was already late delivering. He had been in Amsterdam for more than three months, and TriStar were getting anxious about their nine hundred grand.

He had managed to trim it down to 200 pages by the third

draft, when his then agent called to say TriStar wanted him back, pronto. He flew back to Los Angeles with his precious work, had it typed up and then delivered copies to Danny DeVito's Jersey Films and TriStar. Within the week, he was called in for a conference with studio executives. There were problems. It was still overlength, but the main trouble concerned some of the scenes. They had marked the one where Vincent (the role eventually played by John Travolta) shoots up heroin:

'No way,' said TriStar production boss Mike Medavoy.

'You don't get it,' Tarantino pleaded. 'It's a funny scene. Trust me.'

They didn't. Nothing funny about a guy sticking a needle in his arm!

The next day, TriStar pulled out, insisting that while they admired Tarantino's work and the acumen of Jersey films, it just wasn't their kind of material. Or, as translated by DeVito: 'IT SCARED THEM SHITLESS.'

He wasn't long without a backer, however. Miramax films, who had taken the US rights to *Reservoir Dogs*, came riding in and replaced TriStar with exactly the same $900,000 deal. They had, after all, made a lot of money out of Tarantino's first movie. They gave him a tight $8 million budget for the movie which meant the stars would be playing for peanuts and a profit-share and, once in production, he would have to complete the shoot in ten weeks. Tarantino said yes to everything, and went on his way to begin piecing his movie together.

By then, everyone in Hollywood knew about it and was talking about it – and a lot wanted to be in it. One who didn't expect to get a call, not for one single moment, was John Travolta, the faded icon of the 1970s who was once compared to Brando by the esteemed critic Pauline Kael but whose comeback from 1980s obscurity with the *Look Who's Talking* films had been short lived. It so happened that Travolta was handled by the same agency that Tarantino had just moved to – William Morris, where the star man was Arnold Rifkin, who handled Bruce Willis, Harvey Keitel and Quentin Tarantino.

The fact that they all ended up in *Pulp Fiction* had all the hallmarks of an agent-led carve-up package, but Rifkin insisted that this was purely coincidental. This is their story, and they're sticking to it:

Tarantino says he always had Travolta in mind, though not originally for the part of Vincent. He had first assigned that to Mike Masden, one of his stars of *Reservoir Dogs*. Masden pulled out because he was already committed elsewhere and Tarantino rang the William Morris Agency to locate Travolta. He then sent him a copy of the screenplay with a note suggesting that he paid particular attention to the role of Vincent. Travolta's reaction was cautious, even though his career was on the floor at the time. If there was a single actor in Hollywood who could demonstrate to Bruce Willis the fragility of stardom, it was he. 'The telephone had stopped ringing,' he told me in 1995. 'I mean..it had *stopped*. I had come through a difficult time. I had been languishing so long that I thought I had reached the end of my career. Nobody wanted to know. When Tarantino offered me the role in *Pulp Fiction* I thought, "Poor boy! He doesn't know that they won't accept me." '

That wasn't his only worry. As poster boy of the Los Angeles chapter of the Church of Scientology, the role in Tarantino's movie troubled him and with the quiet humility for which he was then renowned – a far cry from the entourage-equipped prima donna of *Saturday Night Fever* days – he explained his dilemma. Quentin insisted that it would all be told with humour, and Travolta was persuaded.

Harvey Keitel was already on board, to play the role of Wolf. He was one of the producers of *Dogs*, and its star, and there was no way he was going to be left out of *Pulp*. Next, Tarantino cast Butch, the washed-up boxer who redeems himself. He had Matt Dillon pencilled in for that one, until he met Willis one Sunday afternoon at a barbecue in Keitel's back yard in July 1993. Willis had heard about *Pulp* and had already mentioned it to Keitel when he called at the Willises' place, from three mansions away on Malibu beach, to collect his daughter who often went there to play with Rumer.

Willis said he'd love to work with Tarantino. Keitel invited him to the barbecue the following day and, in the meantime, took him a copy of the screenplay to read. Willis would have dearly loved the role of Vincent, already assigned by then to Travolta. Tarantino, who had never met Willis before, immediately saw him as Butch, largely because it was a character well away from anything he had done before, just as Travolta's was.

Tarantino offered it there and then, but explained that he could only pay the scale fee of $1,685 a week, with a profit-share at the end. 'Fine by me,' said Willis, and it was left to Arnold Rifkin to settle the paperwork.

Filming was set for a ten-week shoot in the autumn, to be completed by the end of November. Willis had a good feeling about it. 'I've never met anyone like him,' he told Keitel. 'The movie is already there, in his head. He knows every scene, every twitch. This guy is magic.'

No one knew then just how much Willis would need a touch of that magic to rub off on himself: he was still heading downwards – and he still hadn't touched bottom. While Tarantino went off to prepare the final screenplay and sets, Willis was working on his next two movies, due out in mid-1994. By then, he had seen the test-screening of *Striking Distance* and, if he was honest with himself, he would know that it would do nothing for him. Nor would the two immediately ahead help, either. Indeed, they merely added to his troubles.

His sense of direction and purpose seemed to have deserted him completely; the material could not have been worse. But to give him the benefit of the doubt, the first of the impending disasters might not have been immediately evident. To begin with, the producer/director was Rob Reiner, fresh from his success with *A Few Good Men* – the man about whom Willis had once said he would give his right arm to work with. That opportunity had arrived.

Reiner, for reasons known only to himself, was pressing ahead with a screenplay called *North*, based upon a novel by Alan Zweibel. It came along soon after MacCaulay Culkin had scored an international hit in the *Home Alone* movies and no doubt this one, being another child movie (which were in vogue at the time, as in *Honey I Shrunk the Kids* and *Honey I Blew Up the Kid* etc.), was raised by hopes of similar success; in other words, it was commercially driven. The plot reverses the *Home Alone* scenario and, instead of having the parents going off and leaving the boy, it has the boy who goes off and leaves the parents.

It is one of the continuing mysteries of Hollywood as to why experienced men like Rob Reiner, whose track record includes *When Harry Met Sally* and *Misery*, get hooked onto something which is so infinitely poor. Why couldn't he see it? Or was he, as director, to blame? While Willis might not have been able to weigh up the pitfalls from his role as a kind of narrator, Reiner had no such excuse.

The film stars Elijah Wood, a fine young actor who was first rate in *The Adventures of Huck Finn*. Here, he plays a boy with wealthy parents who pay him such little heed that he decides to go into court to divorce himself from them. He then goes on a world-wide search for a couple to adopt him.

Enter Bruce Willis. He is the boy's guide and the film's guide, a curious character who appears in various disguises including an Easter bunny, a cowboy, a beach bum and a delivery driver. He is neither amusing nor helpful as any of them. But we need not waste further space describing this catastrophe of a movie; an aberration for Reiner and another drag-down for Willis. Even accepting that this is a comic fantasy, the whole idea is too incredible – not to mention inaccurate and not a bit funny in its portrayal. How it ever got made in the first place is beyond comprehension. Perhaps the author's mother, lover or favourite aunt had temporarily become head of the studio – there can be no other possible explanation! Whatever the reason, audiences were not fooled. It was a box office disaster.

And so we move quickly on, as did Willis. It would be nice at this juncture to redress the balance, but things were going from bad to worse. Willis obviously believed that *Color of Night* would secure a reversal of his deepening crisis. He had been involved with the project from the beginning through his own production company, Flying Heart, thus he had an interest at both ends of the spectrum.

His company had joined forces with Cinergi Productions, founded in 1989 by another hotshot producer, Andrew J. Vanja, who was about to loom large in Willis's life, just as Joel Silver had done before him. Willis's close friend and aide, Carmine Zozzora, president of Flying Heart, and his brother, David Willis, represented his interests as co-producers as the movie was packaged up in the search for backers. No major studio came on board and Vanja's Cinergi took the lead interest.

Zozorra and the younger Willis were the lesser mortals among a high-powered five-man production team led by Cinergi's Buzz

Feitshans, a sharp-shooter among big-action Hollywood movies who, like Joel Silver, talks in fast, unfinished sentences . . . 'Gonnabe massive'. Feistshans, anonymous to the movie-going public but a man of power nonetheless, came up in the Roger Corman school of exploitive film-making. He was the editor of one of Martin Scorsese's earliest movies, *Boxcar Bertha*, but soon found his mark among the wham-bang brigade as producer of several of the biggest 1980s movies of Schwarzenegger and Stallone including *Conan The Barbarian*, *Total Recall* and all three of the *Rambo* series.

The movies he had been involved with lately were, like Silver's, high-budget productions, aimed at a mass market; by the mid-1990s they had taken almost $2 billion at the box office. He was not a man noted for any kind of delicacy in his output: straight-forward, hard-core, knock'em dead, blood-splattered action and he was good at it; one of the best, in fact. And so, *Color of Night* was coming from a stable that had no pretentions of pussyfooting around with deep and meaningful plots or pandering to the sophisticates.

Given the success rate of Buzz's past output, and given that it was surely going to be aimed at a certain level in the market place, Willis was optimistic about the outcome. Once again, it *looked* good. From the beginning, it was set up as a sensational movie, in the most extreme sense, with one eye cast firmly in the direction of thrillers with a twist, like *Basic Instinct* and *Jagged Edge*, but it seemed to be aiming at the lowest common denominator.

It had murders, nudity, straight sex, lesbian scenes – all the titillation that they could pile in and handle with the subtlety of a sledgehammer. That would include Willis himself going full-frontal nude. The director chosen to handle this conglomeration of heavy-handed marketing clichés was Richard Rush, who used to be a decent director but hadn't made a film for fourteen years – his last being *The Stunt Man* with Peter O'Toole in 1979.

Color of Night sees Willis playing a New York psychologist. He talks hard to one of his patients and she suddenly hurls herself through his office window and crashes to the pavement several storeys down. He flies to Los Angeles to recover from the shock, though why anyone in trauma would choose that place for recuperation is a mystery in itself. He visits an old friend, another psychologist, and joins one of his therapy groups, which contains a collection of oddball characters. So, when the LA doctor is promptly murdered, Willis and the rest of the group all become Agatha Christie-style suspects.

Young British actress Jane March must have thought her ship had come in when she was cast for her co-starring role alongside Willis. It was only her second movie (the first was the Anglo-French production of *The Lover*). She must have been sorely disappointed with what was required of her, and with the final outcome.

She arrives out of the blue as Willis's love interest and quickly joins him in a swimming pool sex scene containing frontal nudity by Willis (as opposed to a view of Michael Douglas's flat behind in *Basic Instinct*). Later, Jane is involved in a lesbian love scene with Lesley Anne Warren – shades of Sharon Stone. Both scenes were heavily trimmed by the US censors, which provided a publicity blast for the movie.

Much would, of course, be made of these fleshy exposures and especially Willis's decision to go full-frontal. Although cut from the US version, Willis's willy rapidly became a topic for the media – in fact, there wasn't much else to say about the picture. Neither was it much improved when the seventeen minutes of footage deleted from the US print were restored for the video and laserdisc versions, showing Willis completely naked.

When he was sent out on the road to promote this sagging saga, he actually boasted in an interview: 'We spent half our time running around naked on the set,' demonstrating that, when he needed the publicity, he knew how to deliver a choice headline or soundbite. It didn't help much.

The film took only $19 million on the American theatre circuit and, whether he liked it or not, the bottom line remained the judge and jury for his paymaster. Willis, on the basis of that other old Hollywood adage 'You're only as good as your last movie,' looked to be hovering perilously close to his sell-by date.

It was left to Demi to provide a more positive insight into the Movie Family Willis in that winter of 1993. By then pregnant with their third child, she appeared on the David Letterman Show and, amid the hysterical whoops and cheers from the audience, she was announced as the 'most successful actress working today'. The basis for that assessment was not so much a comparison with her peers as the fact that 'her last two movies have earned almost HALF A BILLION DOLLARS'. The audience screams with delight. Money. Money. Money. It's the American dream, and she is now its epitome. She sits there, small but drop-dead stunning, and talks about her work and her family: 'Bruce is fine, working hard, as usual' and they really strive to spend quality time together with the children.

A month or so later, Demi took steps to ensure that she would not be forgotten during her absence, once more through pregnancy, by returning to the pages of *Vanity Fair* – something which she had said would never happen again. But, there she was, splashed across six pages of the December issue under the headline 'DEMI'S STATE OF GRACE'. She revealed that she had formed a new production company, Moving Pictures, naming her friend Suzanne Todd as its president and David Willis as an executive. It would, of course, produce her new picture, *The Scarlet Letter*, coming up in 1994, after the next baby had been delivered. 'Having it all,' she said, smiling wistfully, 'just means having things that make you happy.'

Bruce, at that moment in time, might not have agreed.

14 In the Nick of Time

QUENTIN TARANTINO was riding to the rescue, and he knew it. His quickfire demonstration to the Hollywood big shots of how a good movie can be made in ten weeks, and not a cent over the minuscule $8 million budget, was completed in the autumn of 1993. He planned to have a print of *Pulp Fiction* ready for the Cannes Film Festival, the twelve-day binge of movies opening at the end of May. That very fact was more important to Willis than he realised at the time. Rob Reiner's disastrous *North* and Willis's main hope, *Color of Night*, would be promoted there, too.

Willis would take a hefty clout from both and but for Tarantino would have been like a punch-drunk boxer floundering on the ropes, waiting for the knock-out punch. Although he still faced a bad time with the media, and a huge mauling from the reviewers, by the time those two turkeys went on release everyone would have had the benefit of observing his 30-minute performance in *Pulp Fiction*. It had a remarkable countering effect, and redeemed his reputation. It had them all saying that Willis can do it, given the right material and *direction*.

A foretaste of the critical reaction that would arrive on the release of *North* and *Color of Night* occurred at a press junket in Cannes, ahead of the opening of the two movies in the US in July and August. It was held in a massive seaside hotel ballroom, packed with 400 international journalists and movieland executives. There was a screening of clips and then canapes and drinks were served prior to the press conference. Willis came in wearing sloppy casual clothes and looking decidedly jaded. The reception he received did nothing to improve his mood. He took his place on the stage and his English co-star, Jane March, sat nervously beside him.

There were a couple of tepid questions to answer. Then an American woman journalist yelled from the floor: 'Don't you feel awful guilty after a while, taking money for making SHIT LIKE THIS?' Willis looked up, glowered and, quick as a flash, retorted: 'I bet you sat up all night thinking of that question.'

The exchange brought the press conference to an abrupt halt. Willis got up and marched out, stopping only to chat to a couple of film people. Later he explained, 'I'm not going to sit there and take that kind of shit from anyone. She was being rude for the sake of it. Well fuck that and fuck her. Sure, I don't expect everyone in that room to like me, but those that don't shouldn't come to the screening and try to embarrass me in front of a crowd of people. But then, I come to expect it. I live with it all the time. When you get big, people just want to knock the shit out of you.'

Quentin Tarantino agreed with his assessment of the situation. Although Willis did not need the emergency career resuscitation that John Travolta required, he had come to the point of a curious love-hate relationship with his audiences. 'He was losing his street cred,' said Tarantino frankly, 'and because he was usually up there on his own, he always took the hit if a movie flops. Meanwhile, the director moves on.'

Four months work on *Color of Night* produced nothing but brickbats, yet the movie which detained him for just sixteen days would set the Cannes Film Festival alight. Those few days, Willis admitted, were like being in heaven. It was an experience that few actors of Willis's status – even accounting for his flops – would have been prepared to take on. The motivation was more personal than just a career move. Quite simply, he wanted to work with Tarantino. He told him he would play any role in the movie.

When filming began in the autumn of 1993, Willis was undoubtedly the biggest name among the cast yet he was playing one of the lesser roles. There were to be no divisions of rank, status or temperament; no special treatments, or flash limos ferrying the actors and no entourages of make-up artists. It all had the atmosphere of an amateur drama group production, devoid of any Hollywood casting agency packaging or any other deals.

In spite of the rumours of a casting carve-up by the William Morris Agency that represented Keitel, Travolta, Willis and Tarantino, Quentin insisted he had personally selected the entire cast purely on the basis of how he saw them in a particular role – and not for their box office appeal or any other commercial factor.

He said that no one would have chosen Travolta but himself; he even had to fight the backers to get him on board. He talked to just about every notable Hollywood actress under 35 before he took Uma Thurman to dinner at his favourite restaurant, Toi's on Sunset Boulevard, and decided, within minutes, that she would be Mia.

The nightmare for Tarantino, though, as he began to put the movie into production at hurtling pace, was getting his movie filmed between the work schedules of his small but precious gathering of Hollywood stars including Samuel L. Jackson, Christopher Walken, Amanda Plummer and Tim Roth. Then there were 75 sets to build. He had secured the services of many of the crew of *Reservoir Dogs,* including cinematographer Andrzej Sekula, costume designer Betsy Heimann, production designer David Wasco and editor Sally Menke.

Wasco and his wife Sandy were working around the clock to meet the deadlines. 'What we did,' he explained, 'was to provide the background, Quentin's particular vision of Los Angeles, for what was basically a film of dialogue. Our mission was to provide the surroundings and the tools for the actors, to help them become their characters. It was a very precise task from our point of view.' Tarantino's quest for exact detail was demanding in itself, right down to the particular type of storage box he wanted for drug dealer Lance (Eric Stoltz).

The largest of the sets, Jack Rabbit Slim's diner, was built inside a 25,000 square foot warehouse in Culver City where they would create, as Wasco put it, 'the fifties on heroin'. The controversial drug scenes required particular attention. Uma Thurman's task was especially difficult: she would join Travolta in their protrayal of heroin addicts – something which had made TriStar back away from the movie. Thurman was deeply worried about the harrowing sequence where she overdoses and is then injected with adrenalin, directly into her heart. The special effects team came up with all kinds of gadgets to give these moments realism, such as hypodermics with needles that plunged inwards and a fake chest strapped to Thurman's body for the heart injection scene.

'We've gotta keep up the humour,' Tarantino kept telling them. 'Treat it light. Don't take anything too serious.'

Thurman was also worried about one of the other most discussed scenes in the movie, where she would dance with Travolta. Thurman had a last-minute attack of stage fright. She was convinced she would make a fool of herself and pleaded with Tarantino to change it.

'Forget it. Nobody will give a fuck if you can't dance. I'll show you.'

'*You'll* show me?' said Thurman, mystified.

'Wait till we shoot the scene . . .' Tarantino told her. 'All will become clear.'

On the morning of the dance routine, he brought in a video of Jean-Luc Godard's *Bande a Part* and fast-forwarded it to a dance sequence. 'Just do it like that,' said Tarantino. 'No fancy steps. The dancing doesn't have to be perfect. Just imagine you and Vincent are on a dancefloor having a good time. Enjoy it.'

That was pretty well the theme of his direction, and for Willis as the boxer, Butch, it worked exceptionally well. Willis enjoyed the relaxed, informal atmosphere of the set. The only time he became irritable was when they had to go out on location and film some scenes in a motel room. He was, said Tarantino, paranoid that the tabloids would get a picture of him going into some seedy joint with a girl who wasn't Demi and, movie or no movie, the picture would be run anyway, just as it was in Rome with Andie MacDowell.

Initially, Willis had been somewhat solitary, retiring to his trailer after his work, but he soon fell in with the crowd. He organised a weekly raffle for the crew, for four pots of $50 which he donated. Willis did not insist upon any of the more usual facilities, such as seeing rough cuts of his performance. 'It was,' he said later, 'the most creative process I have ever been involved in. We worked on a level of focus and detail I have never experienced before.'

He did not, in fact, see the first rough cut which was audience-tested by the backers, Miramax, in a small Los Angeles cinema in March 1994, ahead of its appearance at the Cannes Film Festival. Tarantino went along himself to introduce the film and asked those in the audience to put up their hands if they enjoyed his debut movie, *Reservoir Dogs*. A large number shot up. Then he asked if there were any who liked the Merchant Ivory film,

Remains of the Day, and a fair smattering of hands went up. 'Get the fuck outta this theatre,' shouted Tarantino, but added quickly, 'Only kiddin'.' It was a joke that might have misfired. The author of that movie, Kazuo Ishiguro, was a member of the panel of judges at the Cannes Film Festival – where *Pulp Fiction* would be competing for the coveted Palme D'Or.

Next stop Cannes, and the big jamboree and hoopla.

The promotional effort for Willis's *other* movies, *Color of Night* and *North*, was already under way and studio hands were walking around in baseball hats and dark blue sweatshirts bearing the logos. Both were already being assigned to the also-ran league, along with quite a few others on view that year.

Those present from the beginning had judged it to be a fairly quiet start to the twelve-day festival, almost sedate. It was crowded, of course, with the 30,000 temporary immigrants jostling with tourists along the packed promenades of the Côte d'Azur. The movie community is always there, en masse, for the deal-fest: producers, distributors, actors and journalists along with all the usual hustlers, hookers and general hangers-on. The bars and the restaurants were jam-packed. In every corner of every hotel, someone was talking deals. Some decent little movies, and a few bigger ones, from various countries around the world were on view. Celebrities were few that year, and largely second-rank.

Isabelle Adjani had made a nice presentation for her starring role in Patrice Chereau's *Queen Margot*, and Britain's Terence Stamp was camping it up for his drag role in *Priscilla, Queen of the Desert*. Clint Eastwood was also there, serving as president of that year's festival jury. For a while it seemed as if this 47th movie jamboree would sidle off without much ado. That was until Tarantino arrived with Sam Jackson and Travolta on the last Saturday night of the festival. Willis was delighted to have them with him in the hostile climate that surrounded *Color of Night* which brought only heartache and anger for its star.

Tarantino flew in with a suitcase full of redemption for Willis. Ironically, however, Quentin's luggage went astray on the first night and Bruce had to provide him with a promotional bag of *Color of Night* goodies – he ended up wearing the sweatshirt and baseball cap. Meanwhile, the rest of the cast of *Pulp Fiction* were preparing for their big entrance. Virtually overnight, the movie became the hottest ticket in town.

At the press conference that followed, he brought John Travolta, Bruce Willis, Samuel L. Jackson and Uma Thurman onto the stage to face an inquisitive band of over 1,000 journalists for a forty-five-minute Q and A which, almost in its entirety, was directed at Tarantino himself. The blood-soaked action, the disparate sex and the realism of the drug scenes naturally became a focus for a barrage of questions about violence in the movies. The answers were the standard Hollywood responses that push the question aside too easily. 'If you ask me how I feel about violence in real life,' Tarantino shot back, 'then, I will tell you I have a lot of feelings about it. It is one of the worst aspects of America. In movies, violence is cool. I like it.'

He didn't sound all that convincing and Willis, whose own movies are built on the same ingredients (there was a body count of 264 in *Die Hard 2*), chipped in: 'Quentin uses violence as a tool. It's a reflection, maybe, of a violent world . . . but there's nothing in movies that can compare with real-life horror.' If there was a defence in this instance, it lay in the tongue-in-cheek way Tarantino approached it in *Pulp Fiction* and in the confidence of his storytelling, which displays a particular talent for exploding heavy scenes at unexpected moments.

The ten-member jury included Catherine Deneuve, who may have remembered one of her own early appearances there, in 1965, as the star of Roman Polanski's first film outside of Poland, *Repulsion*, a macabre, unashamedly ugly but brilliant movie that the Cannes organisers rejected as an official entry. It was screened anyway, and in a curious way that movie of the diminutive genius provided a distant echo to the arrival of Tarantino; in many ways, he was the modern Polanski.

Just as Cannes did not want to show its approval of Polanski's nasty little masterpiece, so this jury, along with a large number of international film critics, had ample reservations about giving tacit approval to a work so cleverly interwoven and crafted yet which could be seen as glamorising such awful anti-social behaviour.

The signal would, in the end, come from the jury. If they approved it, the film would be a hit; if they didn't, it might well be dismissed as so much trash. But, after a week of studying the

22 other entries – largely made up of Third World angst, tales of woe from 30 years of life in Maoist China and familiar fables of immoral behaviour in continental Europe (all beautifully performed) – *Pulp Fiction* was like cutting Sunday school to go to a rave. In other words, it was no contest and it would have been a fallacy to ignore the breadth and the comic impact of Tarantino's shock-blaster.

In this 150-minute movie, he weaves four tales into one and extracts best-ever performances from the key players, Travolta, Willis, Thurman and Sam Jackson, the Bible-spouting sociopath. What is especially interesting is the influence of Europe: his hard men are reminiscent of the French gangster films of the sixties, moulded with the luridness of the pulp fiction of the thirties and all transformed and wrapped up in modern freakishness.

The dialogue, as much as anything, stops the movie and then carries it on. The characters talk, off-the-wall and in their own particular way, in long diatribes about nothing in particular, about things that have nothing to do with the plots: dialogue that is there for no reason, and which most directors would have cut out of a screenplay. Example: the discussion on how Parisians order a quarter pounder because in France they don't have pounds and ounces, they have kilos. Or, how you would order a Big Mac in Amsterdam.

Just as Willis had surmised on the day he met Tarantino, the director produced every shot from his brain, constructing the movie in such an indirect way that it was impossible to tell what was coming next. There is not a formulaic character in the entire movie, and none of the actors produces the character that might be expected of them.

John Travolta, as lowercase hitman Vincent Vega, is a Travolta never seen before. His scene with Uma Thurman prior to her overdose is a bizarre classic. She is the wife of the mob boss who instructs Travolta to take her out for the night. They go to Jack Rabbit Slim's, the 1950s theme restaurant where Ed Sullivan is the master of ceremonies and Buddy Holly is a waiter. Later, when she overdoses on heroin and they decide to inject adrenaline straight into her heart, Eric Stoltz shouts at Travolta: 'You brought her here, you stick in the needle! When I bring an OD to your house, I'll stick in the needle!'

Funny scenes, but not for the faint-hearted. Bruce Willis appears in the movie for around 28 minutes and he is not the Bruce Willis, in any shape, manner or form, from previous incarnations. The boxer Butch Coolidge is an inspirational creation, unlike anything he has ever done. He has an excellent sequence with Maria de Medeiros who plays Fabienne, his girlfriend, and this performance was probably more studied than anything else he had done in his life.

Tarantino waxed lyrical about Willis. 'He's the only guy who could have done this, the only contemporary actor who suggests fifties – with that Sterling Hayden, Robert Mitchum or Aldo Ray man's man look. Bruce playing Butch made the role deeper.'

The audiences, as well as the critics, noticed. Tarantino tells a story that confirmed, for him, that he had made the right choice with Willis. He had been invited by Richard Linklater, director of *Before Sunrise*, to give a screening of *Pulp Fiction* at a coffee house in Austin, Texas. 'When the credits role,' Tarantino recalls, 'the kids actually started booing Willis. Then, after his scene in the movie where he goes back to save Marseilles (Ving Rhames), they cheered and gave him a standing ovation. Bruce totally won over that Austin coffee-house hippie-slacker crowd.'

If there is a 'missing link' in this story of Bruce Willis, the actor, it has been in the area of what might be described as role intensity. He never had the training of the famous New York method actors like Brando, Pacino and De Niro. Nor had he ever been able to observe any one of them at work, close hand. There has been little evidence from Willis of any kind of meticulous role preparation – that kind of preparation for which Pacino and De Niro are renowned (the latter to the point of obsession and minuscule detail, absorbing everything he can about the character).

These performers, in the true traditions of method, first breathe in the character and then exhale their own creation of it: whatever role they are playing, the audience sees them as the character rather than the star. Willis had seldom been able to achieve this effect, largely because the kind of parts he played seldom called for such intensity or variation. With the exception of Emmett Smith in *In Country*, his characters were simply a variation of two themes: he was either a reincarnated David Addison or Detective John McClane.

In *Pulp Fiction*, it was different. He had a real character to get into and the result was surprising. There were no Willis trademarks; he was calm and alert and demonstrating a depth that some would have said did not exist. Anyway, it was sufficient to overcome the bad press he was getting – and would continue to receive – for *Color of Night* and, in the spin-off hype that surrounded Tarantino's movie, Willis's credibility was miraculously restored, and enhanced.

Pulp Fiction won the Palme D'Or with a nine-to-one vote by the judges. As Clint Eastwood made the announcement in the festival hall, Tarantino leapt from his seat and rushed towards the stage to receive his award. There, he was joined by Willis, Travolta and Jackson for a group hug, and the future of *Pulp Fiction*, and all its players, was assured. They began filing their largely glowing assessments of the movie around the world and the result is now written large in Hollywood history. There were a few carping comments about Tarantino plagiarising past movies and books, and there was also a dispute over the original authorship of the scenes involving Willis: his friend, Roger Avary, claimed that he was the 'full-on' author of one section and, indeed, his name was later included in the credits.

However, numbers become the focus in the next phase. Buoyed up by the reaction at Cannes, Miramax plunged in with an $8 million promotional spend – as much as the movie itself cost to make. It grossed more than $250 million at the box office. Although it was not released into the cinemas until October that year, Willis received the immediate benefit of the reviews from Cannes, as indeed did Travolta, who was suddenly a big star again. His own thespian rebirth was more remarkable than the effects on Willis's career. The actor who, a few months ago, couldn't get arrested was suddenly Golden Globe and Oscar nomination potential, and the offers piled in.

His salary went up accordingly and, after working on *Pulp* for a few thousand dollars, the William Morris Agency hung a $7 million price tag on his head, and then rapidly increased it to $10 million, $15 million and then to $20 million in 1996. Travolta, with the now typical humility, gave the credit to Tarantino: 'He helped me find myself again.'

Willis summed up the effects on himself in one word: 'WHAM!'

His career had been kick-started again, and by the end of the year he had four movies in the frame, including another with Tarantino. The tactic of taking lesser roles, which other stars – and particularly those in the action genre like Stallone and Schwarzenegger – would never do, had paid off at long last. It was repeated again later that year when he was offered a place in Paul Newman's latest movie, *Nobody's Fool*, with Jessica Tandy and Melanie Griffith.

It had echoes of his struggling days, when he was tending bar back in New York, when Willis won an uncredited bit-part in Newman's *The Verdict*. Newman was his hero then, and at the top of the Hollywood tree. Now, a mere decade later, it was Willis who, in spite of the recent setbacks, was a bigger draw than Newman though, of course, he could not hold a candle to Newman's body of work. Such are the vagaries of Hollywood and fame.

Willis, however, showing unaccustomed humility, laid praise on the 70-year-old star saying, 'what a terrific experience it is to be working with my own icon'. It was, as his record shows, indeed a rare experience to be witnessing the techniques of an actor of such stature.

This fact alone represented one other 'missing link' in his own progression – the relative dearth of true Hollywood stars he had worked with. Because he had come straight in at the top – a leading player – he'd missed out on the experience that most up-and-coming actors in Hollywood enjoy – that of repeatedly working with clusters of stars. To this point, and after nineteen movies, you could still virtually count on one hand the major names whose work and preparation he had witnessed first hand.

This little statistic also pointed up another: the success of most of those movies in which he had taken the lead rested largely upon his name being on the marquees. There were, quite simply, no other stars of real note in the majority of his major films. In those that there were, like *Billy Bathgate*, *The Bonfire of the Vanities* and *Death Becomes Her*, he was in a supporting role – usually quick-fire, in-and-out filming in which he experienced none of the atmospherics of working in a group during an elongated shoot.

The film with Newman gave him one more window-dressing opportunity, to show that there was, behind the rough and tumble, a better actor struggling to get out. It was written and directed by Robert Benton, whom he worked for in *Billy Bathgate*. Newman plays a character ten years younger than his own age, an unemployed construction worker who has spent his life rebelling against convention. Willis takes on a small character role as Newman's exploitative boss.

It was not among Newman's best, nor did it fare well in the cinemas. But Willis came out of it well. *Time* magazine went so far as to describe his performance in *Nobody's Fool* as 'astonishingly good'. The critics seemed, at last, to be warming to the idea that he could play other characters besides David Addison, a role which still haunted him five years after the show ended.

The whipping boy had, quite suddenly, become flavour of the month. He needed that, as he admitted to the *Daily Mail*'s Lester Middlehurst: 'I try to do a wide range . . . but my more successful ones have been action movies. I've had some bad reviews lately, but I don't look to the critics for conformation or revalidation of my work. I know when my work is good or bad and so do the audiences.'

He wanted variation, just as Stallone and Schwarzenegger sought to diversify so that if action movies ended, their careers wouldn't. They found the switch harder than Willis because they were aligned to those roles in both their physical appearance and their limited spoken range. In a way, these developments from his appearance in *Pulp* and *Nobody's Fool* demonstrated the major difference between his own work and theirs. He could get out of his more commonly perceived character when he was given the opportunity and the right direction.

They also highlighted the difference between his sole-star roles and the onscreen company of his wife, who was now firmly positioned up among the most heavenly names. After the birth of their third baby (a third girl, Tallulah Belle after Tallulah Bankhead), she zoomed back on her ambition trip and once again leapfrogged her husband in box office standing.

In 1994, with the commercial success of *Indecent Proposal* still winging its way around the world on bountiful video sales, Moore was signed for $5 million to give Michael Douglas a hard time in the film of Michael Crichton's tense tome, *Disclosure*. Douglas, incidentally, was getting $12 million and Demi made a note of the numbers for future reference. Why should he get more than twice her fee? The dealmakers and the packagers seemed unable to let any picture rely on the audience-attracting qualities of any woman actor. She was planning to try to alter that with her own movie, which she was currently researching. Based on the classic novel, *The Scarlet Letter*, the central character, Hester Prynne, was, ironically, America's prototype feminist.

There was nothing feminist about Moore's character in *Disclosure* – just straightforward, menacing sexuality. The issue of sexual harassment in the workplace was a political hot potato of the time.

Film-wise, there was not a lot new in the concept. The harassing of women has been one of Hollywood's most resonant themes. Equally, film-makers have always been intrigued by sexually active, powerful women in film stories and many men had been subjected to their whims long before harassment became such an issue. But, after several high profile cases in the US, the term sexual harassment became a '90s buzzword. At which point, Michael Crichton wrote the outline of the plot for his next novel (and film script) on the back of a cigarette packet. It read, simply: 'Sexual harassment of a MAN by a WOMAN in the workplace.' Terrific, said the studio execs. Go away and write it, quickly, before someone else does it.

So, in the summer of 1994, while Willis was experiencing the duality of success and failure, his wife's continuing profile, was assured of going higher and higher as she began work on what was the most unashamedly politically incorrect movie of the time. It was bound to achieve maximum impact in the then current climate of gender wars.

Although Moore wasn't the first choice of director Barry Levinson – she came in to replace Annette Bening who dropped out at the last minute – her association with the movie captured the imagination of American writers and, for that matter, the public. The story of Moore, the tough cookie in charge of her own life as portrayed in three major articles in *Vanity Fair*, had a certain affinity with the character she was playing, at least from the standpoint of her single-minded approach to her career.

Sexual harassment, however, was not on her personal agenda: she relied on straightforward strength of will. Tales from the set regurgitated her now familiar demands for a double-sized trailer and a private jet to carry her to location filming in Seattle. But then, as she said herself, why not? Douglas had the star treatment written into his contract, and he was getting twelve million big ones to boot! Still, it provided some juicy phrases for the writers who came to watch and observe the action during filming in accord with Douglas's normal policy of an open set. He welcomed the pre-publicity, always mindful of his back-end slice. Demi was playing, they pointedly pointed out, the 'woman who is capable of anything if it means she will win,' and 'the woman you'll love to hate.'

Moore dismissed them, distancing herself from the character: 'I've met women like this. They see all men as fair game and they enjoy it that way. But that's not me. No way.' Nor did she have the appearance of a vixen who was about to have Douglas for breakfast. After more long workouts and punishing pre-dawn five-mile runs, her post-pregnancy body was once more lithe and slender, her hair long and hanging loose. She didn't look her 32 years, until she got into character – and her whole demeanour changed.

It was another *big* movie to add to her body of work. It was heavily promoted, with world-wide television and poster campaigns, showing her wrapped threateningly around a cornered and coy Douglas (re-playing his male-in-peril with his usual style). The enforced chemistry worked well. Moore was far better in this one than in her previous outing with Robert Redford. The whole thing added up to a glossy Tinseltown production that was guaranteed, like most of Douglas's movies since *Fatal Attraction*, to cause a stir. And, of course, it did. *Disclosure* took well in excess of $230 million in international box offices receipts, thus confirming Moore's status in the top five actresses of the year. In box office totals alone, she had now outstripped her husband by almost half a billion dollars!

By then, Willis himself had turned back towards the pinnacle with a promising selection of new projects. He needed them . . . badly. In the previous year, he had done three films: *Pulp Fiction* took sixteen days of his life, *Nobody's Fool* took two weeks and *North* took twenty days. After completing *Pulp*, he had gone ten months without making a movie – his longest period of 'rest' since he came to Hollywood.

Now, Tarantino wanted him for another small part, this time in *Four Rooms*. Terry Gilliam signed him for his own upcoming large one, *Twelve Monkeys*, and Willis announced that he would be going back on his previously (and publicly) stated determination not to make another *Die Hard* movie – the third in the sequences was going ahead.

Everyone was asking what had made him change his mind. The script, he said, looked inviting. And ... SO DID THE MONEY.

He boasted that he had ran his head past a supermarket barcoding pricer. And what did it show?

$15 million!

It was a new record fee, and the revelation attracted much attention. In fact, it was only part of the story ...

15 A Tale of Two Movies

FIFTEEN MILLION DOLLARS to reprise *Die Hard*? It sounded easy: Willis strolling effortlessly into his day job, playing Detective John McClane, they said. The ducking and diving behind the scenes and that fact that, at times, it is necessary to generate one's own employment, is never that obvious. Nor was it when, a few weeks later, the announcement came that Demi Moore was to star in a new version of *The Scarlet Letter*, to be directed by Roland Joffe. One innocent columnist, apparently very familiar with the Nathaniel Hawthorne novel but not the inner workings of Hollywood, went into a lengthy discourse on Demi's suitability for the role and wrote: 'One can see at once why Roland Joffe has selected her to take the lead in this movie.'

Demi *selected* by Roland Joffe? Bruce back in his day job? It wasn't quite like that.

Here's the deal: Willis hasn't anything on his calendar for months ahead, but he does have a script that has been bouncing around Hollywood for some time. He reads it and he's certain it will convert into another *Die Hard*. At the same time, Demi Moore, for quite different reasons of ambition and the desire to make a film with some kind of serious statement, is studying a screenplay based on *The Scarlet Letter*. She wants to turn it into the umpteenth remake of the classic 19th-century novel. The two projects are being worked up separately by His and Hers production companies. The two movies will cost a combined total of around $140 million to make, out of which they will each want a substantial, guaranteed fee as the starring actors, plus a piece of the action on the rights.

Both projects were being mapped out in the early months of 1993 yet, as is the way of Hollywood, it would be almost eighteen months before they went into production.

Moore knew that she faced a battle to get her movie made. It was not high box office material and, as the star, she would be carrying the picture. Hollywood moneymen do not like risking all on the ability of one female actress to draw them in; men, yes; women, no. Demi, it would be said, had been part of a package of stars in all her recent successes. Could she stand alone? There were many doubters.

Willis, for various reasons, also faced an uphill journey. Joel Silver was no longer close to Willis: they had parted company after *Hudson Hawk* and hadn't made a movie together since.

Fortunately, another New Tycoon was looming large in their world. They had got into bed with Andrew Vanja (Andy to his friends), the Big Boss and founder of Cinergi Pictures and a recognised ace at marketing movies. He was an old rival in the blockbuster marketplace of Silver and was glad to have connected with Willis and Moore. He was the man to make their dreams come true, in spite of the fact that he had taken a beating as executive producer of *Color of Night*.

Vanja was looking for big projects. His company, Cinergi, was little more than four years old, although he'd been around Hollywood for years. Like Willis, he'd come a long way in the last decade. He had launched his career in the entertainment industry with his purchase of cinemas in the Far East and had then founded Panasia Films in Hong Kong before forming Carolco with Mario Kassar in 1976.

In less than four years, Carolco became one of the top three foreign sales. In 1982, he was a founder member, and then president, of the American Film Marketing Association. During the same year, Vanja and Kassar made their film production debut with Stallone's *First Blood*. *Rambo: First Blood Part II* was released in 1985, generating more than $300 million world-wide, making it – at that time – one of the most profitable films in history.

Vanja and Kassar went on to other action hits such as *Rambo III* and the hugely successful *Total Recall*, but their output wasn't entirely in the mass-market genre. The success included *Mountains of the Moon*, Bob Rafelson's story of the explorer Richard Burton, and Alan Parker's *Angel Heart*, with Robert De Niro. Vanja sold his interest in Carolco, which was fortunate for him because it hit financial troubles a few years later. He then founded Cinergi, in December 1989, and signalled his big-budget intentions by announcing he was making John McTiernan's *Medicine Man*, starring Sean Connery, which, in the event, did not do as well as expected. His next two productions, *Tombstone*, with Kurt Russell and *Renaissance Man*, starring Danny DeVito, hadn't quite hit the mark either. Nor, of course, had *Colour of Night*.

Vanja was looking for the Big One – enter the Movie Family Willis.

From their joint offices off Sunset Boulevard, the two Willis projects were coming along nicely and were ready for moving on to the moneymen. In Bruce's corner was Carmine Zozzora, president of his company, Flying Heart Films Inc. He was an old friend of Willis's, going right back to his struggling days. He went out west in 1985, got a job as an assistant producer on *Moonlighting* and had been Willis's close confidante and aide ever since. He had taken acting or production roles in five of Willis's movies.

Across the hall was Suzanne Todd, president of Demi's company, Moving Pictures – a title chosen to identify with the kind of films she wanted to make. Todd and David Willis were in the planning stages of *The Scarlet Letter* in which Demi had allotted herself the leading role of Hester Prynne, the married woman who scandalised puritanical 17th-century New England by having an illegitimate child. For refusing to name the father (the local priest), Hester was adorned with a scarlet letter A for adultery.

Meanwhile, Willis and Zozzora were developing a screenplay by Jonathan Hensleigh, whose previous credits included Disney's *A Far Off Place* and *The Young Indiana Jones Chronicles*. His original script had the title of *Simon Says*, an action-adventure story about a white New York City cop who, in a game of Simon Says, is ordered to go to Harlem by a psychopathic criminal. There, the cop meets an African-American named Zeus Carver who aids him in his battle against the madman.

John McTiernan, who directed Willis in the first *Die Hard*, read it and agreed with Bruce that the story's New York cop could easily become John McClane. It was one of several scripts that they had read with a view to bringing McClane back to the screen. The others had been rejected but Hensleigh's story seemed to have all the necessary elements. Willis and McTiernan were particularly intrigued by the script's clever solution to the challenge of creating a new and different *Die Hard* adventure.

Willis explained at a post-filming press conference that the script was vital to the continuing theme that made McClane an unusual hero of the eighties and nineties; he would maintain an audience following while others of the same genre had fallen by the wayside. 'I've made the choice of playing him as a guy who doesn't want to be doing what he has to do in these films,' said Willis. 'I think the interesting thing is that McClane's in situations where he has absolutely no other choice but to do the things he has to do: jump off a building, swing in the window on a hose, jump on the wing of an airplane, jump on to a train that he knows is about to explode. He's a policeman with a sense of duty to the public – I think that's what's made him so popular. The stories have an emotional heart, set against the background of heavy action. It's entertainment but with a message that good guys still do win.'

Hensleigh's script was the key to everything. He recalled: 'They shipped the script to Andy Vanja. Within 48 hours we had all decided to make *Simon Says* into a third *Die Hard* – subject to some adaptation to fit the original story themes. For example, McClane's wife is not put into peril as she had been in the previous *Die Hard* films, but is instead an offscreen presence. This time, we tried to raise the emotional stakes through the two central and very disparate characters so that they formed and became the emotional core of the movie.'

With Andrew Vanja and his Cinergi people, Willis's team began working on the package and, from the outset, they aimed it at a higher level than the previous two *Die Hard* movies, with a strong supporting cast and a story that had a far broader setting: whereas in the past, McClane's battles were fought in a skyscraper and an airport, this time the terrorist, Simon, virtually holds hostage the entire city of New York.

On Willis's suggestion, Samuel L. Jackson, who starred with him in *Pulp Fiction* and was thus HOT, was cast as Zeus Carver, the man who shares the 'emotional core' with McClane. Next, they went for a big-name villain, for the role of McClane's tormenter, Simon. McTiernan, being mindful of the excellence that Britisher Alan Rickman had brought to the first *Die Hard*, sought an actor of similar quality and depth.

They played around with a number of names, until McTiernan came up with Jeremy Irons, who needs no introduction but, for those who have been on Mars for the last few years, he is the multi-award-winning British star of *Brideshead Revisited*, *The French Lieutenant's Woman*, *The Mission*, *Reversal of Fortune* etc., etc. 'I found the role intriguing for two reasons,' said Irons. 'It was my first involvement in the action-adventure genre which is fascinating in itself, although one treads with caution. Second, the character was quite a different villain – one of those men who is very highly intelligent and who loves playing games. I think if you are a duellist in life, you like games, you like duels, and you're always looking for good opponents. Simon thinks McClane may be a good opponent.'

Irons also has a beautiful conspirator, Katya, and in this role director McTiernan cast singer-songwriter Sam Phillips – for no other reason than the fact that he'd seen and liked her photo on the cover of her latest album, 'Martinis and Bikinis'. Yet she does not get to speak. Because a bomb had destroyed Katya's voice box, singer Phillips makes her acting debut as a mute. 'I think they liked the irony of it,' she said.

The Cinergi production people went to work on the costings for the bigger-than-ever special effects and the locations. At the end of the day, they came up with a bottom line figure that was higher than any previous *Die Hard* movie. They moved the whole package over to 20th Century Fox, where Murdoch's moneymen eyed it with caution. Several months of negotiations and rights selling lay ahead. Originally scheduled for filming at the back end of 1993, it was delayed for a further six months. Then, encouraged by Willis's born-again status, Fox finally approved a budget of $90 million and filming began in the late summer of 1994.

By then, Moore's own project was also coming to fruition, courtesy of Andy Vanja. Cinergi Pictures would co-produce with Demi's company, Moving Pictures. She would take the starring role and Gary Oldman was signed to play the priest. They 'adjusted' the story to make the movie more commercial and, of course, there had to be a happy ending. To this they added the brilliance of Robert Duvall, playing the heavy character role of Hester's husband and, with it all neatly packaged, Andy Vanja went off to find a studio that would underwrite the $50 million needed to make the movie.

Back in the Willis corner, *Simon Says* was now retitled *Die Hard With a Vengeance*, and he was joined by Sam Jackson, Jeremy Irons *et al* crashing around New York for the location work. The trailer will set the scene: Detective John McClane thought he'd seen it all. He's back in New York and about to face his most unusual foe yet – a twisted genius named Simon – who plans to engage McClane, and the city of New York, in a deadly game. Simon says: John McClane is about to have a very bad day ... Jeremy Irons, thin-lipped and staring eyes, is Simon, a terrorist with a penchant for high explosives and a particular dislike for John McClane.

With shades of the Riddler in *Batman Forever*, he plays word games and sets little intelligence tests that provide the thriller element to the plot. Will they be resolved in time? Even so, the dialogue is no challenge to the Royal Shakespearean actor; this is sit-back-and-enjoy-the-ride material which makes its point before the audience has had time for the first handful of popcorn. With the Dolby surround-sound turned high, the cinema will shudder as if it is just a few blocks away from the mass opening explosion. Just to show he means business, the nasty Mr Irons has blown up a Fifth Avenue department store with exceedingly spectacular effect – a cacophony of collapsing masonry, twisted metal and flying cars. To ensure that the authorities are aware of his plans, he telephones, in a polite manner, to claim responsibility.

In Britain, where such events are not exactly uncommon (though, granted, the IRA does not have the benefit of Hollywood special effects geniuses), audiences have long since come to terms with American insensitivity on this score. What Willis and his co-conspirators had not accounted for was that, even as the film was being prepared for release, America itself would experience such real-life terrorism first hand. The Oklahoma city bombing occurred in April, an explosion so devastating in its death toll that it dwarfed the usual British bombings.

Even so, with such an event still so vivid in the minds of the public, British film-makers might have thought twice about releasing the movie. For those not entirely carried away by disbelief, the Oklahoma bomb hung uncomfortably over the picture for its duration. What saved it from total embarrassment was the movie's pure, unadulterated escapism, in which Willis, Jackson and Irons excel. For once, here was a high-octave movie that was as much led by performance as by its spectacular content.

Jeremy Irons, normally seen as suave sophistication itself, provides a character whose impact on the movie is reminiscent of Jack Nicholson's performance as The Joker in the first of the *Batman* series. He seemed to have a good effect on Willis, too, who turned in his best-yet portrayal of McClane.

As Hensleigh explained, there had to be an emotional core and, since McClane had no wife to save this time (she having divorced him since all that trouble in Washington D.C.), Hensleigh offered a foil to McClane in the shape of a positively reluctant partner, a racist black shopkeeper from Harlem named Zeus. Samuel L. Jackson and Bruce Willis, who shared no screen time in *Pulp Fiction*, now become a perfect acting combination; an inspirational choice. While McClane, in the manner that all *Die Hard* fans know well, shoots first and thinks later, Zeus is a calm, intelligent thinker. The racial discord between them is not heavily hung, but is sufficient to add to the terrific tension between the two men as they try to work out Simon's little tests and riddles before his next big bang.

We discover that he has hidden his bombs in various crowded public places, and one in a school. And if that wasn't enough, while they are attempting to find the explosives, racing hell for leather through the streets of Manhattan, Simon's next objective becomes clear: he plans to relieve the Federal Bank of $140 billion in gold reserves.

The Oaklahoma memory apart, it is all pure Hollywood fantasy that completely succeeds in its object of providing huge action, with plenty of laughs thrown in. It's not in the least an important movie, in any way at all. But neither does it have that pretension, which many of its kind try to convey – as in the forever stern and earnest Stallone pictures where he always seems to be involved in largely humourless matters of great importance.

This tale is told with a twinkle in the eye and tongue firmly in cheek: just straightforward entertainment; violent but not especially gruesome with clattering dialogue of a kind that you wouldn't find in a Tarantino movie, but in the end it doesn't matter. The movie is what it is and, far from going into decline as many sequels do, the *Die Hard* series strengthened with each one.

Willis's attention to this script turned out to be something of a proving ground for him and his performance was altogether better. *Die Hard With A Vengeance* was also the most successful of his movies. It took $354 million in world-wide box office receipts which, apart from the $15 million he received for his actor's fee, provided him with an additional handsome return from the profit-share deal. Willis, as his family joined him once more for the Los Angeles opening, could mimic Cagney: 'Top of the world, Ma . . .'

Demi, meanwhile was pressing on with *The Scarlet Letter* and, in a way, her task was considerably more difficult than her husband's. She had battled on through adversity and, at times, the possibility of rejection, as she sought to bring her 'moving picture' to the screen. The tenacity with which she pursued the project is worthy of closer examination.

Not for her, initially at least, a common tale pandering to popular taste – although, eventually, she had to submit to the vagaries of commerce. 'I never saw it as a star vehicle for me,' she said. 'It was never going to be a blockbuster, although obviously you don't set out to make a movie that loses money.' Her dream project was saved by Andy Vanja's willingness to throw his weight and his company behind it and, eventually, everything was in place to begin filming, just as Willis finished his movie. Disney's Buena Vista had taken up the American rights and, with a $50 million budget secured, Demi's movie began to roll.

One of the major discussion points from the outset had been the difficulty in transforming a fairly dense literary work into a watchable movie. As Moore later admitted during a television chat-show promotion appearance, it was a 'very uncinematic' book but she was convinced it could be made into a highly watchable film with 20th-century implications. Set in the late 1600s it was written by Nathaniel Hawthorne in 1850 and remained, because of its repeated movie exposure and attention in the literary world, the most famous of his numerous novels. It was supposedly based, in part, on his own experiences. When he was four, his father died at sea and his mother, in straitened circumstances, moved from their home in Salem, Massachusetts, to live in an isolated farm house on the edge of a wood in Raymond, Maine. Here, she was the subject of local gossipmongers.

Director Roland Joffe also concluded that, although the novel was largely seen as a story of 17th-century morals, the film had to demonstrate that it emerged from 'a time when the seeds were being sown for the bigotry, sexism and lack of tolerance we still battle today'.

Transferring the thoughts and inspirations from the minds of literary characters to the screen, however, is a notoriously difficult quest. Films of many great novels, especially, as previously mentioned, those of F. Scott Fiztgerald, have often foundered through it. Even the direction of Elia Kazan, a screenplay by Harold Pinter and a star of Robert De Niro's calibre could not make a success of *The Last Tycoon*, and neither could Robert Redford with *The Great Gatsby*.

Many had tried in the past to convert Hawthorne's celebrated melodrama to the big screen. It is, in fact, the most filmed book in history although most of the movie versions were made during the silent era – a medium to which it was clearly more suited. There had been ten previous versions; the best was in 1926, starring Lilian Gish and Lars Hanson. Then, it was easier. Long passages without dialogue, during which not a lot happens visually, could be covered by a precis of the author's words flashed on the screen.

To make the transfer in line with 1990s technology, and to meet the commercial expectations of the marketing people, the screenplay would have to include those ingredients that are supposed to attract modern audiences – sex, nudity, voyeurism, violence and a happy ending. That meant taking some very serious liberties with the original book.

Demi Moore, at least, fitted exactly the author's description of her character: 'Her face was beautiful from regularity of feature and richness of complexion. She has dark, abundant hair so glossy that it threw off sunshine like a beam.' This is what attracted Moore to the book in the first place; she could visualise herself, exactly, as this early model for the feminist movement – Hester Prynne, the first woman in history to get an A rating, in this case for adultery. Moore's purpose was to transform it all into a morality tale with modern applications.

Moore, as is her style, had considerable input into the creation of the movie although, according to one of her co-stars, the British actress Joan Plowright, she did not 'interfere'. There had been some speculation that Laurence Olivier's widow, playing the role of free-thinking Harriet Hibbons, might clash with Moore. The scenario of one of Britain's finest classical actresses brushing with a relatively untrained popular star with a prima donna reputation was an interesting subplot to the making of the movie. But Plowright insisted: 'She is very natural and very honest in seeking where she wants to go with a part. We were just two actresses at work. No nonsense. I must say that she behaved very well. She was very likable. I saw none of that movie star behaviour although, of course, I'm sure she's capable of that.'

Moore said her intention from the outset was to 'make a movie that was as good as it could be'. She was quite happy, once again, to make a feature of taking her kit off, allowing Joffe's camera to rove across her naked body while she was caressing herself. The stripped-off form of a skinny-dipping Gary Oldman is a less compelling sight, fine actor though he is.

These scenes were the invention of screenplay writer Douglas Day Stewart, who suffered from the distinct disadvantage that, when the novel opens, Hester Prynne's adultery has already occurred. The story involves a young wife who arrives in puritanical New England minus her husband, who is feared dead. She begins her new life alone, taking a cottage at the edge of the community. One day, Hester is strolling through the woods and happens upon a man bathing naked in a pond. It is the young Reverend Dimmesdale (Gary Oldman), spiritual leader of the community although, without his clothes on, that fact is not immediately evident.

The book eloquently describes the lusting thoughts of the young woman, starved of love and manly attentions. But how does it transfer to the screen? Scriptwriter Day Stewart now introduces the attractive slave girl, Mituba (Lisa Jolliff-Andoh), to serve that purpose and, rather too conveniently, to add a touch of voyeurism. She prepares Hester's bath tub and then, while her mistress is caressing her body with soap and thinking of the naked body of the reverend, she observes all through a peephole – yes, the old hole-in-the-wall trick.

The scene of a girl of a different race observing the lily-white naked form of Hester is there for one reason only – to provide the audience with an additional thrill and the merest hint of lesbian thoughts. Mituba is watching again when the sexy reverend calls upon Hester and they commit their sinful act on an uncomfortable bed of dried beans in the barn. The slave girl now strips off and gets into her mistress's bath holding a lighted candle. As the illicit love scene reaches its body-crunching climax, Mituba lets the candle sink beneath the water, extinguishing it with a hiss.

Hester, of course, is now pregnant and when she refuses to name her seducer, the local bigots insist that she wears a scarlet letter A on her bodice. Her daughter, Pearl, is born and grows up as a troublesome child, although this secondary plot-line in the novel is more or less disregarded in the screenplay.

The drama heightens when Hester's long-lost husband turns up in the form of Robert Duvall (brilliant as ever in a strong character role) and attempts to discover who has been tampering with his wife. In the novel, when all is revealed, the Reverend Dimmesdale, gripped by a fatal seizure, confesses his sins on his deathbed, crying out, 'His will be done! Farewell!'

Nothing so ordinary is good enough for a Hollywood movie. Day Stewart, who, through Gary Oldman, has turned this rather despicable character into a romantic hero, turns Dimmesdale into a campaigner for tolerance and sexual freedom. When Hester is about to be hung, he grasps the rope, in a final act of attrition, and pulls it around his own neck. Fortunately, a band of Indian savages happen to be passing at the time and attack the village. And so on, to a rather fatuous ending.

In attempting to apply whatever message the movie was supposed to convey, the emotions of guilt, so implicit in Hawthorne's novel, virtually disappear. Even so, there were some good performances, especially from Moore, Oldman and Duvall who were as convincing as the material would allow. But this dusty old novel, which had proved itself to be beyond the powers of Hollywood in the past, was not satisfactorily dealt with this time, either. With Demi Moore's then current box office clout (following the hype of *Disclosure*), it attracted plenty of interest among the critics who, by and large, gave a fairly indifferent reaction. Some were positively hostile. It faded quickly from the cinemas, taking a mere $12 million in the US which was, naturally, a major disappointment to Moore herself – not to mention her co-producers and backers who had splashed out fifty million green ones, plus the promotional spend.

She collected her fee of $5 million regardless and, although *The Scarlet Letter* was a personal disappointment, careerwise it didn't matter a lot – her upward mobility was already assured. Demi Moore, the sometime feminist philosopher, female chauvinist, $1 million dollar wife, ghost hunter and nude madonna, was about to plunge herself headlong into fresh controversy and public attention – in another shirt-ripping adventure, this time as a strip artist.

For this role, Moore would receive the all-time record fee for a female actress. Demi, it appeared, had told the producers she wouldn't take a penny less than $12.5 million for performing such an act.

And she got it.

To the Willises' tale of two movies, we may add one more for that year. It marked Bruce's return collaboration with the man of the moment, Quentin Tarantino. The new one was *Four Rooms*.

The idea sounded good: Tarantino and three other directors would make the movie in four segments which would feature a collection of Hollywood's hot darlings. We would see: Madonna playing a witch in a rubber mermaid dress; Jennifer Beals being bound and gagged by her husband; someone throwing up over Tim Roth; the producer, Tarantino, taking a starring role and Bruce Willis making a bet that involves cutting off someone's finger.

But most of all, we would see this aforementioned line-up of talent making a rather embarrassing spectacle of themselves in a hastily constructed self-indulgent romp that in parts, is too banal for words. The four stories are set in a strange Los Angeles hotel, the Mon Signor, on a New Year's Eve. Tarantino, freshly nominated for an Oscar, was in charge and, because of that, everyone in Hollywood's hip crowd wanted to be in it. Those lucky enough to be selected surely must have wished, afterwards, that they hadn't been.

The link between all four sketches is Tim Roth in the role of the hotel bellhop, Ted, and one can only admire his courage in the way he camped it up. Indeed, they all try their best, even Jennifer Beals, whose role entails the need to chant a couple of dozen synonyms for the word penis.

The four directors are Allison Anders, Alexandre Rockwell, Robert Rodriguez and Tarantino himself. Their individual segments were of variable quality, and only one was truly funny – Rodriguez's *The Misbehavers*, with Antonio Banderas. Willis has his cameo performance in *The Man from Hollywood*, directed by Tarantino and also starring Tarantino as a spoiled new movie star who has taken over a suite with his strange friends. It promised a good deal more than it delivered – a disappointing waste of his very obvious talent.

The whole was one more example, if ever it were needed, that in Hollywood, all that glistens is not necessarily gold.

16 No Monkey Business

NOW, HE'S IN A HELICOPTER, flying from New York, over his home state of New Jersey, on his way to Philadelphia – an hour or so away from his boyhood home. Terry Gilliam is waiting there to shoot some scenes from his new movie, *Twelve Monkeys*. Willis, heading towards his 40th birthday, takes the opportunity of peering down on his home town of Carney's Point, nestling in the semi-circle that is Penns Grove, the place where he became a famous streaker. The 'copter, gliding at 125 miles per hour, goes in as low as it can for Willis to pick off those familiar dots on the landscape.

He has more than an passing interest. Down there, amid the urban sprawl, are some very large pieces of masonry that are of particular interest to him. Gilliam can wait; a diversion is at hand that takes him back to the place of his childhood – an all-too-infrequent sojourn arising, on this occasion, from his recently revived status and affluence.

Showbusiness is a business, Bruce Willis once said in answer to a query about the expansive fees and wheeler-dealer activities that he and Demi Moore were getting into. In 1995, the couple were looking at multi-million dollar earning possibilities encompassing the movies, the Planet Hollywood chain and a growing hoard of real estate and property developments. First, the movies: their own production companies were developing more than a couple of dozen possible future projects between them, though not all as vehicles for themselves. They were buying up books, scripts and screenplays and were treading cautiously in that Hollywood deal-making minefield which so many stars try to negotiate, with varying degrees of success, in an attempt to become the controllers of their own destiny.

Some do it for the art and to further their own careers; others are attracted by the dollar signs on the cinema box office tills and the prospect of tapping into international rights, television deals, video, laserdiscs, soundtrack CDs and the other merchandising products that come out of the bigger movies.

Willis had made his opinions on that subject quite clear. He and Moore – and she, especially, on the movie production side – wanted to build on their activities as film-makers as well as actors. They were also diversifying – strongly – into other areas. By that year of 1995, their respective positioning in the industry had undergone rapid and remarkable consolidation. Bruce, in particular, had come from a point where, in 1993, his career was definitely on the skids, to a position of considerable strength and renewed power. He was also beginning to get something he had yearned after for years: Respect.

With their joint millions, their financial state had never been even close to precarious but, with their kind of lifestyle, even they had to top up their funds, otherwise their capital would simply drift away – as many have discovered in the past. They were big spenders and had huge outgoings in tax liabilities, agents, managers, their three homes and a vast personal staff. However, the possibility of it 'all ending tomorrow', in terms of star status, had been virtually eliminated with their recent strong screen performances.

In the previous eighteen months, they had, between them, bolstered their bank balances by well in excess of $50 million. Although the basic art of movie making may still get a look-in somewhere along the line in the deal-making machinery, finance, as we have seen, had become the predominent feature. And so it was on this front that the mid-1990s saw a considerable expansion in Taking Care of Business, as the money settled around this now 'truly golden couple' in ever-increasing circles.

As mentioned earlier Bruce and Demi had already been ploughing money – an estimated $8 million – into some prime real estate in their adopted hometown of Hailey, in the Sun Valley. In the spring of 1995, they were focusing their attentions on their latest acquisition, the town's old art-deco Liberty cinema which had hit hard times after a new four-screen theatre had opened not far away in Ketchum. The Liberty, first opened in 1938, was a grim, rundown box of a place with peeling paintwork, broken seats, no screen curtains and an old projection system that often broke down. The Willises bought it at a knock-down price and began a stylish remodelling.

Demi placed herself in charge of the decor, hiring the services of interior designer Colin Cowie. Between them, they came up with a thorough revamp, with new interiors of gilt and glass that matched the building's original era, and rich colour schemes of burgundy and bronze trimmed with matching velvet curtains, hung around the screen. Bruce shipped in $150,000 worth of new electronics and state-of-the-art sound and projection systems. There were two projectors: one to show modern movies, the other to be brought into service for old classics and Saturday morning movies for the kids. The cinema was set for re-opening with a local premiere of Bruce's next movie, *Twelve Monkeys*.

It was one more piece of redevelopment at Hailey that raised the eyebrows of the locals. Nostalgic self-indulgence or true business? The motivation for acquiring five major properties on Main Street was never quite clear. Across the street from the cinema, they had started building on a parcel of land where they planned a museum to house Demi's collection of 2,000 dolls and Bruce's horde of vintage cycles.

Next, they would begin restoring a large, decaying block which they would rename the E. G. Willis Building, after his grandfather. It would be remodelled to include professional offices, craftsmen's studios and a fifties-style Shorty's Diner. Plans for a 65-room hotel were still on the drawing board.

Now, the scene switches . . . to New Jersey, and Willis's home town where, around the same time, a mysterious company suddenly began making its presence felt by bidding for a collection of rundown properties.

Screwball? What's Screwball? *Who's* Screwball? Rose Maurice, the Neighborhood Preservation Program Coordinator in Penns Grove wanted to know – and so did the town's mayor, Paul Morris. The name began cropping up in May 1995, particularly on the waterfront where the local planners had just given the go-ahead for a massive clean-up and regeneration programme.

Inquiries made on the company's behalf through a local law office had made no mention of the true owners of Screwball

Properties Inc. Indeed, company representatives had gone to some lengths to keep quiet the fact that its sole owner was a famous local boy made good: Bruce Willis. At the time, Penns Grove was in the process of picking itself up off the floor. A few years earlier, the borough administrators had launched an aggressive campaign to revive the flagging riverside town.

Mayor Morris explained that the decline of local industry had forced the town's main employers, Du Pont and the nuclear power plant, to shed thousands of jobs, resulting in a major negative impact on local prosperity. Added to that, the big new shopping malls across the river in Delaware (which had no sales tax) were hitting local traders badly. Large sections of the town had fallen into decline and, in 1993, Penns Grove was ranked by the Federal Office of Management and Budget as New Jersey's second most economically challenged municipality, behind Newark. Trade was then so slow that the state gave it permission to levy only half the standard six per cent sales tax.

As the regeneration programme got under way, Penns Grove began attracting private and federal money to renovate the bad housing areas and the downtown shopping area. Next, the authorities began a study on the riverfront development and produced plans to build a 100-berth marina and commercial centre. 'It wasn't just a dream,' said Mayor Morris. 'By the beginning of 1993, we had in place loans and grants from federal sources and private investors for the acquisition of riverfront property. We were in the process of negotiating to buy the land when suddenly, this company called Screwball came on the scene.'

It appeared that Bruce Willis had heard of the development plans while on a visit to his father, still living in a trailer home with his wife Alma. Whenever Bruce came alone, he stayed in the trailer and slept on a pull-out bed. His father said it was 'like a sanctuary to him.' He even kept a closet of old clothes there.

All that was about to change.

In May 1993, Bruce's Screwball company began buying up large tracts of property in Penns Grove, first making a bee-line for the riverfront property that Mayor Morris and his town hall colleagues had planned to develop themselves. Within a month, Screwball Inc. had purchased the cen ral feature of this proposed development, a piece at the end of West Main Street and an eleven-acre parcel of land that stretched back from behind the river into the south side of the town – all for $475,000. Next, the company bought the old Penns Grove National Bank building on West Main Street, a fine old marble-trimmed building. To that was added the local Freemasons' Hall so that the company owned almost an entire block of the main thoroughfare. Then, Willis paid $175,000 for one of the most prestigious local homes, a two-storey stone colonial-style house with white columns adorning the front entrance which was once owned by the town's doctor.

The properties were all carefully selected. Although they were mostly looking tired and in some cases, in disrepair, they were not unattractive. Nor were the local townsfolk upset by the Willises' intervention in their development plans. Rose Maurice, who was at the centre of neighbourhood preservation plans, said, 'True, we had only just finished our waterfront study when Mr Willis came to town and bought up the property before we were able to, but I don't think that's a bad thing. His coming here with investment money could make things happen faster. He has the financial wherewithal to get things moving that may have taken years through local government. It has given us all a pretty good morale boost.'

No one in the locality remembered seeing Willis on his property inspection trips, remarked Rose Maurice, whose brother was at school with him. In fact, the last time she saw him personally was in her own schooldays – she was in a store when there was a commotion outside: a naked youth went streaking by.

The colonial house was earmarked for his father, and a complete remodelling was begun immediately. He hired a former classmate from Penns Grove High, Mark Murphy, to do the work and asked him not to speak publicly about the project. 'As I understand it,' Murphy would say, 'he just came back for a visit one day and heard that there were some things going on, a few properties available, and moved on it.'

The house was completed within three months and Bruce's father and his wife moved from their trailer home into the grand little mansion. Coincidentally, living across the street was Rick Cowles who runs BrunoWatch, the unofficial Bruce Willis site on the world wide web, which attracts a healthy input from Internet subscribers around the world. He had lived in Penns Grove for ten years and, by another strange quirk of fate, had been brought up in Roswell, New Mexico, not far from the trailer park where Demi Guynes spent her early childhood.

Rick worked for several years at the local nuclear plant where Willis used to be a security guard on the night shift; there are still many workers in the locality, he says, who recall him blasting them over the PA system with his harmonica. Like many others affected by the recession of local industry, Rick was moved to the company's plant at Newark, having to commute daily. However, the town remained linked to those old traditions that came with a blue-collar, male-dominated society, with values that came from the Catholic influences of the many Irish and Italian immigrants.

'In that respect, the town hasn't changed a great deal,' said Rick Cowles. 'It was and is a very male-orientated place, with the father firmly the head of the family, even during troubled times. The town has come through a bad patch. There were quite a few depressed areas of the town which fell upon hard times as local industry declined. It began back in the fifties, when the Delaware Memorial Bridge was opened. The traffic that used to come into the town for the ferries was diverted, bypassing Penns Grove completely. That and the loss of jobs at Du Pont and elsewhere hit hard. But lately, there has been a lot of beautiful restoration work here. There are some fine Victorian properties which give a flavour of the town as it used to be; it is a very pleasant place to live. I personally wouldn't live anywhere else and I can quite understand why Bruce wants to get involved here.'

Willis set to work on his ambitions for his waterfront property, along with the other plots of land and buildings he had purchased in the town. At the time these words were being written, only the work on his father's new house had been completed. Plans for his other properties were still progressing through the various stages of approval, governed in part by onerous laws and restrictions over development on the riverside wetlands. His ideas, however, for the blocks of property he now owns in Penns Grove are grandiose and have been estimated locally at costing in excess of $50 million. They include a marina, a hotel, an open-air market, a novice theatre for local productions, an amphitheatre for professionals, a restaurant and an estate of 50 new homes.

'The town is glad to see him back,' said Rick Cowles. 'He is not a regular face among us, but that's understandable from the demands on his time in recent years. There are many, of course, who still remember him as a bit of a clown, a loud, vigorous young man. He kept up his friendship with a few from schooldays, and some of them – and of course some members of his family – went with him to Hollywood. Generally, he has an inner circle of people he can trust. From everything I know about him, he is a very intense individual with a strong personality. He is not a politician, however, and can upset people with his directness. He shoots from the hip and speaks with an honesty that is also refreshing.' Cowles himself soon discovered that. In the autumn of 1996 he had to close down his unofficial BrunoWatch site on the Internet after a warning letter from Willis's lawyers.

Willis's other, more high-profile business activities were also booming – namely the involvement of himself and Demi Moore with Planet Hollywood. In the four years since the company was founded, Planet Hollywood grew to 24 company-owned and six franchised units in nine countries throughout North America, Europe and Asia. In 1995 they extended the concept to two other theme chains – the Official All Star Cafe (sports-based restaurant-merchandise stores) and Marvel Mania (comic book-themed restaurants and stores), wheeling in more celebrities, including Andre Agassi and Monica Seles.

The company expected to have a total of 51 restaurant-merchandise stores set up in 16 countries by the end of 1996, including 45 under the Planet Hollywood logo. In its accounts for 1995, the company showed total revenues of $270.6 million. This figure was expected to double within two years, and to be heading well beyond the $1 billion a year mark by the millennium. Robert Earl, one of the co-founders, had himself become one of Britain's wealthiest businessmen with a 28.8 per cent stake in the company at the time he prepared it for public flotation. Willis and Moore – as members of the original small group of celebrities who were granted share options – remained among the largest stakeholders (17 per cent of the company is jointly owned by the celebrity group). Thus, they were quietly delighted when the company was floated in the early months of 1996 on New York's Nasdaq market. Shares rocketed quickly from the $18 issue price to $25, valuing the company at $2.7 billion – and the celebrities' stake at close on half a billion.

Willis and Moore will also reap the massive financial benefits as Earl proceeds at pace with his publicly announced plans to turn the company into a $20 billion global empire to challenge the likes of Disney and Time-Warner. 'I want to create the largest and most successful leisure company in the world,' he said expansively after the flotation launch of Planet Hollywood. The city does not disbelieve him and his showbusiness partners are, naturally, encouraging him.

In his 25 years in the business, Earl has a record of company hits, including the foundation of the Hard Rock Cafe chain, now owned by Britain's Rank Organisation. Planet Hollywood, with its star turns and support, has become his most sucessful venture yet. His plans for the future include themed music and live-entertainment restaurants, along with superstores which will sell 1,000 items of Planet Hollywood merchandise. It is hardly surprising, therefore, that Willis and Moore are willing attenders to the cause – hyping the company for all their worth, which is plenty!

If Earl succeeds in his ambition to turn Planet Hollywood into the leisure mammoth he believes it can become, they will be sitting on top of a joint pile worth something approaching $1 billion, regardless of what they make in movies.

But . . . back to the dream factory . . .

Terry Gilliam waited patiently for his star to arrive after his boys' night out with old friends in Manhattan. He had taken a weekend break from filming *Twelve Monkeys* to return to his other old stamping ground – that of his struggling-actor days – visiting his friends and the bars where he started out. Now, he could stay at his 'crib in the sky', the luxurious $8 million pad which takes up the top four floors of a residential tower on Central Park West. From there, he can look across that familiar skyline to his old place, his first place, in Hells Kitchen, a few hundred yards and half a lifetime away.

Gilliam was in Philadelphia, one of the several location scenes for the movie that would provide Willis with one more rung on his ladder towards acting respectability – although he didn't know it yet. They were a curious pairing: an art-conscious director and a whizz-bang star associated with the razzmatazz of the Hollywood that Gilliam is known to detest. Yesteryear's *Monty Python* rebel-in-chief, his hair flecked with grey and hanging loosely above his shoulders, looked like an ageing hippie. It had been four years since he made his excellent *The Fisher King* with Robin Williams and Jeff Bridges and his fans were getting withdrawal symptoms. His films have a particular appeal and often a 'cult' feel that, he admits, means they are not always financially successful. He is one of the few directors on earth whose work – good, bad or indifferent – can never be ignored, regardless of the category in which it might be classified.

Gilliam, the 'token Yank' on *Monty Python*, has always had a tempestuous relationship with the film world within his native America. Although the *Monty Python* series ran for only four years, the film *Monty Python and the Holy Grail* (1975) paved the way for the team's popularity in America. *Monty Python's Life of Brian* (1979) was his most controversial movie: involving a peasant mistaken for the Messiah, it aroused the ire of Christian fundamentalists. His battles with Hollywood have been even more spectacular.

Time Bandits, his 1981 film which was apparently made for children, contained violent scenes and involved a boy and a band of dwarfs time-warping through history to steal valuable artifacts. In the inevitable falling-out with his backers, Gilliam was asked to make amendments – so he threatened to burn the only copy; a course of action he would favour above any compromise.

Ironically, he had been brought back to life after his long lay-off since *The Fisher King* by Universal Pictures, the very same studio with whom he had a monumental punch-up in 1985. They refused to release his cut of *Brazil*, the Orwellian fantasy. They wanted to slice 40 minutes from the running time and put a new ending on the film because they considered the existing one was too depressing.

As Universal had put up two thirds of the $15 million budget, they felt entitled to insist; they said the movie was unreleasable. Gilliam stood his ground. He arranged for a clandestine screening and the Los Angeles Film Critics Society named it the best film of the year and Gilliam best director – even though the film had never been officially released.

He badgered Universal to release it and he supported his campaign with advertisements in magazines. They eventually agreed to distribution but displayed it only half-heartedly in the

US where it took only $4.3 million. But, even though it had been tampered with, it became a cult classic.

His third battle came with *The Adventures of Baron Munchausen*. It was budgeted at $20 million but costs escalated to $40 million although it received four Oscar nominations, it dropped dead at the box office. Hollywood regarded Gilliam as a renegade, uncontrollable, and so he remained until revival time came around with *The Fisher King*, which won an Oscar for Mercedes Ruehl as best supporting actress and four other nominations, including one for Robin Williams.

Hollywood forgave and forgot, and offers came pouring in for movies he did not want to make. Finally, he admits, he accepted *Twelve Monkeys* because 'there was nothing else remotely acceptable and I was a great admirer of the writer, David Peoples [*Blade Runner* and *Unforgiven*]. I couldn't miss this; the sheer complexity of it was a challenge.' It is the story of a convict in the year 2035 who volunteers to make a time-trip back to 1996 to try to discover the origins of a plague that has destroyed the world and forces the survivors to live underground.

Gilliam agreed to do the movie on one condition, that the ending was written into his contract – so that Universal could not change it. He, for his part, agreed to their input into the casting process. Studio executives were keen to have a couple of star names to aid the commercial aspect of a film such as this. Gilliam was well known for insisting that actors ditch their star attributes and follow his orders. 'One of the first things I told Robin Williams,' he says, 'was whatever funniness is here is going to be based on pain.'

He would do the same with Willis, whose selection surprised the star himself. 'The studio started throwing names at me, and then Bruce's name came up. He was really keen to talk to me about doing it,' said Gilliam. The director himself wasn't sure about Willis; he was, after all, 'making commercial movies'. They had met briefly once before, when the director was casting *The Fisher King* and Gilliam liked him enormously – but was that sufficient reason to cast him in the movie?

Willis flew to New York to see Gilliam, to pursuade him he could take this role. 'If there was one thing that attracted me to Bruce,' Gilliam says, 'it was a scene in *Die Hard* in which he's picking glass out of his bare feet and he's on the phone to his wife and he starts crying. He had all the macho but also the vulnerability. I talked with him about the scene. He explained that the crying part was his idea and I thought there was a lot more to Bruce than what was seen on the screen and I thought that if he could divest himself of his smart-ass tricks and clever attitudes he might be able to find the lonely, lost but extremely dangerous style deep inside him that was James Cole. Bruce asked me whether I was worried about the "baggage" that he would bring to the film. I was impressed by his concern to make a good film and not a Bruce Willis vehicle. Also, I like the idea of altering the public's perception of him, so I said, "Let's do it." It was potentially dangerous and even disastrous if it had failed. But it didn't.'

Gilliam took even longer to be convinced about Brad Pitt who was Hollywood's new golden boy and who had just been voted by *People* magazine the Sexiest Man Alive. 'It was a very strange time, when these superstars were begging to be in this movie,' Gilliam said. It was neither something he was used to, nor something he wanted. In all his earlier works, the film was the star. It was a new and confusing experience. Willis had convinced him he could do it, then Brad Pitt tried to do the same. Gilliam refused to meet him.

Eventually, Pitt flew to London and got to meet Gilliam. 'During the course of dinner he convinced me he could do it. He just wanted to prove that he could do things which are different, and he is trying to escape from the blonde, blue-eyed bimbo chapter.'

The born pessimist that he is, according to his producer, Gilliam had the feeling that the only reason he was agreeing to hire Pitt was that he had 'sold out' by having Bruce: 'I thought, now here is a chance really to endanger this project and put Brad in. He is going to take this character and make a mess of it, a hash of it. That is what I was feeling. We got him together with a man called Stephen Bridgewater, and he and Brad sat down. Stephen later rang me and said: "What have I done to you to deserve this? Brad cannot do it. He's got a lazy tongue, he can't hold his breath for more than five seconds, he's got no ability to speak fast or annunciate properly." Then he started working harder and became more confident. We were arranging for him to go to psychiatric hospitals and watch schizophrenics and talk to other doctors. He even had himself interviewed by a psychiatrist, in character. He worked amazingly hard, and is a very diligent, earnest guy. When you see that first scene where he is introduced, that was the first day of shooting. It's extraordinary, and by the end of the day he couldn't move. He'd been ticking, twitching and jerking all over the place.'

Willis, in his now familiar way, took much less than his normal fee to work with Gilliam, as indeed did Pitt. If they had both asked for their normal fees, it would have eaten into a major slice of the budget for the whole movie, which was set at a rigid $28 million, not a penny more.

Gilliam laid down only three ground rules for Willis to follow: no smirking, no steely-eyes business and you can't do that little moue. Fine said Willis. It was more or less the same straightening out that he had received from Quentin Tarantino and he was ready and eager to ditch the wisecracking, motor mouth, smirky ways that have dogged his career and his performances for years. 'Terry was so prepared,' said Willis when the movie was in the bag. 'He has the entire film shot in his head before he gets to the set. It was a brilliant experience for me.'

The movie was inspired by – and not, as some suggested, a remake of – the French short film, *La Jetee* (which was composed of still photographs). The writers, David and Janet Peoples, had seen it and the producers had bought the rights to it. Many critics would wax lyrical about this link, but didn't understand that they really had no basis for doing so. 'It was a totally different concept,' said Gilliam, 'and making the film was rather like the film itself, a totally unnerving experience. We all helped each other, because we all kept getting lost.'

So they gathered on location for the first scenes, to be shot in Baltimore. For Willis it was not so much a case of finding his way through the complexity of the screenplay, but more a case of finding himself. His goal was clear: to take a smack at the system that would like to keep him in his place as a blue-collar toughie and then let him rot when the need for blue-collar toughies expires.

He was intent on finding the missing link between art and commerce that had so far eluded him in spite of the various attempts we have seen so far. The difference this time was that he was dealing with a director – not the producers; for once it was the art of movie making that was leading the adventure, not the money. It was also Bruce Willis as never seen before, unattractively decked out in filthy brown overalls, with a dirty face and a shaven head. Brad Pitt, looking like the reincarnation of a young Robert Redford, called him O Mighty Bald One:

'Oh yeah,' said Willis mockingly. 'Well try this kiddo: you're *it* now. You're the *thing* that fame creates. It's your turn. And I'm going to watch. You betcha!'

As to the movie, Gilliam was, as he put it, working towards his usual aim of leaving explosive shards somewhere in the brains of his audience, things that they can't forget, things that stay with them for years. It didn't need to be shocking, either. Gilliam will cite scenes from *Singing in the Rain*, *Funny Face*, *Seven Brides for Seven Brothers*, as well as clips from *Taxi Driver* or *Goodfellas*. One of the great moments in *Twelve Monkeys* that illustrates his point is when Bruce Willis hears Fats Domino singing 'On Blueberry Hill' on the radio: 'The expression on his face of sheer childlike joy is one of the high points for me,' Gilliam said.

The Peoples' screenplay anchors itself in a future world to launch for the central plot lines which are set in 1990 and 1996. Willis plays a convict, Cole, who volunteers to travel back in time to save the world from a deadly plague. He is among a handful of survivors living in a subterranean hell in a time when animals have reclaimed the world's surface after the death of five billion people from the deadly plague. The art-and-life syndrome comes curiously into play again as the movie is being shot – just as it did with the Oklahoma bomb after Willis had just completed *Die Hard With A Vengeance*. This time, there was an outbreak of the deadly virus ebola, claiming hundreds of lives in Africa.

Willis is sent on his travels back through time in the hope of finding the origins of the plague virus, although the writers make no attempt to turn back the clock. The rulers of his domain accept that the disaster has already happened and cannot be prevented; they are seeking only a treatment to give immunity to the survivors. Willis first lands in 1990, bruised and dripping sweat. No one believes his fantasic story, that he is a visitor from a future time or that people will start dying of the plague soon, and they cast him into a mental hospital. There, he meets a woman doctor (who will become his love interest when he returns again in 1996) and Brad Pitt's character, an animal rights activist for a group whose logo contains twelve monkeys in a circle. He also has a father whose laboratory may be harbouring the source of the deadly virus.

The movie is anything but a straightforward thriller. It is a complex tale that needs two or three viewings, at least, to get the full drift. Typically, nothing is ever what it seems, and that is good. Gilliam allows the whole bizarre nightmare to move along with marvellous flexibility. He also garnered from his actors some outstanding individual performances, and among them, Willis's stood out. Gilliam was not dissatisfied, and gave him full credit – for he may have anchored a movie that could so easily have spun out of control.

The exercise, from Willis's point of view, achieved all that he had hoped for: critical acclaim in an important movie that also did well commercially. It was by far one of the most analysed, most dissected, most studied pieces of its time, especially in the film schools and universities. Gilliam himself gave more press conferences and short talks on this film than any he had made in the past. Acres of media space was devoted to it – but for all the right reasons as far as Willis was concerned. Ruthlessly stripped of all his gimmicks and tricks by Gilliam, Willis came out bare, an actor. Whereas *Pulp Fiction* halted his decline, *Twelve Monkeys* provided substantive proof that, even in a difficult movie with all its complexities and time-warping movements, Willis could do it.

And so it was that in December 1995, and with some pride, he staged his own 'world premiere' of *Twelve Monkeys* at his own little cinema, the Liberty, in Main Street, Hailey, Idaho. The remodelling work had been completed just a few days earlier. Willis had laid on a small reception in the lobby for guests. It was a low-key crowd, largely devoid of Hollywood personalities, although Jean-Claude Van Damme was present. It was largely for the locals, who gathered to sample the opening night party fare of lobster, cold shrimp and crepes filled with caviar and crème fraîche.

At 7.30 p.m., Bruce himself swung open the inner doors to his cinema and called out to the assembled guests:

'You can come in now.'

And . . .

'Oh . . . one more thing . . . the Hershey bars are free.'

17 Lots More

THE BOUNTIFUL RESULTS that came directly from the revitalisation of Bruce Willis following his appearance in *Pulp Fiction* were only now becoming evident. Behind-the-scenes manoeuvres were remarkable by any standard. Producers and directors were queuing to hire him for prestigious, big-money movies long before his much-improved status was consolidated by his performance in *Twelve Monkeys*. Indeed, even as he finished filming for Terry Gilliam, he had agreed terms with New Line Pictures to head a strong cast for their upcoming $70 million production of *Last Man Standing*.

It was a major coup for Willis and was quickly followed by another – the announcement that he would take the lead in the secrecy-shrouded project *The Fifth Element*, to be directed by Frenchman Luc Besson and backed by the giant Sony Corporation. It would be an expensive production, one which was rumoured to have been earmarked a jaw-dropping $100 million spend on special effects alone – which meant that they were projecting, and expecting, international gross figures approaching half a billion dollars. The fact that Willis should be chosen to head the cast of two of the major big-spend productions on the Hollywood calendar of forthcoming attractions speaks for itself.

From a personal standpoint, they would be important and crucial movies. Both would give him the opportunity – as Tarantino and Gilliam had done – to develop some strong characterisations, which he seriously needed among his repertoire in that never-ending search for professional respect. With three other projects already in the pipeline for 1996/97, his movies were stacking up towards his very obvious desires in that direction.

In a way, the title of his new one, *Last Man Standing*, was a very apt description of Willis's position in the action-adventure genre. So often grouped in that regard with his friends and business partners, Sylvester Stallone and Arnold Schwarzenegger, Willis was involved in a personal and private little battle to outdo them, to move out of and on from the shackles of categorisation. Although never really one of the body-oiled he-men, Willis was, nonetheless, regarded as a blue-collar hero, a territory in which Stallone was once king (first as the mumbling Rocky and then as the silent Rambo).

Arnie, the speaker of short, sharp sentences and unchallenging dialogue, was similarly 'positioned' by the cognoscenti and both he and Stallone had tried, and failed, to break out of their self-created moulds. For Willis, it became, as we have seen, a career-threatening stranglehold that had to be broken. As one studio executive told me: 'They all made fortunes; for years they have had the biggest pay-days in Hollywood history, especially Sly and Arnie, but where do they go from here? How many times can they play the same character in a plot that is just a variation on a theme. Willis, in one sense, was weaker but actually the weakness turned out to be his strength. He's going on to much better things; he's confronting the future with a lot of thought. He's gonna be Mega.'

In that direction, he was matched by the even more clear-cut ambitions of his wife. As Willis began work on *Last Man Standing*, embarking on the most exhaustive research he had ever undertaken, she too faced an action-packed schedule with four more pictures dead ahead, culminating in *Striptease*, which was being hyped with sensational pre-publicity months before it even went into production.

She kicked off her quartet of films with another of her own productions. There was a hint of back-room dealing when she linked up with New Line Cinema – the same company that had lined up Willis for *Last Man Standing*. Here, another project had been hatched by her own company, Moving Pictures, under the supervision of company president Suzanne Todd and in which Moore herself would again take the dual roles of producer and co-star. The movie was *Now and Then* and, once again, she had insisted upon overall artistic control.

It is the story of four girls from a small town who, in their youth, made a pledge to 'always be there' for one another. They stage a reunion 25 years later when one of them is pregnant and needs their support. With evident shades of *Stand By Me*, it was not a successful vehicle for Moore. She was joined by Melanie Griffith, Rosie O'Donnell and Rita Wilson – the adult stars seen only in the opening sequences. As the story revolved around them as children, the movie was really in the hands of the four talented young actresses, Christina Ricci, Thora Birch, Gaby Hoffmann and Ashleigh Aston Moore. The four adults were given so little screen time that they might have been labelled guests stars.

Director Lesli Linka Glatter said she wept when she first read the script because it captured that 'delicate evolution from girlhood to womanhood, and you so rarely find that'. It did not, however, strike the same chord at the box office. It lacked the psychological undertones of *Stand By Me* but, even so, it was a further demonstration that Moore – like Willis in his early days – was prepared to take on lesser projects for her personal satisfaction. The niche market for the smaller movies which, like *Ghost*, might just take off is an area often ignored by the Hollywood high-rollers. And Moore, to her credit, was prepared to tackle projects that fell into that mould, seemingly without fear of any side-effects to her mainstream career. *Now and Then* was on the circuits at the same time as Willis's *Twelve Monkeys*.

By then, he was already filming *Last Man Standing*, which was still being viewed in the Willis camp as a major coup. The movie had a long history and an intriguing tale developed around it which is worthy of recall. It was inspired by, and adapted from, Akira Kurosawa's 1961 Japanese classic *Yojimbo* which when translated means bodyguard. That story follows the exploits of a wandering 19th-century samurai whose profession has suffered with the collapse of the Tokugawa regime and the abolition of feudalism in 1860s Japan. With social chaos breeding crime and violence, he strays into a town which has been overtaken by savage corruption and is now terrorised by two warring factions who control gambling and prostitution.

Fast forward to 1964: the same story was used by Sergio Leone as the inspiration for his film, *A Fistful of Dollars*. This was the movie that started the spaghetti western craze and brought Clint Eastwood to international fame as the violent avenging stranger who cleans up a Mexican border town.

Three decades later, the story, like all good classics made a comeback and was once again in the frame. In 1985, the Armenian-born, English-educated, London-based designer, entrepreneur and successful retailer, Arthur Sarkissan, headed west with his pile, intent on financing and producing movies. Three years later, he acquired the remake rights to *Yojimbo* from Akira Kurosawa. The project took six years to get off the ground but, by 1994, and with mainstream production company New Line Cinema now backing him, Sarkissan had commissioned a screenplay which set the story in the era of 1920s America, during Prohibition. At this point, they approached writer/director/producer Walter Hill, a leading stylist in the action genre of the contemporary cinema, to head-up their team.

Hill had a long list of credits, including movies from the Laurence Gordon/Joel Silver stable. His early movies, featuring some of his best work, included the 1975 Depression-era drama, *Hard Times*, with Charles Bronson and James Coburn, which he wrote and directed. He continued to direct works from his own scripts, including the tense and clever thriller *The Driver*, with Ryan O'Neal. His biggest commercial success came with the buddy action-comedy, *48 Hours*, which brought Eddie Murphy to fame. He also produced the 1992 sci-fi classic, *Alien*, to which the adjective 'unforgettable' can, for once, be correctly applied.

Hill was also known for his fascination with the American western, which had clearly influenced his work – as it does so evidently in *Last Man Standing*. As producer of such films as *The Long Riders*, *Geronimo: An American Legend*, *Extreme Prejudice* and his (pretty awful) biopic, *Wild Bill*, he was awarded the prestigious Golden Boot and the Western Heritage Award from the National Cowboy Hall of Fame in recognition of his contribution to the movement.

With such a background, and as a devotee of Sergio Leone, Hill was surprised by the approach from Sarkissan and, when told of the plan to remake Kurosawa's story yet again, he simply asked, 'Why?'

Hill was frank enough to admit, ' I could not see at first that it needed retelling. They had to convince me that there was a way to use this story as the basic material and still make some kind of sense in its own right, as a new movie.' Hill agreed to mull it over and eventually agreed to write and direct the movie – after devising a provocative new storyline. 'I would not have made this film had I not been completely satisfied that Mr Kurosawa was in favour of somebody doing an adaptation,' said Hill. 'Once that condition was met, my challenge was to make the story work in an American context. By setting this film against the backdrop of Prohibition, an era unique to our country's history, we could tap into a slice of Americana.'

Hill then set about creating his own milieu and, on a grander scale, did what Tarantino had done in writing *Pulp Fiction* – which was to trawl not only history but also the dime novels and tales from that now familiar era. He was intent on making *Last Man Standing* 'literally a hymn to the tradition of fictional American tough guys. What we came up with is an American gangster film that is also a passionate and reverential adaptation of a classic story which one does not take lightly.'

It was, then, fortuitous that at the very moment that Sarkissan and Hill were beginning their collaboration they were able to witness the rebirth of Bruce Willis in *Pulp Fiction*. He came out of the screen at them like a salesman handing out a business card. Willis was their man and around him they placed, with strategic precision, the diverse talents of Bruce Dern, Christopher Walken and David Patrick Kelly.

Willis portrays the mysterious drifter who in previous incarnations had been the Japanese actor Toshiro Mifune and Clint Eastwood. Hill was well aware that they were proceeding down a well-trodden path of movie tales about notorious gangsters like Al Capone, Lucky Luciano and Frank Costello who had all risen to power during the bootlegging era. He was also aware that he would have to place his action in a setting well away from the popular locations of Chicago in order to recreate the original scenario of *Yojimbo*. They needed a small, wild town.

They researched the roots of bootlegging, which actually dates back to the early 1800s. Then, Indian traders commonly used liquor as a bartering weapon. It was considered to be a medicinal cure-all, a hair tonic and a perfume as well as being just booze and it was traded for furs, pelts and leather. The trade was illegal even then and frontiersmen would stash the 'joy juice' in their boots. And so the term 'bootlegger' became the commonly accepted definition for anyone engaged in the illegal transfer of liquor. It took on its more common usage with the Volstead Act of 16 January 1920, which banned alcohol across the United States.

The Prohibition era became the most colourful and influential period of 20th-century America and the subject of many movies, perhaps best typified by the double-act of James Cagney and Humphrey Bogart in *The Roaring Twenties* and, more recently, with *The Untouchables*, starring Kevin Costner and Sean Connery. In the thirteen years of Prohibition, around 1.3 billion gallons of mob-controlled liquor were consumed by an eager American public, not including the home-made brew concocted in millions of bathtubs.

Apart from the famous escapades of Rum Row, where booze was shipped in to the east coast of the United States, a good deal of the imported liquor came through towns and cities close to the unguarded borders of Canada and Mexico. Crime lords soon emerged and, instead of achieving its aim of moral cleansing – as the promoters of Prohibition in the Women's Christian Temperance League intended – it brought wealth, power and influence to the denizens of the underworld.

Millions of dollars earned from illicit booze were quickly diverted to fund gambling, racketeering and prostitution. A curious bonding emerged between gangsters and society at large as millions of Americans, from all walks of life, were thrust together in the sudden demand for the demon drink. It was the supreme irony that what began as a campaign for purity did, in fact, create the greatest criminal bonanza in modern history and resulted in a criminal structure that would remain to haunt the American law enforcers down the century.

Common thugs thrived, even well away from the cities like Chicago, where shoot-outs and gang wars flourished. Many small towns were virtually taken over and corrupted by mob influences.

Thus, the new slant on an exceedingly well-documented era of history is that it is set in one of those outposts of the Prohibition era – the fictional community of Jericho, on the Mexican border. On this imaginary location, Hill overlaid the story of *Yojimbo*, substituting Willis's character for the lonely 1860s Japanese samurai.

As Sarkissan explained: 'The mob got their best booze by

smuggling it across the border. It's silly to think that Al Capone himself would have been in some lonely outpost north of the Rio Grande arranging these lucrative shipments. While Capone and his henchmen were two thousand miles away, their lieutenants and armies were swinging deals, corrupting officials and hijacking booze from the competition. The West didn't know the meaning of the word "wild" until these guys blew into town.'

So they had the setting ... and now for the rest of the adaptation.

Enter Bruce Willis as Smith, the mysterious drifter who wanders into a rather odd town named Jericho at the height of Prohibition, looking for a place to spend the night. He ends up as the counterpoint in a savage war between rival gangs. Hill admits he deliberately wrote the Willis role to provide a 'minimalist' approach to Smith's character. He conceived the protagonist as a man whose actions speak louder than words. That is evident from the early stages of the picture. Smith packs two guns, shoots them at the same time, and never misses with either. Naturally, the body count will be high; a small laptop might be an advisable accessory in order to keep count. Quite early in the film, Smith takes on a dozen heavily armed opponents in one sitting – and kills them all before they can get a good shot at him.

Hill wanted Willis to appear 'curt' against the other players in the film, leaving the unabashed pulp narrative to fill in the gaps of the personality and motivation of the enigmatic character. 'Smith plays the percentages as he understands them. That means you trust no one; you give nothing up to anybody unless it's absolutely necessary, and you watch your own backside,' Hill explained.

Willis, although on a tight rein as far as the script was concerned, was given a good deal of freedom by director Hill to develop the role for himself, more so than on any previous picture. 'Walter gave me the opportunity to fool around with this character,' said Willis. 'I was trying something I hadn't ever done before, developing the psychology of the character. Smith has done some things in the past that have been bad. But he also does some things in the story that qualify as being heroic. I wanted him to be a thinking man's character. A guy who questions whether he's doing the right thing. Everyone has a moment in life where they make a choice to stick their head in something that is not their business.

Sometimes you come out okay, other times you get slapped. Smith has to choose between right and wrong. He's not a hero and he's not a villain, and I liked the ambiguity in that.'

Smith swings into action when he discovers local power is divided between two ethnic groups, one Italian and the other Irish, who are currently enjoying an uneasy truce. He plots to bring them back into conflict and make a pile from the eventual mayhem. He is first offered $1,000 to work for the Irish gang leader. 'A day or a week?' he asks. 'I'm worth it. I'm good.' As a hint of things to come, Christopher Walken as the leading lieutenant jealously guarding his position, lets rip with his machine gun, spraying bullets around the room, and then coolly asks: 'That good?'

Christopher Walken, best known for his Oscar-winning performance in *The Deer Hunter*, and Bruce Dern join Willis as the movie's other most potent characters. Dern is Jericho's corrupt Sheriff Galt, whom Hill patterned after the petty policeman in Kurosawa's *Yojimbo*. The character, according to Dern himself, was a mainstay in the Walter Hill school of film-making. 'Walter likes to write about big, strong men. Galt represents the apathetic law enforcement in Jericho. And, like everybody else in town, he has his price. In Walter's movies, all the big strong men who have been accorded a certain kind of officialdom have weaknesses. That's one of his creative signatures.' Dern's character makes money selling information to both sides in the best traditions of corrupt Prohibition policemen.

Hill likes familiar faces around him and many of his crew are retained from movie to movie. This was Dern's third collaboration with Hill, although the director had never before met Walken, who was cast, according to Sarkissan, because 'we needed someone with a strong presence to counterbalance the imposing presence of Willis.'

Walken's role of Hickey was modelled on the character of Unosuke in *Yojimbo*. He becomes a malevolent trigger-happy Irish enforcer who puts fear into the town of Jericho with random firings of his tommy gun. He is the principal opponent of Smith. 'There's an electricity between our characters when we finally meet face-to-face,' said Walken, whose character, like Smith, is a man of few words but which Walken delivers with a throaty brogue.

Making movies usually throws together a group of diverse characters and this production was no exception. This point is illustrated by the inclusion of the actress who plays the main love interest among all of this male posturing. Karina Lombard portrays Felina, a naturally stunning Tahitian born beauty, who is the imprisoned girlfriend of the Irish gangleader. He will kill anyone who so much as looks at her. Smith, impressed by her plight, is immediately attracted to her.

Lombard is a classy actress. Her maternal grandparents were Lakota Indians from South Dakota. Her father, a Swiss-Russian heir to a European fortune, moved his children to Spain when she was just a year old. A decade later, she passed through a series of Calvinist boarding schools across Europe, graduating from Vinet in Lausanne before moving to New York at age eighteen. She won acceptance at the famed Actors Studio before a highly successful modelling career developed when acclaimed photographer Bruce Weber discovered her for an ad campaign on Native Americans. Oliver Stone chose her for a small role in *The Doors* and, soon afterwards, she won a life-changing role as Tom Cruise's seductress in *The Firm*. Later still, she became Brad Pitt's wife in *Legends of the Fall*.

To this unusually (for Willis) interesting array of talent, Hill and Sarkissan added the skills of veteran costume designer Dan Moore, production designer Gary Wissner and Oscar-nominated set wizard Gary Fettis (*The Godfather III* and *Apocalypse Now*). They were to conjure up authentic costumes and backdrops for the Prohibition era. They went into deep detail. 'It was my idea, for example, to use different colour schemes to define the two gangs,' Wissner explained. 'I saw one gang as more of a blue-collar crime family. The other was more sophisticated, more culturally rich.' In partnership with Moore, they went on to use reds and browns for the Italian mob's wardrobe and set decor while creating the Irish hoods in a colder, blue-grey domain.

Moore went further with the costumes, so that the Italian and Irish hoods were each allotted specific fabrics and textures for the design and manufacture of the 250 suits needed for the principal cast during filming. The Italians were dolled up in typical broad pinstripes while the Irish were dressed in tweeds and plaids. He topped off their period look with homburgs, fedoras and caps according to their rank in the gangland order. Most were made in

Hollywood, but the costumes for Willis were designed, cut and sewn in Rochester, New York, so that he, the stranger among them, stood apart. His hats were given a wider brim and crown and he was the only character in the film to wear a blue suit.

It was one of the most detailed research operations Willis had ever been involved in, a new experience in so many ways, even for him. He came out of filming in the early spring of 1996, convinced that he had delivered a performance that was among his career best. How would it fare with the critics? He professes to take their opinions with a pinch of salt, even though it remains a fact – as he knows from deeply wounding personal experience – that a clutch of poor reviews will seriously damage the health of any movie. Seven months would pass before he would discover his fate on this one. Demi Moore, meantime, was suffering from a bout of bad reviews of the kind that have dogged Willis's life.

Indeed, the Willis household was in a state of high tension that summer of 1996 as he and Demi awaited the response to their work, as had so often been the case with the His and Hers movies that followed each other into the cinemas. That winter of 1995/96, she had followed his *Twelve Monkeys* on to the circuit with the February release of *The Juror*, a much-hyped production brought to the screens by Robert De Niro's old friend, Irwin Winkler. He was the man who made possible the Martin Scorsese classic *Goodfellas*, along with his less popular *New York, New York* and *Raging Bull*. On the other hand, he also produced Stallone's five *Rocky* movies. This time it was an attempt at a John Grisham lookalike called *The Juror*, in which Moore co-starred with Alec Baldwin.

She was as glamorous and fetching as ever, but also very gloomy as if she knew, as she plodded through the turgid scenes, that this one was a no-no. She suffered some serious vitriol at the hands of the critics. Richard Schickel, film critic of *Time* magazine was among the several who pulled no punches. 'There are two kinds of lousy movies: those made by morons and those made in the firm belief that we are the morons. The former are forgivable – poor dears, they don't know any better. The latter, of which *The Juror* is a particularly egregious example, are infuriating. They leave you feeling you've been patronised and bilked by people nursing entirely unearned superiority complexes.'

Moore plays a young single-parent, seemingly eager to devote a few weeks of her life to help decide the fate of a Mafia boss accused of a murder conspiracy. Soon, she and her son are being stalked by hit man Baldwin who states that, unless she persuades her fellow jurors to free the mafioso, she and her son will be killed.

Director Brian Gibson, who did rather better with the Tina Turner biopic, *What's Love Got to Do with It*, failed to raise this movie from the dead. According to Schickel, audiences would be left wondering what possessed them to 'go spending $7.50 a pop on this kind of numbing drivel.'

That hurt. And Demi's disaster could not have come at a worse time. She, like her husband, was on tenterhooks, waiting for the release of her own Big One, *Striptease*. This was the movie that paid $12.5 million, persuaded her to get her kit off again, and turned her into the highest-paid female actress in history. She had filmed around the same time that Willis had been working on *Last Man Standing*, but it would beat his movie into the cinemas by three months.

Her last three movies had not been successful and the brow-beating she took from *The Juror* was sufficient for the Hollywood pundits to suggest that much more than money rested on the outcome of her stripping venture: her future was at stake. She was in the same position that Willis had found himself in – first, she had set a new record for money, and second, the 'three flops and you're out' penalty was hovering over her head. Long before the release of *Striptease*, commentators were saying it was make-or-break time for Moore. 'This has to work,' said Martin Grove, a Hollywood columnist, 'otherwise, Demi may have to get a day job at Planet Hollywood. It's hard to justify $12.5 million when you're not packing them in, and lately she hasn't been.'

But they all knew, too, that the kid's got guts. Moore herself was aware of the pressure bearing down on her. Apart from the commercial aspects, the mounting criticism and the amazement concerning her fee, the movie itself posed both a challenge and a threat. There was probably not another female film star in the Hollywood A-list who would have taken it on, risking embarrassment and the ogling of millions. But then, as someone pointed out, she had already disrobed in six of her movies, and appeared naked on the cover of *Vanity Fair*. There wasn't much left of her that the movie-going public hadn't already seen. But it wasn't as simple as that. The whole tenor of the movie was one of raw, steamy sexuality. It was not just a question of stripping. Moore was best known for acting roles that displayed the cool, often hard-as-nails bravado of the modern woman and she was anchored in a feminist rather than feminine approach.

She went about the task with her usual cool, tough approach, motivated in part by her vanity, but mostly by her single-minded determination that had become so evident during the progression of her career and her marriage.

Like Willis in his preparation for *Last Man Standing*, she had done her homework. Carl Hiaasen, author of the hilarious novel on which *Striptease* is based, was surprised and impressed. She had obviously read his book from cover to cover and then 'struck out with a journalistic appetite researching the stripping business.' As filming began, so did Demi's now familiar routine of fitness and mind exercises. While on location in Florida, she was up before dawn to run along the beach, even on the days when she faced three gruelling hours of dance rehearsal or a session with her personal trainer in the special trailer fitted-out with $15,000 worth of gym equipment.

Some days, she spent two hours in yoga positions, deep in meditation. Calmness prevailed. She could show anyone how to ride out life's stormiest moments, and did so quite literally. One night, during September, a loud and scary thunder storm with zig-zagging lightning struck the Florida coastline. While other members of the cast lay fretting in their beds, Moore went running in the rain, then took a swim in the ocean. 'She was amazing, almost shocking in the way she handled everything,' said one of her supporting colleagues, Siobhan Fallon. Director Andrew Bergman agreed: 'Everything is a matter of Demi trying to have a sense of empowerment. Given her early life, you can understand it.'

She had set up her temporary home in her trailer, decked out with family memorabilia. The nannies herded the children, although the eldest, Rumer, was also part of the movie. She was making her acting debut as the daughter of Demi's character. Demi was unperturbed about her daughter seeing her mother perform, although she was kept away from the more raunchy moments – as when she did a hot and sexy number on the movie's night-club stage in Fort Lauderdale. For that sequence, 200 male extras crowded into the room to play strip club patrons. 'The fee was minimal,' said one, 'but there wasn't a man among us who wouldn't have done it for nothing. She was terrific.'

The atmosphere was electric. With the extras seated at tables around the catwalk, the cameras rolled and Demi made her entrance to the blaring sound of an Annie Lennox song, 'Money Can't Buy It'. Moore swaggered to the catwalk dressed in a man's suit, specially adapted for an easy tear-off. She was only a few minutes into her routine when the audience of extras began whooping and screaming. Uproar! They wanted realism but this was too much. The director yelled 'Cut!' The scene was reshot and Moore, once again, went into her routine.

The filming of *Striptease* naturally attracted a good deal of media attention, prodded by the studio publicists and the simmering angst of the Hollywood backbiters, who were still smarting over her $12.5 million pay-day. It soon became apparent that Moore was in for a rough ride. The magazine treatment of her became almost as hostile as the pre-press criticism dished out on her husband's movie, *Hudson Hawk*. Apart from the speculation that if she flopped on this one, she would be in trouble, the analysts and the tabloids took the opportunity of examining her standing with the movie-going public. Several commentators remarked that the picture would do nothing for her low-popularity rating among women.

She lacked the qualities of warmth and vulnerability of, say, Julia Roberts or the respect attached to the likes of Jodie Foster. She was generally cast as a real-life hard-faced, self-seeking bitch. *Allure* magazine, for example, took her to task with a venomous review of her style and her tough demeanour. In a long article, she was chided over her 'preternaturally perky breasts'. The writer went on to describe her as a 'famously buff mother of three despised by unbuff mothers of three everywhere'.

Another suggested that it was all to do with her background, a throwback from an awful childhood and her wild, uncontrolled youth – and was it possible that her mother, Virginia, would star in the sequel, old age stripper? That reference was a clear side-swipe to the time Virginia went nude in 1993 for *High Society* magazine, imitating her daughter's heavily pregnant state in the *Vanity Fair* photographs.

The media disquiet was heightened by word leaking from the studio as the movie neared its release. Reaction from test audiences was not encouraging. The producers ordered a reshoot of some of the scenes, including scenes where Moore's co-star, Burt Reynolds (in white wig), turned violent. The danger signs were more or less confirmed when the movie was released in America in June 1996. A fairly mixed bag of reviews and unimpressive box office statistics pointed up a certain confusion about the movie.

The original novel, in which the characters were funny and witty, was pretty well adhered to – with the exception of Moore's role. There had been a certain tampering, to give her a seriousness that excused the need for her to become a striptease artist – she loses her daughter (Rumer) in a custody battle and only resorts to stripping to earn money to fight the case. Moore's usual persona of steadfastness was not to be undermined. And she was definitely *not* funny. There were some very good performances, especially from Burt Reynolds, and the hilarious supporting characters rescued the film from disaster. For all the hype, the miles of newsprint and Demi's own pontificating in the promo interviews, it was a major disappointment.

Three months later, it was Willis's turn as *Last Man Standing* went on release. He fared rather better. The movie was not wholeheartedly received by the critics, many complaining of its gloomy, repressive atmosphere for which director Hill was blamed. But that said, Willis's performance was recognised as being one of his best, and certainly the most outstanding performer in this particular film. Now, it is perhaps no longer necessary to record that he had disposed of the smirk and all the other familiar trademarks of so many of his films.

Willis the actor, as opposed to Willis the one-act wonder, is shining through and this is, indeed, a suitable point to leave this interim account of his life and times. There is no doubt that his place in movie history is settled; he will go on in the mould of the famous names from the past and, at last, it is possible to link him, through his performances, to old Hollywood and fine actors, with whom he can now be justifiably compared. Comparison, in Hollywood's way, is the mark of success. It adds weight to the pedigree he needed and sought: some meaningful entries on the CV that are not all bluff and blunder.

It was always going to be a long slog. He came from nowhere, had virtually no real training as an actor, did very little theatre work and had no history at all of graduating through support roles in movies. Willis came in near the top and, in that, he was pretty unique. The pressures and the problems that we have seen in his personal life and his attitudes were matched only by the unmitigated resentment of this upstart by the Hollywood establishment. To that they added antagonism and a general dislike of the woman with whom he chose to share his world, Demi Moore. 'They deserve each other,' was not an uncommon jibe on the party circuit. Behind the nastiness that continues to surround him and Demi is the jealousy, engendered by the Willises' financial clout. If they did, indeed, 'deserve each other' then they also surprised everyone by making it work.

As everyone close to them knows, it has been a tempestuous relationship; they fight a lot and have occasionally been known to come to blows. But, by Hollywood standards, it looks a fairly stable marriage though, as Willis himself said, 'there are no certainties in matrimony'. Moore maintains that 'the children are our glue, and we're each other's best friend. Those two facts see us through tough spots.'

And the money.

They both figure in the Forbes list of top-earning entertainers. Willis alone, according to Forbes, earned more than $35 million in eighteen months during 1994/95 and, as this work was being completed, he was said to be negotiating a new Hollywood all-time record fee of $25 million for one picture – *Die Hard 4*.

Willis, more than any other actor in Hollywood, became the epitome of the modern male star of the last decade. He moved in a movie world that was alien to those who remained dedicated to the artistry of performing, simply because he knew no better. He was gathered up by people in power at a time when drastic changes were occurring, especially on the artistic front.

Once, the power, the strength and the star-making potential was in the hands of fine directors. They were the backbone of the movie business; every one of their movies was like a painting and carried the artist's signature. The stars, as Polanski once crudely put it, were just the monkeys while the organ grinder sat bawling his instructions from behind the camera. Josef von Sternberg was less insulting, but made the same point: 'I regard actors as marionettes, as pieces of colour in my canvas.'

That has not altogether disappeared, but the emphasis has changed. Producers and deal-makers really took over in the 1980s and actors themselves, led by the example of Warren Beatty (himself inspired by Orson Welles), wanted a bigger piece of the action.

Willis had none of these connections with the past, none of the hand-me-down contact from days gone by because he did not move in those kind of circles. He has, throughout his career, been getting in and out of bed, metaphorically speaking of course, with the Big Men who spout megabucks, megapromises and mega-everything; often overbearing men who control the pictures from beginning to end, regardless of the artistic whims of the man who happens to be directing.

Willis, for a while, fell into the trap of self-importance; his wife was even worse. Old-timers marvel at the way some directors have been treated by the modern breed, and conjecture with wonderment what horrors would have befallen them in the Golden Age, at the hands of directors like Billy Wilder, Otto Preminger, Alfred Hitchcock, John Huston, and even Polanski, if they had tried the I-am-the-star routine upon them.

Today, studio bossess are subjected to the forces of external powerbrokers who pander to the stars. Travolta (who has become as pleasant a chap as you could hope to meet since his experience of failure and rebirth), found it impossible to work with Polanski on *The Double*. He said goodbye to $17.5 million and caught the next plane home. Polanski is not that bad a person; he is just a perfectionist who happens to stand by that rather old-fashioned view that the director actually directs!

Willis, belatedly, and with the assistance of Tarantino and Terry Gilliam, seems to have been shown a side of movie-making that had eluded him, or that he had ignored. He also now appears to appreciate that, in order to earn respect, you have to have respect. The future looks decidedly bright.

They have it all: the minders and the entourage, the bodyguards and the security – all very necessary these days when stars are not

stars without their own personal stalker. They have their $3 million white stucco mansion on the beach in Malibu, a fourteen-room pied-à-terre on Central Park West, their $5 million six-bedroom, seven-bath ranch house on 48 acres in Idaho, a large chunk of Penns Court, New Jersey, a mass of other real estate and a handy portion of Planet Hollywood.

Willis could pack it all in tomorrow if he wished. But he won't. He was infected by the acting bug in his youth and he would go anywhere for a gig. From his poverty-stricken starting point, success was, for years, scored by his loudness and how much money he had in the bank – not by his performances.

It's good, finally, to record the change.

Filmography

The First Deadly Sin (1980) Filmways Pictures: *producer* Elliott Kastner; *director* Brian G. Hutton; *screenplay* Mann Rubin (*novel* Lawrence Sanders); *photography* Jack Priestley; *music* Gordon Jenkins; *cast* Frank Sinatra, Faye Dunaway, David Dukes, George Coe, Brenda Vaccaro, Martin Gabel, Bruce Willis (uncredited long-shot stand-in)

The Verdict (1982) TCF/Zanuck-Brown: *producers* Richard D. Zanuck and David Brown; *director* Sidney Lumet; *screenplay* David Mamet (*novel* Barry Reed); *photography* Andrzej Bartokwiak; *music* Johnny Mandel; *cast* Paul Newman, James Mason, Charlotte Rampling, Jack Warden, Milo O'Shea, Lindsay Crouse, Edward Binns, Bruce Willis (uncredited walk-on)

Blind Date (1987) TriStar/Blake Edwards: *producer* Tony Adams; *director* Blake Edwards; *screenplay* Dale Launer; *photography* Harry Stradling; *music* Henry Mancini; *cast* Kim Basinger, Bruce Willis, John Larroquette, William Daniels, Phil Hartman, Alice Hirson

Sunset (1988) Columbia/TriStar/ML Delphi: *producer* Tony Adams; *writer/director* Blake Edwards (*story* Rod Amateau); *photography* Anthony B. Richmond; *music* Henry Mancini; *cast* Bruce Willis, James Garner, Malcolm McDowell, Mariel Hemingway, Kathleen Quinlan, Jennifer Edwards, Patricia Hodge, Richard Bradford, M. Emmet Walsh, Joe Dallesandro

Die Hard (1988) Fox/Gordon Company/Silver Pictures: *producers* Joel Silver and Lawrence Gordon; *director* John McTiernan; *screenplay* Jeb Stuart and Steven E. de Souza (*novel* 'Nothing Lasts Forever', Roderick Thorp); *photography* Jan de Bont; *music* Michael Kamen; *cast* Bruce Willis, Bonnie Bedelia,

Reginald VelJohnson, Alan Rickman, Paul Gleason, De'Voreaux White, William Atherton, Hart Bochner

Look Who's Talking (1989) Columbia TriStar: *producer* Jonathan D. Krane; *writer/director* Amy Heckerling; *photography* Thomas del Ruth; *music* David Kitay; *cast* John Travolta, Kirstie Alley, George Segal, Olympia Dukakis, Abe Vigoda, Twink Caplan, Joy Boushel, Don S. Davis; Bruce Willis (voice-over)

In Country (1989) Warner: *producers* Norman Jewison and Richard Roth; *director* Norman Jewison; *screenplay* Frank Pierson and Cynthia Cidre (*novel* Bobbie Ann Mason); *photography* Russel Boyde; *music* James Horner; *cast* Bruce Willis, Emily Lloyd, Joan Allen, Kevin Anderson, Richard Hamilton, Judith Ivey, Peggy Rea, John Terry, Dan Jenkins

Look Who's Talking Too (1990) Columbia TriStar: *producer* Jonathan D. Krane; *writer/director* Amy Heckerling; *photography* Thomas Del Ruth; *music* David Kitay; *cast* John Travolta, Kirstie Alley, Olympia Dukakis, Elias Koteas, Twink Caplan; Bruce Willis, Roseanne Barr, Damon Wayans, Mel Brooks (voice-overs)

Die Hard 2 (1990) Fox/Gordon Company/Silver Pictures: *producers* Lawrence Gordon, Joel Silver and Charles Gordon; *director* Renny Harlin; *screenplay* Steven E. de Souza and Doug Richardson (*novel* '58 Minutes', Walter Wager); *photography* Oliver Wood; *music* Michael Kamen; *cast* Bruce Willis, Bonnie Bedelia, William Atherton, Reginald VelJohnson, Franco Nero, William Sadler, John Amos, Dennis Franz, Art Evans, Fred Dalton Thompson

The Bonfire of the Vanities (1990) Warner: *producer/director* Brian de Palma; *screenplay* Michael Cristofer (*novel* Tom Wolfe); *photography* Vilmos Zsigmond; *music* Dave Grusin; *cast* Tom Hanks, Melanie Griffith, Bruce Willis, Kim Cattrall, Saul Rubunek, Morgan Freeman, F. Murray Abraham, John Hancock, Kevin Dunn, Clifton James

Mortal Thoughts (1991) Columbia TriStar/New Visions/Polar/ Rufglen: *producers* John Fielder and Mark Tarlov; *director* Alan Rudolph; *screenplay* William Reilly and Claude Kerven; *photo-*

graphy Elliot Davis; *music* Mark Isham; *cast* Demi Moore, Glenne Headly, Bruce Willis, John Pankow, Harvey Keitel, Billie Neal, Frank Vincent

The Last Boy Scout (1991) Warner/Geffen/Silver: *producers* Joel Silver and Michael Levy; *director* Tony Scott; *screenplay* Shane Black; *photography* Ward Russell; *music* Michael Kamen; *cast* Bruce Willis, Damon Wayans, Chelsea Field, Noble Willingham, Taylor Negron, Danielle Harris, Halle Berry, Bruce McGill

Hudson Hawk (1991) Columbia TriStar/Silver Pictures: *producer* Joel Silver; *director* Michael Lehmann; *screenplay* Steven E. de Souza (*story* Bruce Willis and Robert Kraft); *photography* Dante Spinotti; *music* Michael Kamen; *cast* Bruce Willis, Danny Aiello, Andrew MacDowell, James Coburn, Richard E. Grant, Sandra Bernhard, Donald Burton, Don Harvey, David Caruso

Billy Bathgate (1991) Warner/Touchstone: *producers* Arlene Donovan and Robert Colesbury; *director* Robert Benton; *screenplay* Tom Stoppard (*novel* E. L. Doctorow); *photography* Nestor Almendros; *music* Mark Isham; *cast* Dustin Hoffman, Nicole Kidman, Loren Dean, Bruce Willis, Steven Hill, Steve Buscemi, Billy Jaye

The Player (1992) Guild/Avenue: *producers* David Brown, Michael Tolkin and Nick Wechsler; *director* Robert Altman; *screenplay* Michael Tolkin (*novel* Michael Tolkin); *photography* Jean Lepine; *music* Thomas Newman; *cast* Tim Robbins, Greta Scacchi, Fred Ward, Whoopi Goldberg, Peter Gallagher, Richard E. Grant, Sydney Pollack; Bruce Willis, Jack Lemmon, Nick Nolte, Julia Roberts, Susan Sarandon, Peter Falk, James Coburn, Harry Belafonte, Anjelica Huston and 56 others (as themselves)

Death Becomes Her (1992) UIP/Universal: *producers* Robert Zemeckis and Steven Starkey; *director* Robert Zemeckis; *screenplay* Martin Donovan and David Koepp; *photography* Dean Cundey; *music* Alan Silvestri; *cast* Meryl Streep, Goldie Hawn, Bruce Willis, Isabella Rossellini, Ian Ogilvy, Adam Sorke, Nancy Fish, Alaina Reed Hall, Michelle Johnson, Mary Ellen Trainor

National Lampoon's Loaded Weapon 1 (1993) Guild/New Line: *producers* Suzanne Todd and David Willis; *director* Gene Quintano; *screenplay* Don Holley and Gene Quintano; *photography* Peter Dening; *music* Robert Folk; *cast* Emilio Estevez, Samuel L. Jackson, Jon Loves, Tim Curry, Kathy Ireland, Frank McRae, William Shatner, Bruce Willis (uncredited cameo as mobile home owner)

North (1994) Castle Rock Productions/New Line: *producers* Rob Reiner, Andrew Scheinman and Jeffrey Stott; *director* Rob Reiner; *screenplay* Andrew Schienman and Alan Zweibel (*novel* Andrew Scheinman and Alan Zweibel); *photography* Adam Greenberg; *music* Marc Shaiman; *cast* Elijah Wood, Jason Alexander, Julia Louis-Dreyfus, Jussie Smollett, Taylor Fry, Alan Arkin, Mark Coppola, Bruce Willis (narrator)

Color of Night (1994) Cinergi Pictures/Hollywood Pictures: *producers* Buzz Feitshans, David Matalon, David Willis and Carmine Zozzora; *director* Richard Rush; *screenplay* Matthew Chapman and Billy Ray; *photography* Dietrich Lohmann; *music* Dominic Frontiers; *cast* Bruce Willis, Jane March, Ruben Blades, Lesley Ann Warren, Scott Bakula, Brad Dourif, Lance Henriksen, Kevin J. O'Connor, Andrew Lowery, Jeff Corey

Pulp Fiction (1994) Miramax Pictures: *producers* Lawrence Bender, Danny DeVito (executive), Michael Shamberg and Stacey Sher; *writer/director* Quentin Tarantino; *photography* Andrzej Sekula; *music* Karyn Rachtman; *cast* John Travolta, Samuel L. Jackson, Uma Thurman, Bruce Willis, Amanda Plummer, Tim Roth, Maria de Medeiros, Harvey Keitel, Christopher Walken, Eric Stoltz, Ving Rhames, Rosanna Arquette, Quentin Tarantino, Angela Jones

Nobody's Fool (1994) Capella/Cinehaus/Paramount Pictures: *producers* Arlene Donovan and Scott Rudin; *director* Robert Benton; *screenplay* Robert Benton and Richard Russo; *photography* John Bailey; *music* Howard Shore; *cast* Paul Newman, Jessica Tandy, Bruce Willis, Melanie Griffith, Dylan Walsh, Gene Saks, Philip Bosco, Catherine Deneuve

Die Hard With a Vengeance (1995) 20th Century-Fox/Cinergi Productions: *producers* Buzz Feitshans and Andrew Vanja (executive), Robert Lawrence, John McTiernan, Michael Tadros and Carmine Zozzora; *director* John McTiernan; *screenplay* Jonathan Hensleigh; *photography* Peter Menzies; *music* Michael Kamen; *cast* Bruce Willis, Jeremy Irons, Samuel L. Jackson, Graham Greene, Collen Camp, Larry Bryggman, Anthony Peck, Nick Wyman, Sam Phillips, Kevin Chamberlin, Sharon Washington, Stephen Pearlman, Michael Alexander Jackson, Aldis Hodge, Mischa Hausserman

Twelve Monkeys (1995) Universal Pictures/Atlas Entertainment: *producers* Lloyd Phillips and Charles Roven; *director* Terry Gilliam; *screenplay* David and Janet Peoples (inspired by Chris Marker's screenplay for *La Jetee*); *photography* Roger Platt; *music* Paul Buckmaster; *cast* Bruce Willis, Madeleine Stowe, Brad Pitt, Christopher Plummer, Joseph Melito, John Seda, Michael Chance, Vernon Campbell, H. Michael Walls, Bob Adrian, Rick Warner, Frank Gorshin

Four Rooms (1995) Miramax Films: *producers* Quentin Tarantino (executive), Lawrence Bender and Paul Hellerman; *writer/director* Allison Anders (*The Missing Ingredient*), Alexandre Rockwell (*The Wrong Man*), Robert Rodriquez (*The Misbehavers*), Quentin Tarantino (*The Man From Hollywood*); *photography* Phil Parmet; *cast* Tim Roth, Madonna, Sammi Davis, Amanda de Cadenet, Valeria Golino, Quinn Thomas Kellerman, Ione Skye, Lili Taylor, Alicia Witt, David Proval, Jennifer Beals, Antonio Banderas, Lana McKissack, Paul Calderon, Lawrence Bender, Quentin Tarantino, Bruce Willis

Last Man Standing (1997) New Line Cinema: *producers* Paula Heller and Walter Hill; *director* Walter Hill; *screenplay* Walter Hill and Ryuzo Kikushima (original screenplay for *Yojimbo* by Akira Kurosawa); *photography* Lloyd Ahern; *music* Elmer Bernstein; *cast* Bruce Willis, Christopher Walken, Alexandra Powers, Bruce Dern, David Patrick Kelly, William Sanderson, Karina Lombard, Ken Jenkins

The Jackal (1997) Universal Pictures: *producers* Sean Daniel, James Jacks and Kevin Jarre; *director* Michael Caton-Jones; *screenplay* Frederick Forsyth (from his novel 'The Day of the Jackal'), Kevin Jarre and Chuck Pfarrer; *photography* Karl

Walter Lidenlaub; *music* Carter Burwell; *cast* Richard Gere, Bruce Willis, Mathilda May, Sidney Poitier, Diane Venora

The Fifth Element (aka The Fifth Man) (1997) Columbia Pictures: *producer* Patrice Ledoux; *director* Luc Besson; *screenplay* Luc Besson and Robert Mark Kaemn; *visual effects supervisor* Mark Stetson; *music* Eric Serra; *cast* Bruce Willis, Gary Oldman, Ian Holm, Luke Perry, Yolanda Garza, Chris Tucker

Index